AF328831

GEOLOGICAL SURVEY OF MICHIGAN.

UPPER PENINSULA

1878 – 1880

ACCOMPANIED BY A

GEOLOGICAL MAP.

VOL. IV.

PART I.   MARQUETTE IRON REGION.
PART II.   MENOMINEE IRON REGION.

BY

C. ROMINGER

STATE GEOLOGIST.

PUBLISHED BY AUTHORITY OF THE LEGISLATURE
OF MICHIGAN

UNDER THE DIRECTION OF THE

BOARD OF GEOLOGICAL SURVEY.

NEW YORK
JULIUS BIEN
1881

ERRATA:

Page 114—line 23, read "the iron-bearing" instead of "this."

" 173—line 24, read "east line" instead of "west line."

" 174—line 27, read "east line" instead of "west line."

" 175—line 5, read "not far" instead of "north, far."

" 220—line 15, read "substance" instead of "susbtance."

" 223—line 6, read "of the Quinnesec ore-formation" instead of "underlying the Quinnesec ore-formation."

" 236—line 13, read "Selden" instead of "Sheldon."

PART I.

MARQUETTE IRON REGION.

TABLE OF CONTENTS.

*To the Honorable the Board of the Geological Survey of the State of
Michigan :*

GENTLEMEN :

Having been asked by your honorable body to furnish a statement of what has been accomplished by the geological exploration
of the State since the beginning of the Survey, and also to designate what in my opinion yet remains to be done, I have the honor
to submit the following for your consideration.

The general structure of our State, of the Lower as well as the
Upper Peninsula, has been as thoroughly examined as time and
circumstances enabled.

Of the Lower Peninsula and of the eastern part of the Upper
(which portions of the State are underlaid by horizontal strata of
the Silurian, Devonian, and Carboniferous periods) we have
acquired sufficient knowledge for all practical purposes. The
greater part of these districts is deeply covered with drift deposits
which hide the older rock-beds ; but from local exposures, from
borings and other artificial denudations of these older rocks, it
becomes possible not only to ascertain the local extent of each of
these formations, but also to positively designate what kinds of
minerals are found in each of these districts, and to indicate where
they may be found in places in which they have not yet been discovered.

The case is altogether different with the western part of the
Upper Peninsula, the structure of which consists of the oldest
known rocks, partly of a sedimentary and partly of a volcanic
origin.

By volcanic action these sedimentary rocks have not only been
lifted from their horizontal position into all degrees of inclination,
and in some places even completely overturned, but have also
been considerably altered so as to again resemble, more or less,

the volcanic rocks from the transformations of which they originated.

While the relative age of the younger horizontal sedimentary rock-beds may be determined without difficulty by the order in which they are superposed and from the organic remains peculiar to each of the successive groups of beds, in the examination of the older upheaved sedimentary rocks, we can no longer rely with any degree of safety upon their order of succession, as their relative position is often changed and even completely reversed by plication of the beds and by faulted dislocation. We do not find fossils in them to guide us in the discrimination of one rock from another ; we can only resort to the nature of the rock itself, and this is a fallacious criterion, as the rocks in question are remarkably uniform in their composition and resemblance ; while on the other hand there are local differences in molecular structure and degree of metamorphosis which cause analogous beds to differ widely in appearance. I thus briefly allude to these difficulties, that hinder the speedy recognition of the geological structure of such a region, in order to show what and how great they are.

In the first volume of the Michigan Geological Reports, Major Brooks gives the results of his examination of these older rocks in the Lake Superior region, and plainly says that he considers his work as merely a fair beginning of a great task yet to be finished.

On me now devolved the continuance of the Survey, and the Report now presented to you embodies the results of my work during three summer seasons in the Marquette district, and of one season in the Menominee district.

The perusal of the Report will show what has been accomplished, and how far our knowledge of this large and interesting country has been extended ; and I will now specially designate what remains to be done, and the reasons for its immediate execution.

The structure of the Upper Peninsula is so complicated, its extent so large, and the greater portion so difficult of access, that considering these facts I believe I have accomplished during the time above stated as much as could be done well ; nevertheless, I am more than ever convinced that years of research are necessary to complete these geological examinations as far as possible, and that even then many points concerning the history of the formation of the earth's crust will remain an unsolved problem, because nature has in part destroyed her own vestiges by building up new structures from their material.

As regards the necessity for an immediate continuance of the Survey, I desire to call the attention of your honorable Board to the fact that a geological examination of a district like the one under consideration cannot be made with expediency, accuracy and a due economy, unless advantage is taken of the work done by the private explorations, which afford the geologist valuable information not otherwise to be had without a great expenditure of time and money.

The State Geologist thankfully acknowledges that much of his Report is based upon information derived from the borings and test-pits of private explorers, and he hopes that he is in some degree able to repay them by such suggestions as he can offer concerning where to explore and where an examination will entail only a pecuniary loss. He believes that during the past year he was able to give advice which saved many times the cost of the annual survey, and that the best encouragement for the development of the mineral resources of our State is by averting fruitless expenditures in futile explorations.

The most favorable time for continuing the survey of this district is, then, while the test-pits remain open, for in a short time the caving-in or filling with water will deprive the geologist of such information as they now afford. Moreover, while these private explorations are going on it is well if the State Geologist can be at hand to give impartial advice based upon scientific principles.

Very respectfully yours,

C. ROMINGER,

State Geologist.

INTRODUCTION.

DURING the progress of the Geological Survey of Michigan, instituted by the Legislative Assembly of 1869, Messrs. T. B. Brooks and Raphael Pumpelly were intrusted with the investigation of the geological structure of the Lake Superior district.

The results of their labors, continued during three successive summer seasons, have been published by the State authorities in 1873, in connection with my own report on the eastern portion of the Upper Peninsula, in two volumes, accompanied with an atlas of maps and sections.

The interesting and valuable documents by these two gentlemen have added a great deal of information to our knowledge of the structure. of that country which we received from the previous reports of a number of able scientific observers, such as Douglas Houghton, Jackson, Foster, Whitney, Whittlesey, Credner, and others ; but even now, if we should ask the authors of these latest Reports whether they consider their work done, and to have given a full, satisfactory description of the geology of the country, I have no doubt they would answer in the negative ; they would say, Our work is a mere beginning ; the time bestowed by us on the investigation of so large an area and of so complicated a structure was totally inadequate to the task, which for years to come will engage diligent observers to accomplish it, and this only partially, never completely, as the different phases of the progressive development of the earth's crust have not all left traces behind them sufficiently distinct to construe from the observable parts a connected history of the events of creation. Creation consists in a constant change of things ; it continually works over the same material, destroying in one place and building up in another, in a modified form and combination. We can therefore never expect to see the vestiges of all the successive transformations which took place during the lapse of ages completely preserved, because the same material was always utilized for new purposes. If we commence to trace from our present time backward the different changes in the surface of the globe, we find for the periods next preceding our days abundant facts by which we are enabled to form an approximative idea of the topography of the earth at these times ; we can understand by their anology with present organisms the full organization of extinct forms of animals or plants, of which only imperfect fragments are found inclosed within the sedimentary rock-beds. But the farther we step back in tracing the history, the more we feel the scarcity of facts to prove our suggestive ideas ; and finally, we are altogether left in the dark, and have to resort to hypothetical speculations, or acknowledge in modesty to have arrived at the limits accessible for the human conception. In the present instance we are not under the necessity to go so far back ; still we have to examine very old rock-formations—rocks supposed to be the earliest sedimentary deposits. The study of more recent sedimentary rocks is comparatively much easier, as we find them in an undisturbed succession piled one upon another ; and most frequently each group of sediments, representing a certain period, incloses also a certain class of animal or vegetable remains peculiar to this horizon, by which contemporaneous formations can be identified with certainty, even if the lithological characters of the rock-beds should be widely differing. The rocks we have to examine are totally devoid of such organic remains ; whether none existed at that time, or whether the conditions for the preservation of such remains were not favorable, is a question about which scientists disagree. In determining the relative age of these rocks, we have nothing to go by but their lithological characters and their order of succession. The first are very changeable, if we compare distant localities, and can be little relied upon ; the other criterion of the age, seemingly infallible, loses much of its importance by the great dislocating disturbances to which these older rocks were once exposed : they have lost their original horizontality, and hold all sorts of inclined, erect, or overtilted positions, making it often impossible to decide which is the upper or lower side in the succession. Moreover, we find these sedimentary beds often considerably altered, resembling, externally and in chemical composition, the crystalline rocks of truly volcanic origin, which likewise form a large proportion of the surface of this region, and which have by intrusion commingled with the altered sedimentary rocks in the most varied manner.

The difficulties in the study of these ancient rocks, indicated by the previous remarks and the incompleteness of our present information about them, were fully comprehended by the members of the Board of the Geological Survey ; they decided therefore to continue the commenced investigations, not alone in appreciation of the economical importance of a thorough knowledge of the geology of this part of the State, which by its mineral wealth belongs to the most favored spots on the continent, but they thought also the pride and duty of the citizens of this commonwealth required it to contribute to the promotion of science in general, with the same liberality as many other States have done and are still doing, and to have so interesting a part of its territory fully examined.

In consequence of this decision the Board directed me to lay before them the plan I intended to follow in making the explorations. My suggestions were to examine with careful accuracy certain small circumscribed districts, so selected as to embrace the most important rock-formations developed in the region, thinking such a course would lead the quickest to a correct recognition of the structural arrangement of the earth's crust, not only there, but over the whole territory where similar rocks compose the surface. This plan met their approval.

Indispensable for the successful execution of this plan is an accurate topographical map on a large scale. The Government maps of the linear survey of the United States, projected on the scale of two inches to the mile, would answer the purpose admirably ; but it is to be regretted that so little attention was paid to the topographical details of the country in their construction, partly by total omission, partly by false representation. The points intersected by the network of measured lines, dividing the surface in squares of a mile in extent, are usually correctly located, but the course of creeks and rivers through the interior of such squares, and the hills inside of the circumscribed lines, were merely located by guess-work, which led to considerable errors. Under these circumstances I was compelled to supply the topographical deficiencies of the maps, and to correct their errors, which is a very slow, time-robbing work, requiring an often repeated crossing of every square mile, noting the distances by counting the steps taken in a certain compass direction, in order to locate the drainage channels and surface elevations in the interior of the sections in their proper positions, which is an important requisite of a geological map, as the nature of the rock-formations composing a spot generally determines the form of the contour lines of its surface, by which the geologist may often be enabled to foretell from a distance what rock-formation he likely will find by visiting the spot to be examined.

While performing this topographical work I came across a number of instructive outcrops, which otherwise might have escaped my observation ; and in so far I feel fully compensated for the retardation of the geological work by the topographical. Doing the work in this slow way, I became satisfied that my adopted plan was, after all, the most expedient way to become acquainted with the structure of the country, and to decipher the much-obscured records of the history of this part of the globe, written on the rocky leaves of nature's book. Those familiar with the labors of exploration will not be surprised if I tell them that, straining all my energies, I could not accomplish more in a summer season than to make the examination of about sixty square miles. I selected the environs of Marquette as a starting-point for my explorations, taking in a strip of land about ten miles in width from north to south, and extending the examination of this belt as far westward as to include Lake Michigamee.

Within the indicated space nearly all the older part of the Lake Superior rock-formations is represented ; it includes the majority of all the iron mines worked in the district, and the numerous artificial openings made by the miner greatly facilitate the labors of examination. Another advantage is the location of the H. & O. Railroad along the centre of the examined strip. The manager of the road, Mr. Sam. Schoch, most liberally offered the State Geologist, during his engagement, free travel over it, and I am happy to have here an occasion to express publicly my cordial thanks for these favors tendered to me as an official of the State.

MARQUETTE IRON REGION.

GENERAL TOPOGRAPHY.

DURING the past three summer seasons I have extended my investigations over about 200 square miles, embracing the environs of Marquette, Negaunee, and Ishpeming, or, more accurately indicated, six townships—namely, Town 48, range west 25, 26, 27, and Town 47, range west 25, 26, 27—were carefully examined by me, and a special topographical and geological map constructed of this district, on a scale of two inches to a mile. Besides, I have examined all the important mining locations, not inclosed within the named six townships, as the Washington, Champion, Republic, Spurr, and Michigamee mines.

The surface of this area is extremely broken and hilly. It rises by degrees from the level of Lake Superior to an elevation of about 800 or 900 feet, but reaches in some summit points a height of 1000 or 1100 feet. The outlines of the hills are generally rounded, notwithstanding their frequent composition of greatly disturbed, often vertically erected rock-beds, which is caused by the powerful abrasion of all the sharply projecting inequalities of the surface during the drift period, in evidence of which we find everywhere on the exposed rock-faces the marks of drift scratches, all corners rounded, and the surface smoothed, or even polished almost as bright as a mirror, particularly if the rock masses are very hard and compact, like quartzites. In addition to this grinding down of the prominences, a great proportion of the then existing unevenness of the surface became levelled out by the débris left on the spot, often to such an extent as barely to leave the summits of the rock-ridges unincumbered, and large spaces are by accumulated drift-masses completely covered, and represent extensive plateau lands.

A disposition of the surface elevations in parallel ranges trending from east to west is plainly obvious, and is in causal connection with the upheavals of the rock-beds in this principal axal
direction of the disturbing forces ; still these mountain ridges are
rarely continuous for any great length, but usually are found cut
up into more or less isolated rounded knobs, clustered together in
rows of the indicated direction.   The ridges never reach an
elevation of more than 200 feet above the surrounding general surface ; usually they are lower, from 50 to 100 feet in
height, and frequently we find low rounded rock-knobs not over
10 feet high, scattered over drift-covered plains.   The shore
near Marquette is partly bordered by rock cliffs 20 or 30 feet
high, which, some distance back, gradually rise into rock-spurs
150 or 200 feet above the water-level ; but the largest portion of the shore is formed by drift bluffs forming distinct
terraces, of which the lower one is about 25 or 30 feet above the
water-mark ; a higher one is found on an elevation of 80 or 85
feet.   North of Marquette harbor, between the Lighthouse Point
and Presque Isle, low sand plains and partly marsh lands surrounding the outlet of Dead River form the shore belt ; a half mile
or more further inland the drift terraces rise, or the rocks come to
the surface, first in isolated smaller knobs, then in larger connected
mountain masses.   The terraces near the lake shore are not the
only ones in existence ; the drift plateaus on higher levels more
remote from the shore are clearly rising in terrace form one above
the other, and the well-stratified alternating beds of sand, gravel,
and clay composing them evince the former stand of the water
to have been 800 and 900 feet above the present level of Lake
Superior.

I recall the attention of the reader to a statement made by me
in the last Report on the Lower Peninsula, where I mentioned the
deposition of well-stratified sand and gravel beds at an elevation
of 1100 feet above the level of Lake Huron.

The undulating summit part of the highlands west of Marquette
locally expands into marshy plains, from which numerous creeks
take their source, or the surface declines more rapidly into kettle-
shaped depressions, filled by splendid bodies of crystal clear water.
More than thirty lakes, from the size of a few acres to over a
square mile in extent, can be counted on the examined district.

Sometimes three or four of them are found in close proximity, one from 5 to 30 feet above the next one, and all connected by creek channels, or more abruptly by rapids and cascades.

The numerous creeks and outlets of the various lakes collect in three principal drainage channels—in the Dead River, the Carp River, and in the Escanaba River. The first two have an eastern and quite tortuous course, flowing sometimes sluggishly through meadow lands; but for the most part they make a rapid descent, and each of them has several beautiful cascades to leap before it reaches Lake Superior. Dead River enters it two miles north of Marquette; Carp River two miles south of the town; Escanaba River flows southward into Lake Michigan. The head branches of the three rivers approach each other very closely, and two of such opposite streams frequently are fed by the same marsh lands.

The district was once heavily timbered, partly by hard wood, partly by pine; the marshy portions are occupied by almost impenetrable cedar thickets; not so often by tamarack, by alder-bushes, or other lacustrine trees and shrubbery. Since the settlement of the country the forests have been pretty well cleared off in the vicinity of the mines and furnaces; large parcels of timber land have also accidentally suffered destruction by fires and wind storms, but very little of the cleared lands has been cultivated and tilled, as agricultural pursuits have so far not been considered equally well remunerating as the working of mines. Many of the clearings have therefore already recovered their forest nature by a vigorous new crop of seedlings of poplar, maple, and other trees of rapid growth. Other places once covered by fine forest trees growing on a thin crust of soil with a rocky underground, after being accidentally destroyed by fires and wind storms, could never recover; the little crust of soil became speedily washed off by the rains, and the naked usually drift-polished rock faces can often be noticed for miles in length on the crests of ridges still bearing here and there the blackened stump of a gigantic pine-tree, the growth of former times, whose wide-spreading roots entered every available fissure.

GENERAL REMARKS ON THE GEOLOGY OF THE DISTRICT.

With exception of the previously mentioned drift masses, which cover a large portion of the surface, and some isolated patches of Silurian sandstones resting horizontally on other rock-formations, all the remainder of the surface is formed either of crystalline masses of granite, syenite, diorite, and kindred rocks, or else by stratified sedimentary beds, many of which are found in an altered semi-crystalline condition, and all in a highly dislocated position, lifted up into all sorts of inclination, from the horizontal to the vertical, or even completely overturned ; they are frequently found shattered into fragments, which often are subsequently recemented into a breccia, or we find them curved and coiled or corrugated in a high degree, which proves them to have been in a plastic condition at the time of their upheaval. The up-heaving forces evidently acted in a certain constant direction, which coincided almost with east and west ; accordingly we observe the previously mentioned parallelism of the rock-ridges in east and west rows, and with a dip to the south or to the north. Local deviations from this rule are not uncommon, but this does not interfere with the correctness of the general observation of re-gional geology.

Examining the order of distribution of the different kinds of rock, we find the crystalline granitic masses principally confined to the northern and southern limits of the examined territory, while the stratified and metamorphic beds occupy its central portion. The dip of the strata on the south part is almost invariably di-rected to the north, and on the north side to the south, with exception of the environs of Marquette, where the stratified beds have a decidedly northern dip, which probably indicates their being in an overtilted position. According to this we may with propriety consider the examined area as a synclinal trough of granite, which by the upheaval of its northern and southern margins caused the inclosure of the incumbent sedimentary strata between its walls and their simultaneous uplift and corrugation into parallel folds by the lateral pressure exerted from its rising and approaching edges.

We find these upheaved granitic and sedimentary rock-masses intersected in irregular transversal directions by narrower rock-belts of a compact more or less crystalline structure, which evidently represent lava streams subsequently intruded from beneath, which intrusion seems to have occurred at different periods, as we observed one kind of these rock-belts intersecting the other, and both kinds to differ in chemical composition and external aspect.

SPECIAL CONSIDERATION OF THE GEOLOGICAL STRUCTURE OF THE DISTRICT.

The granitic rocks of the Marquette district are, in the Report of Major Brooks, identified with the Laurentian series of the Canadian geologists, and the incumbent sedimentary and metamorphic rocks with their Huronian series. By comparing the descriptions of the Laurentian formation, as developed in Canada, with the granitic exposures observable in Michigan, or specially in the Marquette district, I can not see so strong an analogy between them as to identify them without hesitation ; while I indorse the identification of the other group of rocks with the Huronian, although they differ too in some degree.

The Laurentian rocks are represented as a succession of altered sedimentary rocks of crystalline but tolerably well-preserved laminated structure, principally of gneissoid, partly of granitic character, with interlaminated large belts of limestone, of quartzite, of conglomerates, stratified belts of iron-ore, graphitic layers, and of serpentine, besides a large variety of other accessory minerals dispersed through the various beds.

In the Marquette district gneissoid rocks have a very limited occurrence, while granites of a massive non-stratified character largely prevail. Limestone belts, so characteristic of the Laurentian in Canada, have never been noticed in alternation with granitic rocks in Michigan ; likewise quartzite belts and stratified layers of iron-ore are unknown in such a position, if we except the smaller irregular transverse quartz seams intersecting the granitic rocks and concretionary masses of iron-ore accumulated in fissures and pockets ; finally, of the great variety of accessory minerals abounding in the Laurentian rocks, the granites of Marquette are almost if not altogether destitute.

Great stress is also laid on the discordance existing between Laurentian and Huronian rocks ; and Major Brooks mentions a few localities where he observed a discordance between supposed Laurentian and Huronian beds, but in no instance did he see the layers in immediate contact ; and even if he did, a discordance between rock-beds which have been subject to such great disturbances, as the older rock-beds of the Marquette region, does not prove anything either way. Conformable beds may be thrown by them into a discordant position, and on the other hand a stratum originally deposited in discordance on the surface of another, may as likely by the act of disturbance be pushed into a perfectly conform position with it. As far as my own observations go, I have never been able to discover any positive proof of an existing discordance between the granites of Marquette and the adjoining Huronian beds ; on the contrary, outcrops of the two kinds of rock supposed to represent the contact of the two formations exhibit everywhere a remarkable parallelism in strike and dip, and in a good many localities, where belts of granite are found interlaminated between the Huronian schists, the conformity is perfect ; but I am far from believing that these conformably interstratified bands of granite ever had been formed there as regular members of the sedimentary series ; I consider them as intrusive masses, as I will prove in some of the subsequent pages. To shorten this discussion, I declare at once my serious doubts whether the granites of the Marquette region represent the Laurentian series of Eastern Canada, which I never had an opportunity to study in the field, but which is represented to be a much older formation, pre-existing as a surface-rock before the Huronian sediments began to form, while according to my own observations the granites of Marquette are eruptive masses which came to the surface after the Huronian beds were already formed, and by their eruption caused not only the great dislocations of the Huronian formation, but the half-molten plastic granite masses induced by their contact with the Huronian rock-beds, also their alteration into a more or less perfect crystalline condition, and commingled with them so as to make it an embarrassing task to find a line of demarcation between the intrusive and the intruded rock-masses. The syenitic and gneissoid hornblende rocks connected with the granites differ so little from the crystalline hornblende rocks of the Huronian series, that I look at them merely as differently advanced stages in the transformation of the same material : those nearest to the focus of altering influences are more completely transformed and restored to the domain of the volcanic nucleus ; the more remote strata were less changed, and retained distinct marks of their sedimentary origin ; but if this view is correct, it cannot be expected to find traces preserved of the conformable or non-conformable deposition of the Huronian layers on their substratum. In giving a description of the Huronian rock series, Major Brooks originally divided it in nineteen different groups, to which he subsequently added a twentieth. I cannot agree to accept this method for my own descriptions ; the subdivisions made are altogether too numerous, and also otherwise seriously objectionable. Beginning below with his groups from 1 to 5, he never made an attempt to define them ; we are occasionally informed, by reading the book, that such and such an outcrop represents Group 1, 2, or any of his subdivisions, and this is all. As Groups 7, 9, and 11, certain dioritic outcrops are designated, and considered to be regularly interstratified layers in the sedimentary succession, while I have full reasons to consider them as intrusive masses, belonging to a lower horizon of the Huronian series, which by volcanic pressure have been forced through or between the incumbent rock-beds, wherever a chance for it was offered, and consequently are found one time in contiguity with this, another time with another stratum, as it happened to be the surface-rock of the spot.

Groups 8, 10, 12, 13, and 14, being the ore-bearing rock-beds, are more carefully described, as the special object of Major Brooks' Report was principally the exhibition of the economically important members of the Lake Superior series of rocks.

Groups 15 to 20, intended to comprise a series of younger beds developed in the western part of the Marquette region, are unnecessarily multiplied into vaguely defined subdivisions. Subsequently Major Brooks identified strata of the Menomenee River district as representatives of Groups 15 to 20, which lithologically have no similarity with those of the Marquette district, adding still more to the confusion already existing. Describing the Huronian series, I propose to make the following subdivisions in an ascending order :

    I. Granitic group.
   II. Dioritic group.
 III. Quartzite group.
  IV. Iron group.
   V. Arenaceous Slate group.
  VI. Mica schist group.

In a seventh chapter I have described the serpentine formation, in an eighth the vulcanic dyke-masses, and in a ninth the fissure veins.

The Quartzite group should, according to my present information and views on the structure of this region, be placed as Group IV., while the Iron group as the older formation should be ranged in as Group III. ; but I have not altered the originally adopted arrangement, as in the vicinity of Marquette, which will be first described, the Iron formation is not well represented, and the quartzite rests directly on the dioritic rock-series, and as an acquaintance with the quartzite formation previous to the examination of the iron formation is a help to the proper understanding of the facts concerning the latter.

CHAPTER I.

GRANITIC GROUP.

I HAVE previously stated that the northern and southern limits
of the district are composed of granitic rocks. Granites are also
found interstratified with the Huronian schists, right within the
city limits of Marquette, and in other centrally situated localities ;
but to find the first outcrops of a larger body of granite, forming
a continuous belt trending westward, we have to go a mile or over
north of the town, to the mouth of Dead River. We find also
some islands, called Gull Islands, three quarters of a mile east of
the promontory of Presque Isle, composed of granite ;. they project only about 15 feet above the water-level, are perfectly denuded of soil and vegetation, and offer a fine opportunity to see
various modifications of the granite ; besides, we observe its intersection by numerous dykes of a distinct character. One sort of
dyke intersects the other, and is consequently of later date ;
they will be specially considered in a subsequent chapter.
Presque Isle, an isolated mountain mass comprising one half a
square mile, and of about 150 feet elevation, is, contrary to our
expectation, composed of an entirely different rock-mass, principally of magnesian composition, partly silicates, partly carbonates.
It is to all appearances an igneous outburst, greatly corrugated
and shattered, pervaded by a dense network of sparry seams, and
by asbestine bands with transverse fibres. A great proportion of
the superficial masses is in a state of rapid disintegration, friable
into a crummy sand-mass. This eruptive rock is capped with
Silurian sandstones, the lower ledges of which are a coarse conglomerate, principally made up by rounded pebbles of the underlying rock. The sandstones are not entirely horizontal, but this
is not a dislocation by upheaval, and can with propriety be at-

tributed to an often observed adaptation of sedimentary layers to the undose inequalities of the subjacent surface. A belt of marsh lands surrounds the promontory from the land side, but at no great distance all around it are small granite knobs rising above the sandy plains, and the bay north-west of it is crowded with granitic islands ; the largest of the islands is called Middle Island, or also sometimes Partridge Island ; it has an elevation of about 80 or 100 feet, and is well timbered, but all its circumference is formed by bold cliffs of granite in alternation with belts of gneissoid rocks, and pervaded by many dykes of a dioritic and partly of a doleritic character. On its south side we find also a patch of Silurian sandstones resting on the granite. West from here is a very broken, hilly country, all underlaid by granite. The Dead River winds its tortuous course for a number of miles over ledges of granite. Near its mouth the rock projects only in solitary knobs from 20 to 60 feet in height above the sand-covered lowlands ; a mile west of the shore the ground begins to rise more rapidly, particularly on the north side of the river and south of Campo Creek, which runs parallel with the lower course of Dead River. The interval between the two water-courses is occupied by a granitic mountain body of extremely rugged character ; its summit part is divided into great numbers of rounded knobs and shorter ridges forming parallel rows, with an abundance of rock exposures. The height of the ridge at its eastern termination, near the Marquette powder-mill, is 150 to 200 feet, but rapidly increases westward to an average elevation of about 400 feet. The north slope of the ridge, toward Campo Creek, is little incumbered by drift masses, and offers one of the best opportunities to study the granite of this region, together with its interstratified dioritic belts and the numerous dykes intersecting it transversally. Toward the south the slope is less abrupt ; the rocky summits seen from this direction repose on a broad rolling drift plateau, which terminates toward the Dead River with steep bluffs.

On the north side of Campo Creek a part of the valley is lined with vertical bluffs of granite, but down toward the lake the valley has a rounded drift-covered slope, which on its height expands into a spacious rolling plateau which extends to the lake shore ; but its edge all along the shore northward is lined with granitic rock-bluffs. A mile north of Campo Creek this plateau is crowned with several high peaks of granite. Sugar Loaf Mountain, the largest of these peaks, is not far from the shore, and touches it with its rapidly descending eastern slope.

A mile west of the Sugar Loaf is an equally high granite mountain, called Mount Crispy, on which the Lake Survey has erected one of their stations. It is separated by a deep depression from the Sugar Loaf, which toward the south forms the valley of a tributary of Campo Creek, northward it declines into the valley of another creek flowing through a good-sized lake, before it enters Lake Superior, in the bay on the west side of Granite Point, an isolated knob of granite in a soft disintegrating condition, situated at the end of a narrow land-tongue covered with sand and underlaid by Silurian sand-rock, which latter forms the greatest part of the shore line as far south as the foot of Sugar Loaf Mountain, where granitic cliffs begin.

I observe this large granitic body to be much less intersected by dioritic rock-belts, than I found it in the granitic range between Campo Creek and Dead River, where several subordinate dioritic ridges of considerable extent are wedged in between the crests of granite.

On the south side of Dead River the granites are, for several miles westward from the mouth, not often seen at the surface ; the valley, after leaving the marsh-land with its few low knobs of granite, is generally formed of slowly ascending, rounded, drift-covered hill-slopes, although the river bed is nearly all the while formed of granite ledges in connection with schistose belts of chloritic or dioritic character, which in the more northern exposures are not seen associated with the granite. Farther up stream, near Collinsville and the Bancroft furnace locations, the valley becomes narrower and the drift hills increase in height, frequently allowing the granite to come to the surface on their slopes, and crowned with insular granitic prominences of more circumscribed or of a larger extent. The granite outcrops south of Bancroft's furnace alternate with belts of peculiar hornblendic or dioritic rocks, parallel with the trend of the formation, and are transversely intersected by quite numerous seams of dioritic and of doleritic nature. A conspicuous landmark is formed by a cluster of granite knobs at the section corners between 7, 8, 17, and 18, of T. 48, R. 25. The surrounding country is all a drift-covered, undulating plateau, which westward falls off in abrupt bluffs toward the Dead River valley above the former location of Stone's mill.

The river flows here in curious curvatures through a broad swamp valley, passing repeatedly almost the same spots. At the mill site it breaks through a granitic barrier and through chloritic schists and diorites, conformably interlaminated with the granite belts, and falls in numerous rapids and stair-like offsets within half a mile more than 100 feet, escaping the Narrows at Bancroft's furnace, near its union with a large creek, flowing likewise over granite ledges in hurried descent from a western direction. Entering the valley of this creek, we see it on the north side bordered by high steep drift-hills, which form on top an extensive plateau, spreading in a width of over half a mile in a north-westerly direction beyond the limits of the examined district. The nucleus of these highlands is granite, which occasionally shows itself along the margins of the plains in bluffs. The south side of the valley is superficially formed by drift, and the underlying granite is only seen in the ravines.

At the first bifurcation of the creek the granite divides into a northern and southern belt, and between these, chloritic schists and dioritic rocks occupy an area of from two to three miles in width, which extends for many miles westward; but in the western portion of this belt, which is of a very broken hilly character, a large proportion of the dioritic rocks and schists is overlaid by slaty and arenaceous beds of a younger period of the Huronian area. The northern borders of the schistose belt approximately coincide with the north line of the Town. 48, R. 26. The southern belt of granite follows the course of Dead River on its north side, and is seen in a last outcrop in the S.E. quarter of the S.W. quarter of Sect. 10, Town. 48, R. 26. On the south side of the river the granite exposures extend much farther westward to the west end of the township, and beyond following the south line of Sects. 15, 16, 17, and 18 in a quite prominent knobby ridge; it makes its last appearance near the centre of Sect. 13 in the next township, R. 27; further on, diorites and schists continue the hill-range, and soon also these begin to disappear beneath younger Huronian rock-beds, which almost exclusively cover the north half of Town. 48, R. 27, with exception of the north-east corner, where near the location of the Holyoke mine the older schistose and dioritic rocks occupy the ground. A more isolated body of granite, which, however, evidently forms a continuation of the before-mentioned granite range following the north side of Dead River, projects at the edge of a large drift-covered high plateau in large vertical walls following the south line of Sect. 6, Town. 48, R. 26. Associated with the granites of this locality are chloritic schists and diorites. On the northern edge of this plateau the interlamination of granite seams between the schists is seen in several exposures. Belts of granitic nature are also found interstratified with the dioritic schistose group in the south part of Sects. 1 and 2, Town. 48, R. 26. This rock is generally very compact, fine-grained, and consists principally of feldspar, with small proportions of quartz ; locally the rocks become porphyritic by the secretion of large but indistinctly defined feldspar crystals within the granular, almost aphanitic, ground-mass ; likewise is their transition to gneissoid structure frequently observed by the segregation of delicate micaceous or chloritic laminar streaks in the mass. Besides these granitic belts the schists inclose also large belts of a coarse conglomerate rock in the last-mentioned locality, consisting almost exclusively of bright red granite pebbles of all sizes, with exquisitely well crystallized grain, quite different from the associated granite seams, and of fragments of chloritic schist ; all cemented together by the same chloritic schistose material as the inclosed fragments, but usually an amorphous flinty coating intervenes between the pebbles and their schistose cement.

Turning our attention to the granites which form the south margin of the synclinal basin of the Marquette district, we notice a striking difference in their relations to the surface of the country. While the northern granite outcrops occupy, always or nearly so, the highest elevations, and constitute the most conspicuous ridges, we find the granites on the south rim of the basin always occupying a lower level than the younger Huronian rocks. The granites form the floor of the immense pine plains expanding on the east side of the Escanaba River, and low rounded bubble-like prominences scattered over the sand-covered level are the only places where the rock is found exposed ; north of the plains we see the quartzite hills of the Goose Lake district rise abruptly to the height of 300 feet above them. On the west side of the Escanaba River, along its west branch, the granitic area is considerably more mountainous, broken up into innumerable knobs with sharper contours, presenting precipitous rock-walls ; the summits of these are on a level 200 feet lower than the row of steep hills adjoining them on their north side, and composed of the younger Huronian rock-beds. This granite belt disappears farther south beneath the Silurian deposits, but in a number of localities the iron-bearing Huronian beds also have been discovered to overlie it in the south. The Smith mine is opened in one of these deposits, and several other promising localities have been more recently discovered in this southern granite district.

The topographical limits of this southern granite belt toward the synclinal basin may be described as follows : Granitic seams are noticeable within the dioritic schists exposed on the shore of Lake Superior, near Harvey's furnace, but the first good outcrops can be observed near the quarter-post on the west line of Sect. 1, Town. 47, R. 25. From here it passes through the south part of Sects. 2 and 3, thence, curving southward, intersects Sects. 10, 9, 8, 17, and 18, of the same township, crosses diagonally Sect. 24 of the next western township, follows the north line of Sect. 26, and thence continues in almost due west direction through the Sects. 34, 33, and 32, from here, curving more northward into Sect. 30, it enters the south part of Sect. 25 of Town. 47, R. 27, and trends in straight western direction across the whole township, and is found to occupy again almost the entire Sect. 25 of Town. 47, R. 28. Farther west my explorations did not extend in this southern part of the district. Isolated protrusions of granitic rock-masses are in various places found north of the described rim ; one of these can be observed in the S.W. quarter of the S.E. quarter of Sect. 19, Town. 47, R. 27, overlaid by the iron-bearing beds of the Saginaw mine.

The two granite belts on the north and south side of the synclinal basin differ very little in structural composition ; but in different localities the lithological character of the rocks changes considerably by differences in grain, colors, and relative proportions of the component minerals in the granitic and hornblendic rock species.

The granites of the Marquette district are usually middling coarse-grained, of reddish tints, oftener composed of a magma of incompletely defined crystals imbedded within a granular interstitial mass, than of well-formed completely defined crystals ; its fracture is therefore rather generally of a dull lustre. Red orthoclas, of a milky appearance, in lighter or darker shades of color, is the prevailing constituent, and large bodies of granite are composed of orthoclas mingled with variable proportions of glassy quartz-grains, without mica or any other mineral substituting its place. The micaceous constituent of these granites, where it does enter into the composition, is rarely well crystallized in brightly shining larger leaves, although it occurs occasionally, but usually has a minutely scaly form and a dark green color approaching to chlorite by gradations, or is replaced by hydromicaceous fibroso-granular substance, generally called talcose, from its soft, greasy feel and its lighter color, with partial transparency in thin seams. This latter mineral imparts to the granite an irregular sub-schistose cleavage, causing it to disintegrate more readily than other kinds into wedge-like shelly fragments. Such granites are seen in outcrops near the Marquette powder-mills, associated with schists of chloritic nature ; but they occur almost regularly on the south side of the synclinal basin on the line of contact between the normal granites and the lower quartzite formation, and seem to be the product of metamorphosis of the quartzite, as we find all degrees of transition, from the ordinary quartzite into a regular granitic rock-mass. The least altered beds of the quartzite, are seen pervaded by pale yellowish green streaky seams of hydro-mica, whose proportion of intermixture increases with the progress of alteration. At a more advanced state we find flesh-red feldspar crystals sparingly segregated within the mass, which finally so increase in number as to give the rock the character of a granite or protogine. Examples of such a transition can be observed near the quarter-post on the east line of Sect. 2, Town. 47, R. 25, where a natural section through a quartzite knob exposes the bubble-shaped arched elevation of the ledges, in the centre of which the granite just shows itself at the base in the described modifications of metamorphism, and at a short distance from the place ordinary granites appear in the outcrops. Similar granite-like altered quartzites, beautifully red and white speckled, form large perpendicular bluffs in the south half of the N.E. quarter of Sect. 30, Town. 47, R. 26. Another good exposure of such metamorphosed rocks can be observed on the north side of the lake in Sect. 9, Town. 47, R. 25. Some of the granites have a laminated gneissoid appearance, from the distribution of the micaceous or chloritic constituents of the mass in parallel linear interrupted streaks, but it is doubtful whether this is an indication of a former sedimentary lamination. I have in several instances seen narrow intrusive granitic dyke-masses similarly laminated by the parallel arrangement of the mica scales in them.

Nearly all the granites I observed were mingled with more or less iron pyrites, in dispersed small cubical crystals ; also epidote not rarely occurs intimately mingled with the granitic crystal magma, but more frequently it is found to fill the smaller fissures in the rock as a solid cement mass. Other minerals are altogether uncommon, if ever found as accessories of the granite. On the Huron Islands, 60 miles north of Marquette, the granites, apparently identical with those around Marquette, contain occasionally delicate thin leaf-like sheets of metallic copper seemingly embodied with the mass, but on close inspection they are found to cover the surface of hair-fine fissures in the rock, which suggests to me a secondary deposition of the copper into the fissures by galvanic action. Almost constantly associated with granitic outcrops, we find large belts of gneissoid, well-laminated rocks, consisting of a brightly shining blackish or dark green hornblende in flattened scaly crystals in laminated alternation with similar linear seams of granular feldspar and quartz intermingled ; not rarely also black mica enters into the composition of the rock, or it takes altogether the place of the hornblende and constitutes a genuine gneiss.

The rock is usually compact, not very fissile in the direction of the laminar striation ; if the hornblende in its composition preponderates over the quartz and feldspar, which is often the case, it has a uniformly greenish black or bluish black color, with bright lustre of the crystal facets. More feldspar in the composition gives the rock a delicately white and black striped appearance, which becomes particularly obvious on weather-worn surfaces of cross-sections.

This stratified banded rock, in contiguity with the granite and alternating with it in parallel belts, often becomes completely intermingled and entangled with it. The granitic masses intersect the gneissoid, enter wedge-like between them in the direction of the lamination or transversally, inclosing strips of the gneissoid ledges between the loops of the anastomosing granite seams, and moreover, frequently the so-intermingled masses are curved into the most curious coils and serpentine flexions, which evinces their almost liquefied plastic condition at the time their intermixture took place. A splendid exhibition of these rocks, intermingled in this most singular mode, whose gayety of colors is yet augmented by additional seams of light green epidote, can be seen on the large denuded rock-walls forming the north-west shore of Middle Island, a sight not only interesting for the geologist, but attractive for every one who happens to pass by. Other similar exposures can be seen in the centre of S.W. quarter of Sect. 6, Town. 48, R. 25, but the denudation is not near so complete as in the first-mentioned locality. The southern granite belt is associated with similar gneissoid hornblende rocks as the northern, but frequently we see here the hornblende partially or completely replaced by black mica, which micaceous nature of the rock is in the northern belt less common. South of the Republic mines, gneissoid rocks have a large display, but I have only superficially passed over that district.

In association with the granites, a second form of hornblende rocks is observed, which, unlike the former well-stratified beds, forms crystalline non-stratified masses resembling eruptive dykes. These rocks never cover areas of as large an extent as the gneissoid rocks, but are more sporadically interspersed narrower belts, although some of them are seen in outcrops of considerable bulk. Picnic Islands, a group of low, naked rock protrusions in the bay, half a mile north of Marquette Lighthouse Point, are composed of this kind of rock. Another large dyke of it, 70 feet wide, intersects the granite of Middle Island, and is well exposed on the north-west shore in close proximity to the above-mentioned rock-walls, exhibiting the contorted intermixture of the granite with the gneissoid rock-belt. Seams of granite run across the hornblendic rock, and again the hornblende rock cuts through the granite masses, so that one hesitates which of the two to consider as the intruded and which as the intruder. The priority in age of one over the other can at all events not be very great. The hornblende rock of the Picnic Islands incloses fragments of the Huronian schists exposed in the vicinity, and also the granite seams on the island embrace similar schistose fragments ; their eruption must, according to this, have occurred subsequent to the deposition of the schists. On Middle Island again we find a large doleritic dyke to intersect both the hornblende rock and the granite, which proves, on the other hand, the priority of the latter over the doleritic lava stream.

The rock is a mixture of rather large blackish green hornblende crystals, with variable proportions of reddish orthoclas, besides a white granular interstitial mass of anorthic feldspar, which often seems to be only present with exclusion of the orthoclas, but the hornblende always preponderates considerably over the feldspathic components ; the color of the rock is therefore usually uniformly dark green on fresh fractures, but becomes spotted with white by long exposure to atmospheric influences. By greater abundance of the feldspar, the red and whitish crystals of the feldspar are also visible on freshly fractured surfaces, and the rock is speckled throughout. Black mica is an ordinary accessory component, besides small granular crystals of iron pyrites. Epidote is also found disseminated through the mass, and occurs in great abundance as filling material of fissures in the rock, associated with calkspar, which occasionally contains nodules of copper pyrites. Some of the fissures are replenished by flesh-red feldspar.

The Picnic Islands are, besides the belts of ordinary granitic rock which traverse them, intersected by narrow dykes from three to five feet in width, which consist of a compact minutely granular feldspathic ground mass of dusky reddish gray color, and with an almost flinty fracture. Within this mass are small scales of black mica copiously segregated, and arranged in linear interrupted subparallel seams, which impart to the rock a laminated gneissoid appearance. The lamination is vertical, parallel with the walls of the dyke. We see here a fine example of gneissoid structure developed in a lava mass, and totally independent from a sedimentary arrangement of the material ; the laminated structure of the gneisses is therefore not necessarily a proof of their former sedimentary origin.

On the sandy flats of the mainland adjoining the Picnic Islands, several masses of largely crystalline hornblende rocks are found in the outcrops in intimate connection with dioritic schists ; they contain a large amount of iron pyrites, and the hornblende crystals are more fibrous, with less lustre, than the rock on the islands, and seem to be destitute of feldspar. West of these outcrops, in the S. E. quarter of Sect. 14, Town. 48, R. 25, on the height of a drift terrace, a belt of granite 75 feet wide comes to the surface, adjoined on both sides by well-stratified dioritic schists, which are partly transformed into well-crystallized coarse-grained diorites, or, at all events, the schists are interlaminated with such massive crystalline rocks, and exhibit a transitory gradation from the schistose to the crystalline condition. Many narrower granite belts are observed conformably interlaminated with the schists besides this larger one. The smaller belts are seen in places to wedge out completely, or to divide into side-branches crossing the schists transversally, clearly evincing their intrusive nature. This interlamination of granite seams between the schists can be traced westward for several miles in numerous exposures to a locality in the south-east quarter of Sect. 16, Town. 48, R. 25, where a great number of granite seams of large dimensions is found in alternation with schistose dioritic rocks, and where the true relationship between the two kinds of rock is well exhibited. To omit unnecessary repetition, I propose to describe these outcrops more explicitly in the following chapter, treating of the dioritic group, No. II.

Another class of hornblende rocks, genuine syenites, represent the granitic group in association with ordinary granites in an extensive chain of hills trending westward from the centre of Sect. 23 through the north half of Sects. 22, 21, and 20 of Town. 48, R. 26. They are very showy completely crystalline rocks, in different variations of coarseness in the grain, and of the proportions in the mixture of their constituents, which are a dark blackish hornblende and a reddish gray orthoclas, both minerals in crystals of bright lustre. Quartz is entirely excluded, but the syenites are often associated with belts of the ordinary quartz-bearing granite. Black mica is often an accessory constituent of the syenites, but never in proportions large enough to alter the general hornblendic character of the rock. Iron pyrites is, as in the granites, also in the syenites, frequently disseminated in small grains. This nicely mottled rock, in compact solid masses, would answer for masonry and ornamental monuments better than any other granitic rock in the district, as it takes a fine polish, and is

3

much more easily dressed than the granite. In some localities of this syenitic range, the rock is of a different character ; the feldspar crystals become very large, and form almost the entire mass, while in place of the hornblende, narrow interstitial seams of chloritic schistose nature form the cement for the reddish-colored feldspar ; this rock is full of cleavages and easily disintegrates. With the syenites we find rock-belts associated, which correspond with the hornblende rocks of the Picnic Islands ; they intersect the others in the form of dykes.

One of such rock-belts is well exposed along the north half of the section line between Sect. 22 and 23, Town. 48, R. 26, which differs from similar belts in the same neighborhood by a considerable increase in the proportion of the feldspathic element, and by the substitution of black mica in place of the hornblende ; besides this, the rock contains a large proportion of carbonate of lime, which, being more easily dissolved by exposure to the atmospheric influences, causes it to be very rough and cellulose on the surface in a weathered condition. The feldspar is a greenish-colored anorthic kind.

The hitherto described hornblende rocks, associated with the granites, distinguish themselves from similar rocks occupying a higher position in the series by a much brighter lustre of the hornblende crystals, which in the other mentioned rocks exhibit much less splendor and a somewhat fibrous quality.

Such rocks, of a duller aspect, genuine diorites, composed of a magma of hornblende and feldspar, are frequently found in contact with granite, forming short intermediate parallel ridges, which I consider as eruptive igneous masses ; other similar dioritic rocks, found on the boundary lines between the granitic and dioritic subdivisions of the Huronian series, are at the same time in close connection with the schistose beds of the second group, of which they may be more highly metamorphosed portions, but I hesitate to give a positive opinion on their origin. The previously mentioned dioritic ridges occurring in the granite hills south of Campo Creek, in Sect. 4, 5, and 6, of Town. 48, R. 25, I consider as representatives of the eruptive diorite ; many of the smaller transverse dyke-masses in the same hill range are identical in lithological character with the larger belts : it is a uniformly dark green rock, the greater part composed of a confused mass of hornblende crystals, imbedded in a sparingly existing granular interstitial mass of feldspar ; as accessory minerals we find in it iron pyrites and epidote, besides chlorite. In the outcrops in the N.E. quarter of Sect. 6 the rock is full of cleavage cracks, and readily breaks into sub-rhomboidal fragments ; a portion of it is also rapidly disintegrating, and falls into a crummy sand-mass, accumulating at the base of the exposed cliffs as a talus.

Another different kind of eruptive diorite contains a much larger proportion of feldspar in its composition than the former ; both minerals, the dark green hornblende and the greenish white feldspar, are in sufficiently large crystals to give the rock a speckled appearance. A cluster of low knobs situated on the south side of Dead River, near the quarter-post between Sects. 10 and 11, Town. 48, R. 25, and other knobs on the north side of the river, in the S.W. quarter of S.W. quarter of Sect. 2, are formed of such diorites and connected granitic outcrops. Similar light-colored speckled diorites occur with the granite in the S.W. quarter of N.E. quarter of Sect. 17, and in the S.W. quarter of the S.W. quarter of Sect. 18 of the same town ; in the latter two localities they are also associated with schistose strata. The diorite in the knobs near the quarter-post of Sect. 10, containing a large proportion of reddish orthoclas, in addition to the greenish-white anorthic feldspar, and often also epidote. The smaller clefts in the rock-mass are filled out with brick-red orthoclas or with epidote ; larger fissure-veins, principally filled with quartz and calcspar, contain in addition micaceous iron oxide, iron and copper pyrites, epidote, orthoclas ; and as a last deposit we find, nearly regularly, the space left vacant by the other minerals filled out by chlorite. Some of these fissures exhibit their walls incrusted by botryoidal chalcedony in alternately bright red and colorless whitish banded layers.

The last described dioritic rocks, in larger bulky masses parallel with the formation, and the narrower transverse dioritic rock-belts to be described in one of the subsequent chapters, are very similar in character of the rock-mass, and have, in my opinion, the same contemporaneous origin by volcanic eruption ; they should with propriety therefore have been described together ; but as opinions differ on this topic, I gave the description of the larger rock-belts parallel with the granite, in this place, separately.

CHAPTER II.

DIORITIC GROUP.

THE previous description of the granitic group has made us acquainted with so many rocks of nearly equal composition with the diorites, that it appears almost improper to select for this second division the name dioritic group, in order to distinguish it from the first ; but as I do not intend to indicate by these subdivisions separate distinct epochs, based on a difference in the rock material, but merely wish to draw artificial lines of demarcation for the convenience of description, the name may be applied in this sense, and is justifiable by the great prevalence of dioritic rocks in the so-named subdivision.

The granites, considered in their present surface position, are, in relation to the stratified sedimentary rocks of the Huronian series, actually the younger rock, so far as the intrusion of very large masses of granite between the stratified sediments can be demonstrated by clearly observable facts, and as the other larger bodies of granite inclosing them from two sides are in direct continuity with the vein granites, and lithologically identical with them. The hypothesis of their contemporaneous eruption is therefore well admissible. But supposing this to have been the case, one may ask, Of what nature, then, was the substratum on which the Huronian sediments were deposited ? I answer, Nothing contradicts the possibility of their deposition on a surface of granite already formed ; it is even probable to me that it has been so ; but if we reflect upon the high degree of plasticity and the almost perfect liquefaction which the concerned rocks subsequently underwent, and upon the dislocating forces, causing the softened and, necessarily by this softening process, considerably altered masses to intermingle almost chaotically, we can no more wonder that the traces of the originally existing former relative position of the rocks among themselves are greatly obliterated. The records of these periods in the history of the earth's crust, when oceanic sediments commenced to form and fell back again within the grasp of the central fire-focus, as we can observe it in this case, are wiped out, and most likely all our efforts to ascertain the existing original conformity or discordance between such rocks will be in vain.

From such a standpoint, the various crystalline hornblende rocks found in association with the granites could be considered as remelted, completely metamorphosed, Huronian sediments, on account of their nearest proximity to the volcanic focus ; while those more remote from it did not altogether lose their sedimentary structure, but still became altered, and frequently streams of the lower melted or emolliated plastic masses broke through them, filling transverse ruptures or entering between the ledges parallel with the bedding.

The rock series comprised under the name of dioritic group is made up by a large succession of schistose beds of a very uniform character, which are interstratified with massive belts of diorite differing in structure from the minutely granular, almost aphanitic condition, to a coarsely crystalline form, and being in chemical composition almost identical with the schistose beds.

The name schists, intended for thinly laminated rocks with an imperfect slaty cleavage, is here used in a wider sense, as many of the concerned rock-beds, although laminated, have very little of a slate-like fissibility. Some of the schists have their cleavage parallel with the lines of stratification, but in the great majority of schists and genuine slate-rocks, their cleavage is in discordance with the original bedding plains, and is the result of an immense pressure acting obliquely on the sedimentary layers, and causing a sliding dislocation of the molecules composing them.

The color of nearly all the rocks composing the dioritic group is dark grayish or blackish green, imparted to them by protoxide of iron, partly, perhaps, intermingled as a mere pigment, but principally as a constituent of hornblende, chlorite and mica, which three minerals, with the addition of feldspar and quartz, are the main constituents of all the rocks of this group. Chlorite frequently replaces the hornblende, and often seems to be a product of decomposition of the first ; or, in other instances, a green earthy substance results from it, called viridite. A part of the schists belonging to this group, of a minutely scaly structure with a lubricous fatty feel, often called talcose, are not of magnesian composition, and consist to a great extent of an aluminous silicate, named hydro-mica.

The dioritic rock-belts are usually imbedded conformably with the schists, and not rarely an insensible gradation from the schistose condition to the massive dioritic can be observed. In the exposures the massive body of diorite generally forms a nucleus around which, eccentrically, the inclosing rock-masses assume more and more a perfect schistose structure, without an important change in the material, as by close examination with a magnifying-glass the schists are found to be composed of an aggregation of hornblende and feldspar crystals, imbedded within a chloritic or hydro-micaceous or a minutely granular feldspathic ground mass. Other generally narrower diorite belts intersect the schists transversally, which differ little in composition from the conformably interstratified masses, and may, as I previously intimated, represent the lowest, more completely liquefied portions of the rocks in progress of alteration, which were forced through ruptures in the beds to the surface.

The north belt of the granitic synclinal is, on its south side, found in parallel juxtaposition with the schistose dioritic formation, but exposures sufficiently extensive to allow a detailed study of the rocks in their contiguity have not occurred to me. We see the lower part of the bed of Dead River often carved through dioritic schists in contact with granite masses ; but the denudations are too restricted, partly by being under water, partly by drift deposits which cover the rock in the embankments ; but we can so far notice a conformable parallel trend of the formations and the vertical position of the schists adjoining the granite, besides the interposition of narrow granite belts between the schists. An exposure of this kind is seen near the Collinsville furnace ; at the same spot a doleritic dyke crosses the river and intersects all those beds. South of Collinsville a drift-covered hill land rises, which in its ravines has some granitic outcrops. Farther east, at the powder-mill, looking southward, large sandy plains over a mile wide extend before us ; past them, we see drift-covered terraces forming the foot of an east and west range, commencing at the Lighthouse Point, slowly rising in height to an elevation of about 200 feet, its broad summit dotted with knobby rock-protrusions, consisting of a large succession of well-stratified schists of dioritic or chloritic character, with interspersed massive diorite belts and granite belts, intersected by numerous transverse dykes of various nature. The schists dip under a high angle northward, while in the synclinal arrangement of the strata a southern dip should be expected. The above-mentioned ridge, after its extension for two miles west of the Lighthouse Point, is interrupted by the valley of a creek flowing there in almost a direct northern course along the section line between Sects. 16 and 15, and entering Dead River half a mile south-west of the powdermills. The valley of this creek presents one of the most interesting cross-sections through the schists of the lower Huronian series. Ascending the valley from its lower end, where the creek flows through drift embankments, we meet, about 400 steps south of the northern section-corners of 15 and 16, with several small knobs of granite almost denuded of soil and washed at the base by the creek. Several narrow belts of a gneissoid rock are seen to intersect the granite in dyke form, they are composed of very bright, somewhat scaly hornblende crystals of a blackish color in intermixture with red orthoclas in laminar, interrupted, streaky seams. The intersection of the granite by an identical gneissoid rock-belt, and the intersection of both by a later dioritic eruptive rock-seam is also seen well exposed on the north side of Dead River, opposite the furnace buildings at Bancroft's. A short distance farther up the creek from the granite knobs, which interval is covered again by drift, the dark green colored, well-laminated dioritic, and to a certain extent chloritic schists, begin to form the embankments in high bluffs, presenting a cross-section through the almost vertically erected beds with a northern dip. While farther ascending the creek, we pass for the distance of half a mile through an uninterrupted succession of such schists, all dipping in the same northern direction. This natural section, representing a succession of rock-beds not less than 3000 feet in the aggregate thickness, may possibly not be the real thickness of the schistose beds, and by plication a repetition of the series may have occurred, but no indication of a folding of the rock-beds is observable. The parallelism and uniformity in the dip of the strata does, however, not preclude the existence of folds causing a repetition of the beds, as continued lateral pressure on a fold of the strata will finally bring the layers of both sides into a parallel contiguous position, while the connecting salient arches of the folds are destroyed by abrasion, and the entering arches are buried in unknown depths and not seen. We could without any difficulty recognize the existence of such folds if the lithological character of different horizons in the series would obviously differ, and a repetition of certain marked beds in an opposite order could be observed ; but we find, from one end of the section to the other, a remarkable uniformity in color, structure, and chemical composition of the rocks.

The great bulk of the series is a dark grayish or blackish green, rather hard rock, of delicately laminated schistose structure, but rarely very fissile in this lower geological horizon, or segregated in flaggy layers with even surfaces, and frequently intersected by cleavage seams, causing them to break into rhomboidal fragments. The substance of the schists is a minutely granular mass of feldspar composition, in intimate intermixture with minute crystals of hornblende or partially with chloritic scales, with mica or also with hydro-mica ; the distribution of these minerals in the ground mass is laminar, which gives the slabs the delicately lineated appearance on cross-fractures. A gradual, almost imperceptible transition from the schists into massive diorite belts is particularly observable in this lower horizon ; the higher schistose strata are often more of an aphanitic texture, and chlorite frequently takes the place of hornblende. Imbedded between the dioritic schists of this section, particularly in the southern portion of it, are very even-bedded light-colored flags cleaving into rhomboidal pieces, which consist of a compact granular feldspathic mass, semi-transparent in their splinters, intimately intermingled with fine scales of white mica and with fibroso-granular linear seams of hydro-mica, particularly well noticeable on the surface of the flags. Within this mass larger crystals of feldspar and of quartz are often segregated, which makes them resemble the porphyritic dyke granites which in the same localities are found interposed between the schists, but the described beds seem to be real members of the sedimentary series. They are observable in the outcrops all along the range, from the creek to the Lighthouse Point, at which place the light-colored, hard, even-bedded flags, with rhomboidal cleavage, are particularly well exposed on the north side of the lighthouse building. Proceeding in the valley of the examined creek farther southward, we see the dioritic schists exposed in continued succession without an obvious change in their character, but soon we find on the west side, a short distance from the creek bed, high rock-bluffs rising, which are formed of granite, alternating with the dioritic schists in frequent repetition of broader or narrower belts conformable to the schists as they usually appear ; but on closer examination these regularly interstratified granite belts may at once be seen to change direction and to divide into side-branches, cutting transversally through the adjoining schists, which positively proves their intrusive nature. The narrower branch seams of the granite belts are usually imperfectly crystallized porphyritic, while the larger bodies are completely crystalline, composed principally of feldspar and quartz, with scantily interspersed chlorite in place of mica. The parts of the schist in immediate contact with the granite have sometimes suffered no visible alteration, but in other instances, for the distance of a few lines, the substance is somewhat altered, generally by change in color. This same locality, with its numerous granitic seams, exhibits also very beautifully the gradations of the schists from a well-laminated aphanitic mass into a massive crystalline dioritic, and the intersection of schists, diorites, and granites by other transverse dioritic rock-seams, which differ in appearance and composition very little from the conformably interstratified seams of diorite ; but all of these rocks again are cut through by doleritic dykes, well distinguishable from the dioritic dykes by their dark blackish color.

South of these granite exposures, after having passed over some of the ordinary schistose beds, we meet in the succession with a belt of a banded, well-laminated quartz schist, inclosing within its mass an abundance of minute granules of magnetite, which, in certain of the narrow alternating seams of the banded ledges, amounts to fifty or sixty per cent of the rock-mass.

A number of test-pits, uncovering this rock-belt in this spot, and in others on the opposite side of the creek, were not rewarded with success in finding a commercially valuable deposit of iron-ore ; the strata exposed in the pits are frequently found in a much corrugated and distorted condition. The same ferruginous beds we find exposed in the rock-bluffs on the north side of Michigan Street, within the city limits of Marquette ; they are contaminated there by a large proportion of iron pyrites, mingled with the magnetite On the north side of the ferruginous beds, dioritic schists adjoin, which merge with a bulky rock-mass of crystalline diorite, forming the north end of the bluffs. Two or three hundred steps west of this locality, we find, on Michigan Street, at its intersection by Front Street, between the dioritic schists, lenticular seams of calcspar and of sparry carbonate of iron ; the ironspar is partly decomposed into a dark reddish brown friable ochraceous mass. The schists at this spot are very even-bedded and hard, cleaving into sharp-edged rhomboidal fragments, which answer a good purpose in construction of road-beds, and are quarried there for use in the streets of the city. East of the bluffs, exposing the ferruginous and pyritous ledges, in the prolongation of Michigan Street, a low knob projects over the plateau land, consisting of interwoven crystalline blades of hornblende with a micaceous fissibility, and of a moderate proportion of red orthoclas crystals, besides an abundance of interspersed pyrites granules ; the rock seems to be an analogon of the Picnic Island rock, and intrusive of the surrounding schists.

The so far described rock-series, characterized by its hornblendic composition, and therefore all of a dark green color, commences to change if we follow the succession of layers farther to the south. Lighter colors begin to prevail, and the schists become more fissile, slate-like, approaching clay slate in aspect, or else resembling novaculite. Some of the layers are intensely tinged with red oxide of iron, and irregular belts of hematitic iron-ore are interstratified with them. Such an ore-belt was one of the first discovered iron mines in the district—the Harlow mine, also called Eureka mine, situated on the north side of the Houghton and Ontonagon Railroad, only two miles west of Marquette ; the mine is abandoned since the discovery of the much richer ore deposits farther west. Leaving the dioritic schist quarries on Michigan Street, and going south toward the slope of the hill above the Grace furnace, we pass on the way several quarries or pits in which lighter-colored softer schists of argillitic character are exposed, similar clay slate-beds compose the bluffs above the furnace, varying in color from green to whitish, and from brown to red ; some of them have a bright silky lustre from micaceous or hydro-micaceous scales, copiously mingled with the mass ; at other times the micaceous component forms a coating over the cleavage plains like a varnish. Alternating with these beds are seams of cellulose, sometimes cherty and ferruginous quartz ; they continue down to the lake shore, but are not well uncovered there. West of the described locality we find in Ridge Street, where it passes over a steep hill, exposures of similar argillitic schists near the south slope of the hill, and north of these a large belt of novaculite schists more than one hundred feet in width ; then, after short interruption of the outcrops by sand-masses, farther north the dioritic schists follow, all dipping regularly northward. The novaculite belt is at this spot divided into two reuniting arms by a large body of an eruptive diorite of coarsely crystalline structure. The drift-polished, denuded surface of the novaculite exhibits everywhere a much corrugated and distorted condition of the ledges. The novaculite of these and numerous other exposures farther west on the range is a wax-like, yellow, fatty-feeling rock, thinly laminated, and often readily fissile into the thinnest semi-transparent leaves, which have a resinous lustre and a certain degree of flexibility ; it consists of an amorphous or minutely granular feldspathic mass, intimately amalgamated with a soft talcy mineral, which I identify with hydro-mica. Other good exposures of the novaculite are observable on the hills occupying the N. half of the N. E. quarter of Sect. 22, joined on the north side by dioritic schists, on the south side by clay slates. We find them again in the low meadow grounds in front of the knobs of dioritic schists, near the S. E. corner of Sect. 16 ; from here continued exposures can be traced passing the south end of the previously described granite hills, south of the magnetic quartz schists. Farther west, a high ridge, composed of almost vertically erected ledges, projecting in steep bluffs, occupies the central part of the S. W. quarter of Sect. 16, and extends some distance beyond into Sect. 17. These ledges are a continuation of the schistose novaculitic rock-belt, which here, being richer in hydro-mica, has a bright silky lustre, and is often minutely corrugated ; the schists are interstratified with quartzose seams and with ferruginous beds, which in part have the quality of a good hematite ore ; but in the numerous test-pits opened on this range no quantities of the ore could be found to remunerate mining operations. The south slope of this ridge is formed by slaty argillites in various modifications ; on its northern slope dioritic schists become exposed. Near the foot of the south slope a row of low but very cliffy knobs borders it, which consist of a blackish, coarsely crystalline rock, closely related to the doleritic dyke-masses found in other neighboring places ; but while in these a white glassy anorthic feldspar, in combination with blackish brown augite, composes the rock, we find in this other rock a flesh-red orthoclas prevailing over the anorthic feldspar, which is not missing in it altogether. This eruptive rock-belt extends across Sect. 16, from one end to the other, close to its south line. South of here, across the valley, we find the basal part of another high range of hills composed of argillitic, hydro-micaceous and ferruginous schists, with quartzose seams and lenticular belts of hematitic iron-ore, with sparry carbonate of iron, and sometimes also with masses of hard specular ore. The before-mentioned Eureka mines are opened in the rock-belt of this locality. The higher part of the hill-range is formed of dioritic schists and of massive diorite, but a large portion of its surface is covered by drift-deposits, which prevent an observation of the relative positions held by the different rock-beds. We find the slaty and ferruginous beds of the Eureka mine series still farther to the south in circumscribed patches in the north-west corner of Sect. 26, and farther south in the slaty knob close to the brownstone quarries we see them well exposed ; another outcrop is to be seen in the N.E. quarter of Sect. 28 ; but as a general rule all the rock-outcrops within the space of two miles south of the dioritic hill-range, which commences with the cliffs of the Lighthouse Point of Marquette, are, with exception of those mentioned, of a dioritic character, more resembling the strata next south of the granitic rim of the basin than those pointed out by me as Eureka mine series. Beyond this interval of two miles, a marked range of quartzite hills, commencing with high bluffs near the mouth of Carp River, trends westward ; the heavy compact ledges of the quartzite dip south and form with their edges a brisk escarpment toward the north, under which in various localities an outcrop of novaculitic schists can be observed, exhibiting the same dip to the south as the quartzites. In the S.E. quarter of Sect. 29, Town. 48, R. 25, we find the said novaculites conformably underlaid by greenish or bluish slaty argillites in almost vertical position ; and north of these, after short interruption of the outcrops, follow high bluffs of vertically erected ledges of dioritic schists, which inclose a belt of coarse conglomerate, principally composed of granite pebbles in intermixture with schist fragments, and recemented by the same material, and alternate with seams of crystalline massive diorite. Farther to the north the rock-beds disappear under the drift. West of this locality the quartzite range terminates abruptly, and for the distance of over four miles only diorites and dioritic schists can be noticed in the outcrops in that direction, until we strike Carp River, where, in the N.W. quarter of Sect. 33, Town. 48, R. 26, the quartzite reappears, forming a high hill-range, which follows for a while the south side of the river, and then bends more to the south-west, striking the north edge of Teal Lake. The dip of the quartzites is south ; on the north side of the ridge the projecting ledges form high perpendicular walls, beneath which novaculites, and farther down the hill-slope schistose strata, resembling the schists of the Eureka mine, become largely exposed ; some of them are copiously disseminated with granules of martite, or others intensely tinged with hematitic iron oxide ; other greenish hydro-micaceous, and partially chloritic schists, are full of lenticular masses of carbonate of lime and of iron, more or less mixed with siliceous matter ; and abundant quartz seams interrupt the uniformity in the succession of beds, which, farther north, in the embankments of the river, make gradual transition to the ordinary sort of dioritic schist, which compose the hills on the north side of the valley and present numerous exposures.

The description given thus far of a section across the dioritic rock-series of the Huronian group commencing on the north margin of the synclinal basin at the Dead River near the powder-mills, and continuing southward to the quartzite range, trending west through Sects. 35, 34, 33, and 32 of Town. 48, R. 25, has been a simple enumeration of the rock-beds succeeding each other in the indicated direction, without making an effort to reflect on the relative age of these strata. The general northern dip of the rock-series, from Dead River to Marquette Harbor, would indicate the youngest age for the rock-beds farthest north, as they lean on and above the others ; and as the oldest in the series, we had to take the novaculites and clay slates forming the southern hill-slopes near Marquette, as we see them there dipping under the dioritic schists ; but we notice, farther south, dioritic rocks exposed corresponding lithologically with those north of the novaculite belt, and these succeeded again by argillitic and ferruginous beds, like those composing the bluffs at Grace furnace ; still farther south we observe an inverted dip of the rock-beds, and see the novaculites and argillites next below the quartzite formation, which decidedly has a younger age than all the before-considered rock-beds. From these facts we must necessarily infer the existence of repeated plications of the strata exposed within this interval, and an overturned position of the northern part of the layers, as the novaculites and argillites underlying them are beyond doubt the equivalents of those seen on the south side next below the quartzite, and upon the dioritic layers, and represent the uppermost beds of the dioritic rock-group.

The drift-masses covering the largest portion of the surface of the land intermediate between Marquette and the southern quartzite chain, whose eastern terminal point bears the name Mount Mesnard, prevent the actual observation of the above suggested plications of the strata, and the recognition of a certain order in the distribution of the different rocks, which would enable one to determine the relative position which every one of the outcrops holds in the succession of beds. I shall therefore describe the rocks of this area merely with regard to their lithological characters, and the notation of their topographical location.

The rock-bluffs and small islands between the Cleveland ore-dock and the mouth of Whetstone Creek are principally composed of middling coarse-grained diorites, in which the component hornblende and feldspar crystals can be distinguished with the naked eye. The feldspar is in part red orthoclas, and epidote forms almost constantly part of the mixture, besides sparingly disseminated grains of iron pyrites, and sometimes copper pyrites. Epidote is also the filling material of small fissures in the rock, while in other cases it is red feldspar. The larger fissures are generally filled with quartz, or with a singular intermixture of fibrous quartz and epidote crystals, with addition of calcspar, which bands have

often the fibres arranged in transverse position to the walls of the
fissures.   Associated with these shapeless massive rocks are hard
schistose beds of dioritic and chloritic composition, and other
argillitic slates, with inclosed quartz seams, which slaty layers seem
to belong to the upper Eureka mine-series.   We see them well exposed in the quarries on the road to the North-Western Hotel, and
still more extensively on the south side of the diorite knob at the
mouth of Whetstone Creek, where a succession of several hundred
feet of them, in all colors, as green, red, brown, bluish, and gray,
forms the shore bluffs.   In the quarries at the North-Western
Hotel we see the massive, evidently eruptive diorites in discordant
contact with the schistose beds.   The diorite composing the
promontorial knob at the mouth of Whetstone Creek differs considerably from the other diorite masses by a very fine aphanitic
grain and a much lighter pale green color ; its substance is often
not entirely homogeneous, and exhibits, particularly on the
weather-worn, drift-polished surfaces, lines marking a considerable
corrugation and intricate distortion, as if differently shaded rock-
doughs had been incompletely mixed.

The adjoining schists have participated in this corrugation, and
both rocks are pervaded by a network of narrow seams of calcspar
and partially of quartz, which serve as a cement for the fractured,
shattered, less plastic portions of the disturbed masses.

West of this knob, on the south side of the mouth of the creek,
the ground rises rapidly in stair-like, rocky offsets, to a height of
200 feet, and spreads then into broad undulating drift-covered
highlands, which increase in elevation with their distance from the
shore.   The summits of these undulating lands are formed by
numerous rocky knobs and short ridges, partly arranged in parallel
east and west rows, partly in irregular scattered position, some of
them not more than 20 feet high, others projecting as much as
fifty feet over the general surface.   One of the largest of these
ridges commences with a conspicuous isolated diorite hill, situated
at the south-west corner of Sect. 23 ; it is severed by a narrow
ravine from the western continuation of the ridge, which follows
the line between Sect. 22 and Sect. 27.   In this and the other
neighboring ridges or knobs, the main body is formed of a fine-
grained rather light-colored greenish gray diorite in bulky non-
stratified masses, usually surrounded by schistose beds of a dioritic

character ; but the schistose exposures are, in these localities, never very extensive, being, as the more destructible, softer material, removed from the surface by erosion of the exposed parts.

In case of their exposure, a general conformability seems to exist between the schists and the inclosed diorite masses ; but often we see, as in the above-mentioned instance, the schists adjoining a diorite mass completely entangled with it, in a mode which proves a high degree of plasticity of the diorite mass at the time the intermixture took place. The fine homogeneous grain of these diorites is more apt to preserve the traces of a former plastic condition, by a streaky and cloudy lineation of their substance, particularly visible on the exposed drift-polished surfaces, than is the case with a coarsely crystalline rock ; we notice it therefore in this range more frequently than in other localities, with outcrops of coarser grained diorites. Coarse-grained diorites are, however, not missing in this range ; they are generally darker in color than the finer grained rock. A few low diorite knobs in the S.W. quarter of the N.E. quarter of Sect. 27, Town. 48, R. 25, are middling coarse-grained, similar to the rock of the quarries at the North-Western Hotel ; much coarser is the rock in the diorite bluffs of Sect. 29, near the old county road to Negaunee, and in various other localities farther west. Particularly extensive are the dioritic exposures in Sects. 19 and 30 of the town presently considered, and in the adjoining sections of Town. 48, R. 26, which together form one compact body of the dioritic rock-series, crowded with rock-ridges, and not so much incumbered by hiding drift-masses as in the more eastern sections ; therefore a splendid field for examination is offered here to the observer. Although the general character of this large series of rock-beds is very uniform, as it regards the chemical composition, still an endless number of variations in their structure is produced by the different degrees of metamorphism to which these once indubitably sedimentary rock-beds were subjected. In bulk the schistose beds prevail over the massive rocks, which generally form parallel seams wedged in between the schists, sometimes in briskly changing contrast, much oftener linked with the surrounding beds by almost imperceptible gradations in the structure. From all facts which I observed, I must infer, the principal altering agent causing the transformation of the sediments into their present form, has been heat in sufficient degree to allow selective crystalline arrangement of the sedimentary molecules in all of them, and to produce in a portion of them a partial fusion and emolliation, by which the sedimentary structure became obsolesced more or less completely. During the uplift of the superficial rock-crust, more by means of a laterally exerted pressure than by tension from below, the lower softened or even liquefied masses most naturally entered the sinuosities of the less altered beds raised into parallel folds, and consequently appear in the exposures as regularly interstratified alternating seams, while some of the completely liquefied mass occasionally found its exit to the surface through irregular transverse clefts in the covering crust contemporaneous with the general uplift, and therefore such dykes, originating from the same store of material as the larger diorite belts conformable with the formation, scarcely differ from them, except perhaps by a less perfect granular crystallization of the narrower, more quickly refrigerated transverse belts, than the slowly cooled bulky diorite masses have.

It would be tiresome for the reader, to give a lengthy description of all the different rock varieties which occurred to me in the examination of the presently considered area. I only take occasion here to make some remarks on the schists, generally called dioritic schists. Only the smaller portion of the so-named schists consist of the essentially important constituents of a diorite, of hornblende and feldspar, in a form discoverable with the naked eye ; many contain the hornblende in small microscopical crystals ; in other schists, which all consist of a feldspathic ground mass, chlorite replaces the hornblende, either partially or completely ; they are called chloritic schists, but in many of them chlorite is a very subordinate component ; but a large portion of schists belonging to this rock-series, and dark green-colored like the others, has a fibroso-micaceous, fatty-feeling mineral for one of its main constituents, which is probably hydro-mica, and not talc, for which it is frequently mistaken. They are softer and much more fissile than the true dioritic schists ; but as numerous transitory forms connecting these various kinds of schist exist, I have generally made no distinction between them, and have used the name dioritic schist for all the green-colored schistose members of the dioritic group, with exception of clay slates, or others of a different specific character.

The dioritic rock-belt of the Marquette region extends in a width of about two miles for a long distance westward, but a part of it is covered by the younger members of the Huronian series. The general rock-character remains the same. Another already-mentioned area of dioritic rocks is displayed on the north side of Dead River. The strata in this western country are not so excessively dislocated as to be overturned, like those near Marquette ; they lean on the north side, with a southern dip on the granite formation ; and off from it, rarely an intrusion of granitic seams between them is observed. In the upper horizon of the dioritic formation in this western district, the schists frequently inclose brecciated or conglomeratic seams, as a part of the pebbles is angular, another rounded. Such conglomerates are well exposed on the north slope of the hills west of Deer Lake furnace. The pebbles are sometimes crowded, but often distantly dispersed through the mass ; the majority of them consists of granular, somewhat porous feldspathic substance, which on fresh fractures contrasts little from the surrounding schistose mass, but shows itself very plain on weathered surfaces, on which the pebbles turn white or pale reddish. The previously mentioned conglomerate masses, full of granitic pebbles of large size, found within the dioritic schists in the S.E. quarter of the S.W. quarter of Sect. 29, Town. 48, R. 25, belong to the same horizon ; but the likewise previously described much larger belts of a granite conglomerate found in the south part of Sect. 2, Town. 48, R. 26, interstratified with the schists, in close proximity to true granites, are much lower in the series. Other compact but distinctly laminated schistose rocks occupying about the same horizon, exposed on the hills east of Deer Lake furnace, are porphyritic by the segregation of an abundance of white feldspar crystals within a minutely granular feldspathic ground mass, colored dark green by intermingled chlorite ; with them occur more fissile schistose layers, inclosing red and white feldspar crystals copiously intermingled, besides considerable proportions of calcspar, which makes the rock effervesce with acids, and by exposure its surface becomes full of cavities.

Near the southern margin of the synclinal basin the dioritic rock-group rarely forms the surface ; the quartzite formation and the iron-bearing rocks occupy it to the greatest extent, and come in many places in close contact with the granite, or are separated from it by only a narrow belt of schistose rocks, which, by inter-lamination of novaculite seams and of siliceous limestones in irregular wedge-like or lenticular bands, have some resemblance with the Eureka mine-beds, forming the top part of the dioritic series. In some localities, however, as in the bluffs in the south half of Sect. 25, Town. 47, R. 26, a large succession of micaceo-chloritic schists rests on the granite, while, further north, the iron-bearing rock series is found under the drift-covered surface.

Large insular bodies of diorite and of dioritic schists are found in the central part of the basin, where the iron-bearing rocks or other younger Huronian deposits form the surface. These dioritic rocks in the central part of the basin are by Major Brooks represented to be regularly interstratified belts of the iron-bearing rock series, forming part of the sedimentary succession. According to his statements, three distinct belts of such diorite occur. The first and lowest is said to be intercalated between his Groups VI. and VIII., both composed of siliceous and ferruginous schists. The diorite belt itself is called Formation VII. Another diorite belt is located as existing between Formations VIII. and X. The last is a likewise ferrugineo-siliceous group ; this diorite belt is called Formation IX. And finally, Formation XI., another imagined distinct diorite belt, is placed between Formations X. and XII., both iron-bearing rocks.

I consider this as a misapprehension, and am of the opinion that these different dioritic masses are a part of the second sub-division of Huronian rocks, which were forced through the incumbent younger rock-strata at the time the general dislocation of the rock-beds occurred. They hold no definite position to certain rock-beds of the upper series and are, just as it happened, once in contact with one kind, another time with another kind of the beds, and frequently their contact with them is not conformable. The chemical composition and external aspect of these dioritic masses is absolutely identical with the lower rock-complex, and differs on the other hand so widely from the nature of the beds with which they are found interstratified, or rather interposed, that this latter circumstance alone makes it very improbable that so sudden and abrupt a change in the material of regularly succeeding sediments ever occurred three times in repetition ; particularly as a very close relationship exists in the material of the three interposed sedimentary rock-belts, which clearly indicates a slow progressive change in the deposits from below upward, if we think, for argument's sake, the intervening diorites eliminated, and consider the three sedimentary belts in uninterrupted continuity. The parallelism frequently observed as existing between the diorites and the adjoining rock-beds of sedimentary character does not prove anything like a regular succession, as the parallel plication of the entire rock-crust of this country, caused principally by a lateral pressure, offered all the eruptive masses much greater opportunity to enter the sinuses of the folds or the seams of bedding, than to find their way to the surface by rupturing the beds transversally.

By comparison of the diorite masses projecting like islands from the iron-bearing belt which covers the surface of the Negaunee and Ishpeming mining district, with the main belt of exposures of the dioritic group, we find in the first massive, well-crystallized diorites to prevail over the schistose portions, which in the latter compose the much larger bulk of the formation ; minutely granular or aphanitic diorites are almost unknown in the mining districts, while such composed of large hornblende crystals imbedded in a granular feldspathic interstitial mass are locally quite common, generally constituting a portion of larger bodies with a finer grain. In the course of description of the iron-bearing rock-strata, and of other members in the succession of Huronian beds, there will be often occasion given for further remarks on the dioritic formation by their contiguity with it in the outcrops.

A change of material in the sediments, first perceptible in the terminal layers of the dioritic series, represented by the bluffs near Grace furnace, or by the beds of the Eureka mine, is mentioned previously. Rising in the geological horizon, we see argillitic, ferruginous, novaculitic, and quartzose beds taking the lead ; hornblende, the typical constituent of the lower series, almost disappears, and the equally important feldspar plays a more subordinate part in the composition of the sediments ; finally, quartz becomes supreme over all, and for a while it is the exclusive deposit, accumulated in heavy layers, amounting to a great thickness, a proof that great changes must have taken place in the ocean-bed. I have partially given a description of the above-mentioned transitory rock-beds from the dioritic formation to the quartzite formation ; but as the exposures of this series farther west are generally observed in connection with outcrops of the quartzite formation, I propose to make, in further considerations, all descriptive remarks concerning them jointly with the descriptions of the quartzite formation.

CHAPTER III.

QUARTZITE GROUP.

WE are already informed of the extension of a quartzite range
beginning near the shore two miles south of Marquette, with a
knob about 300 feet in height, called Mount Mesnard, and trending
westward for about four miles, where it abruptly terminates ; and
that, after an interruption of nearly five miles in distance in the
same line of strike, another range of quartzite rises, and continues
to the north shore of Teal Lake. The quartzite, after having
formed there a row of vertical bluffs, is finally lost under the level
of the water, but reappears again near the west end of the lake,
and continues to be well exposed almost without interruption westward, to the inlet of Carp River into Deer Lake, and thence bend-
ing somewhat southward, bluffs of quartzite can be followed to the
east end of Lake Cooper, (or near to the quarter-post on the south
line of Sect. 32, Town. 48, R. 27.) where the rock is seen for the
last time as a part of this range.

Approaching Mount Mesnard from Marquette, we first pass, on
the west side of the iron-smelting works and of the gas-house, the
valley of a creek, which is underlaid by horizontal beds of Silurian
sandstone, extensively quarried at this spot and shipped to Chicago
and other large cities as an excellent building-stone. Farther up
in this valley we can see the sand-rock horizontally deposited into
clefts existing between the vertically erected Huronian schists at
the time the deposits formed ; and with some care hand specimens
may be obtained, representing the two vertical schistose side-walls
and the intermediate horizontally laminated sand-rock mass, all in
one piece. South of the quarries a large body of drift-hills, very
much cut up by deep ravines, is to be surmounted ere we come to
the foot of Mount Mesnard, which up to two thirds of its height

is covered by the drift-masses, and even on its summit an abundance of scattered granite boulders and large blocks of the Silurian sand-rock show, in addition to the drift-polished surface of the quartzitic rock-ledges, that the débris of the glacier period passed freely over the summit. After ascension above the drift-covered part of the slope, the first outcrops noticeable are light-colored, rather gritty arenaceous novaculites, unlike the fatty-feeling novaculitic schists with resinous lustre cropping out on the hill-sides of Marquette. Their dip is south, nearly vertical ; next above, in conformable superposition, follows a belt of compact white or white and reddish mottled quartzite in thick layers, amounting to about 200 feet, which composes a separate summit elevation adjoined on the south side by a shallow depression about 150 feet in diameter, which space is occupied by a succession of argillitic and hydro-micaceous schists or slates. The south side of this depression is formed of another thick quartzite belt, which composes a similar crest parallel with the other ; the ledges of this latter are more thinly bedded and interstratified with ferruginous and siliceous slaty seams. ' Conformably superimposed on this second quartzite belt follows a series of siliceous reddish-colored limestones, interlaminated with hard novaculitic slaty seams of purplish color. This limestone formation composes the southern declivity of the hill, and projects in high vertical walls along the margin of the summit part ; some of the almost upright ledges, dipping to the south, are tilted over, and seem to have a northern dip. The much-corrugated limestone beds are full of siliceous seams, partially parallel to the stratification, partially pervading the rock in an intricate network, which seams, resisting atmospheric influences and the lixiviating action of water much better than the lime, project in sharp relief from the surface of the weathered rock, of which often nothing is left but the cellulose siliceous skeleton.

A short distance east of the summit of Mount Mesnard, the more thinly laminated quartzite strata, often ripple-marked on the surface and covered by a film of micaceous or hydro-micaceous scales, are quarried at the foot of the hill, to be shipped abroad for the use of hearthstones in construction of furnaces in Bessemer steel-works. By crossing this quartzite ridge, one and a half miles west of Mount Mesnard, on the line between Sects. 33 and 34, we find on the north slope of the hills, conformably beneath the quartzite belt, outcrops of a coarse conglomerate in a seam of considerable thickness. The conglomerate, of dark purplish iron-color, incloses quartzite pebbles of white and red color, besides novaculitic schistose fragments of various tints ; they are cemented by a paste of similar schistose material, and intermingled with quartz-sand and octahedric crystals of martite. In connection with the conglomerate we find undisturbed beds of fine-grained novaculite schists, colored dark purplish gray by interspersed granules of martite, which sometimes become so abundant in the rock as to impart to it the quality of an iron-ore ; still I have never seen deposits of this kind large enough to give them practical value. The thick quartzite belt leaning on the south side of the conglomerates forms the summit part of the hill, which slopes slowly southward ; and then, at the opposite end of the succession of these large rock-masses, a deep ravine, following the trend of the strata, interrupts the uniformity of the descent by the steep rock-walls of its sides ; it is caused by the erosion of the belt of softer schists seen previously exposed between the two summit elevations of Mount Mesnard. The south side of the ravine is formed by reddish-colored quartzites dipping south in conformity with the other almost vertical rock-beds. The red quartzites are succeeded by a large series of siliceous, calcareous, and slaty beds, all more or less intensely red-colored by iron oxide. The limestones in this locality are partially much freer of siliceous seams than at Mount Mesnard, but still too impure to be used as a marble, or even for the purpose of burning lime. Having descended two thirds of the hill-side, the rock-ledges are found to disappear under the drift-deposits which form the base of the range and, border the bed of Carp River in steep bluffs of alternating clay, sand, and gravel beds, which gravel is to a great extent cemented into a hard conglomerate scarcely distinguishable from the Silurian conglomerates exposed close by in the sole of the river-bed. Entirely analogous sections can be observed by crossing this quartzite ridge in any other place, but while observing the general harmony in the successive deposits, we learn at the same time how much the nature of certain layers can change in comparatively very short distances. I have crossed this ridge all along its extent at intervals of half a mile, and found in every instance considerable variations in the details of the section.

Arrived at the western end of the quartzite ridge, near the quarter-post on the north line of Sect. 32, Town. 48, R. 25, and close to a small lake situated in Sect. 29, just touching the line, we see the quartzite ledges with their incumbent limestone formation descend to the edge of a swamp, and disappear. Following the section line from the quarter-post westward, we come across this swamp. and have repeatedly to ascend and descend the interlocking drift-covered hill-spurs through which the ravine-like, meandering valley of Little Carp River winds its way. On the north side of our course we see high dioritic hills touching the creek valley with their base ; on the south side a broad belt of undulating plateau-lands extends. After a mile's travel, and having just emerged from the creek-bed crossing our way, we find at the quarter-post of the north line of Sect. 31 outcrops of the limestone formation, but no sign of the underlying quartzites to the north of the limestone exposures ; the surface is formed by drift, and not a great way off large rock-walls of diorite rise above it. The siliceous limestones alternating with slaty layers of purplish iron-colored tints continue to be exposed on the north side of the now widening valley of the Little Carp River to the north-west corner of the section, whence the formation crosses the valley and presents itself in conspicuous bluffs on its south side, as far as the Morgan furnace, and a short distance beyond it, where it is buried under the drift. On the opposite side of the creek, in this part of the valley, the diorite, covered at its base with a narrow talus of drift, rises to the height of 200 feet above the sole of the valley in briskly ascending rock-walls. East of the furnace the limestone formation composes several high knobs, which represent a succession of several hundred feet of strata in a nearly vertical position, and exhibiting considerable corrugation of the beds. The limestones are in part quite free of siliceous seams, some fine-grained with conchoidal fracture, others of saccharoidal crystalline structure, and certain beds contain large sparry crystals dispersed in a fine-grained calcareous ground mass, which imparts to them the aspect of a porphyry. Their color varies in different shades of red or gray, or is variegated like Castile soap. While the Morgan furnace was in blast, the limestones were used as a flux with satisfactory results. Belts of cherty layers, of ferruginous argillites, and of silky shining hydro-micaceous schists, are interlaminated with the limestone-beds in often repeated alternation.

Two miles west of the Morgan furnace, in the N. half of Sect. 33, Town. 48, R. 26, the previously mentioned high ridge of quartzite commences, which is supposed to be the continuation of the eastern quartzite chain, lost sight of at the quarter-post on the north line of Sect. 32, Town. 48, R. 25. The quartzites and associated rock-beds form a broad belt nearly a quarter of a mile in width. Thick compact ledges of whitish quartzite dipping south under a high angle, and amounting to a thickness of over 200 feet, form the south side of the hill, and project in large rock-walls ; these are succeeded by an equally broad belt of compact, fine-grained novaculitic or argillitic slate-rock, of a dark purplish iron color, streaked by irregular seams or blotches of yellowish untinged slate substance ; then follows again a large belt of light-colored compact quartzite and other slaty seams, alternating with thinner bedded quartzite ledges or belts of quartzite breccia occur in the succession ; finally, schistose novaculitic strata, cropping out on the north slope of the range, signalize the lower horizon of the quartzose deposits, and beneath them the previously mentioned series of slaty argillites and hydro-micaceous schists, more or less charged with granular martite or with hematite, composes the base of the hill-side. In the east part of this quartzite range we found the quartzites on the south side regularly succeeded by the limestone formation ; here, and west of here, no more of it can be discovered. Singularly, we find westward, all along the quartzite range, a large amount of limestone blocks mingled with the drift-masses, but no trace of the rock-ledges in place ; the quartzites are on the south side of this hill-range overlaid by a large succession of slaty and arenaceous rocks, which have no similarity with the limestone formation or with the associated rock-beds.

Two miles farther west on this quartzite chain, near the east end of Teal Lake, is the location in which formerly a fine-grained compact novaculite was mined for manufacturing hone-stones of a superior quality. The strata are in that place several hundred feet thick, of fine grain and of even-bedded slaty structure ; the greatest portion of the rock is dark graycolored, more of a clay slate nature ; the seams, useful for hone-stones, are composed of a harder, more compact, and lighter colored material ; but a large proportion of these seams is spoiled for the purpose by numerous linear quartzose veins, and by specks of ferruginous substance. The large amount of waste rock to be dug out and handled in order to get a small quantity of sound and perfect pieces, made the business rather expensive ; and after, by some unfortunate accident, the grinding and finishing shops erected at Marquette, near the mouth of Whetstone Creek, were destroyed by fire, the whole undertaking was given up as not sufficiently profitable.

Recently other parties made an attempt to mine hone-stones in Sect. 29, Town. 48, R. 25, but the prospects were not considered favorable, and the place was abandoned again.

Large and very instructive exposures of the quartzite formation and of its connection with the underlying dioritic series are observable at the west end of Teal Lake. The south slope of the hills is formed by a thick belt of compact, heavy-bedded, whitish quartzites, which project in long rock-walls, dipping southward under an angle of 65° to 70° ; north of this belt we find dark-colored slaty rocks richly impregnated with minute crystals of martite in connection with seams of lighter-colored not ferruginous argillitic or novaculitic schists, amounting to considerable thickness ; another thick body of quartzite ledges follows on their north side, which forms the edge of the northern slope of the hill-side, on which a descending section through the lower portion of the formation down to the dioritic series is well exposed ; novaculitic seams alternating with bands of quartzite form the upper part of the slope ; beneath them follows a large succession of silky shining hydro-micaceous slate-rocks, with a crystalline granular aluminous ground-mass in different shades of color, and in some of the seams charged with large proportions of granular crystals of martite and magnetite. These slaty rock-beds are on their north side conformably adjoined by chloritic and dioritic schists with inclosed massive diorite belts, which rock-series composes all the hill-ranges farther north to the valley of Carp River, and those on the north side of the valley. West of the exposures on Teal Lake we find in the bluffs bordering the west side of Carp River, near its entrance into Deer Lake, a coarse quartzite breccia. interstratified with the novaculitic and hydro-micaceous schists in the lower horizon of the series ; this brecciated rock is not an accumulation of rock-fragments variable in character and transported from a distance, but seems to be formed mainly of the shattered ledges on the spot, becoming somewhat intermingled and recemented by siliceous and ferruginous matter. If we follow the brow of the hills trending from there westward along the south line of Sect. 33 to the east end of Lake Cooper, the exposures of the quartzite formation become much more extensive. The quartzite formation forms here the basal girdle of a much higher mountain body of dioritic rocks, which occupies the central part of the above-named section ; and here frequent opportunities are offered to see the intimate connection existing between the two groups, linked together by uninterrupted succession, and by gradations in the change of the material of the rock-beds.

A mile north-west of Lake Cooper is an isolated large belt of quartzites, which trends in north-east direction diagonally across the S. E. quarter of the S. E. quarter of Sect. 30, and the S.W. quarter of the S.W. quarter of Sect. 29, Town. 48, R. 27. The heavy beds of quartzite lean in highly inclined position with southern dip on the side of a ridge of serpentine, towering with precipitous rock-walls above its circumvallation by the quartz rock. A creek washes the base of the quartzite bluffs, and on the opposite southern side of the valley rises another serpentine ridge equalling the northern ridge in elevation. The quartzites are severed from the serpentine by a deep narrow ravine partially filled with talus, which prevents seeing the rocks in their immediate contact. The serpentine ridge on the north side is nearly a mile wide, very rugged, and cut up into a good many smaller parallel crests with intervening ravines. North of the serpentine a narrow belt of dioritic schists, with inclosed, imperfectly crystalline granitoid seams, follows as the adjoining rock, being well exposed near the N.E. corner of Sect. 30 ; thence northward much of the surface is covered by drift deposits ; but south of the quarter-post, on the west line of Sect. 20, quartzites of granular arenaceous structure, partly full of rounded pebbles and conglomeratic, become exposed in association with porous micaceous, thinly laminated sand-rock ledges, greenish yellow or reddish brown, colored by iron oxide ; their dip is northward. Farther north the surface rapidly declines and spreads into extensive marsh-lands, through which one of the head branches of Dead River winds its way ; but a short distance west of the S. E. corner of Sect. 18, in the midst of the marsh-lands, a low wave-like ridge projects, which is composed of alternating layers of a dark sand-rock and of black carbon-colored slates, dipping north. The entire marsh-land and the hills adjoining it are, as far as I could examine them, all underlaid by a similar black slate-rock, with inclosed sand-rock beds. The last-mentioned rock-beds are found to repose directly and conformably on the quartzite formation, in many exposures to be seen on the east and on the west side of this marsh ; the south line of the S. E. quarter of Sect. 24, Town. 48, R. 28, passes over a hill of quartzite, exposed in high perpendicular walls, and overlaid on the north side of the hill by a very large succession of slate and sand-rock beds. A quarter of a mile south of this place, in the N. E. quarter of Sect. 25, is another ridge formed of thick quartzite beds, with some schistose novaculitic layers, which on the south side are in contact with the dioritic formation. Other large quartzite hills occupy the N. E. quarter of the N. E. quarter of Sect. 23, and the S. E. quarter of the S. E. quarter of Sect. 14, Town. 48, R. 28 ; likewise in association with novaculitic and hydro-micaceous schists, and conformably overlaid by dark slates and banded siliceous rocks, which contain in this latter locality a large percentage of iron oxide. Farther to the west I have not extended my examinations.

East of the above-mentioned marsh-land surrounding the head-waters of Dead River, the first exposures of the quartzites analogous to the quartzites of Teal Lake or Mount Mesnard are found in the N. W. quarter of the S. W. quarter of Sect. 21, Town. 48, R. 27, where a short but quite bulky ridge of quartzite leans with its beds dipping northward on the northern slope of a high serpentine ridge, which constitutes a part of the previously mentioned body of serpentine hills, although a swampy valley intervenes between them. North of this quartzite ridge we find a row of other knobs trending north-west, composed of the same rock, which occupies nearly the whole east half of the N. W. quarter of the section. On the east side of these quartzite hills we see the schistose beds of the underlying novaculite series at the surface, and these on their part to repose on dioritic and chloritic schists. On the west side and on the north side, the dark-colored arenaceous slate-rocks, identical with those forming the bottom of the marsh-land, are seen to overlie the quartzite, amounting to a great thickness, and projecting in a separate row of hills with very steep declivity on their north slope. The last-mentioned quartzite outcrops are cut off by a swamp near the north quarter-post of Sect. 21 ; but by taking a north-east course we find them again in the centre of the S.E. quarter of Sect. 16, and from there we can follow the exposed ledges of the rock eastward almost without an interruption to the S.E. quarter of Sect. 14. Here the dioritic rocks, and soon after the granitic, commence to form the surface rock further on in this eastern direction ; but we can find the belt of quartzite outcrops continued by taking a north-east course, at a distance of not over a half a mile north of the quarter-post of the east line of Sect. 14 ; very good exposures are also at the quarter-post on the east line of Sect. 13, at which latter place the direct contact between the granite and the quartzite is plainly observable. From that locality we can follow traces of this rock-belt all along the north side of the granite range trending eastward, and find it well exposed again in the north part of the S.E. quarter of Sect. 17, Town. 48, R. 26, near the coal-kilns and the tram-road of the Morgan Furnace Company, at which place coarsely brecciated seams are seen interlaminated with the other compact ledges of quartzite, leaning with northern dip on the granite hills ; and above the quartzite, follows in uninterrupted succession, a large series of more thinly bedded flaggy layers of a micaceous and ferruginous sand-rock alternating with slaty rock-seams. The slope of the granite range is farther to the east much incumbered by drift deposits which hide the quartzite formation ; but as the next incumbent, arenaceous and slaty rock-beds are constantly exposed in this direction in the bluffs of Dead River, I suppose it to continue eastward as far as the centre of Sect. 14, Town. 48, R. 25, at which locality heavy masses of compact quartzite underlie the said arenaceous-rocks, and repose directly on the granite which composes the summit of the hill range on the north side of Dead River. In this northern belt of the quartzite formation, in anticlinal position with the Teal Lake quartzite range, the lower novaculitic horizon of the group has rarely been noticed in the exposures, with exception of those mentioned as occuring in the west half of Sect. 21, Town. 48, R. 27, where this part of the formation, consisting essentially of the same argillitic and hydro-micaceous material as in other localities, is a harder, more compact rock, delicately marked with linear striæ of lamination, but not always very fissile in this direction, cleaving sometimes into rhomboidal, but often into very irregular fragments, contrary to the lamination. The color of the rock varies from light greenish white to drab or brown, or from light reddish tints into a blackish purple ; generally narrow seams of various colors alternate with each other. The dark purplish seams are richly impregnated with granular crystals of martite, or also magnetite, and often we see the ledges extremely distorted and corrugated by their upheaval. The visible thickness of the exposed ledges amounts to more than 300 feet ; upward in the succession, the intercalation of quartzite seams connects them gradually with the quartzite formation, and descending, we see a similar gradation and connection with the schistose part of the dioritic series exhibited by the increase of chlorite in the composition of the ledges, and by their change in structure from a regular banded sedimentary lamination to an irregular schistose or slaty lamination independent of the sedimentation. In this locality the intersection of these novaculitic schists by a large doleritic dyke is likewise to be observed, of which I intend to give a more explicit description in the subsequent chapter on eruptive volcanic rock-belts.

Returning to the shore, three miles south of Marquette, we find the south side of Carp River valley likewise formed by high quartzite ridges, larger in extent than those on its north side. The intermediate space of the valley is generally covered by drift deposits, and beneath them by Silurian sand-rock, which is in several places denuded in the bed of the river and in the bluffs at the shore. The quartzite formation comes also to the surface on this space at and near the shore line, on the south side of a small creek which enters the lake not far from the supposed N.E. corner of the S.W. quarter of Sect. 36, Town. 48, R. 25, whose place is in the lake. The white compact quartzite ledges, in a nearly vertical position, barely project with a rounded drift-polished surface from the edge, and from the top part of a drift terrace. A spur of the outcrops forms a small rock promontory projecting into the lake, at which locality the discordant superposition of the Silurian sandstones and conglomerates on the upright quartzite beds, and into the clefts existing between them, is well exhibited. In a quarry opened in the bluffs near the creek-bed, fine slabs of quartzite can be obtained, covered with micaceous scales, and wrinkled on the surface by ripple marks. The high ridge of the quartzite formation commences close to the shore, and exactly in the N. E. corner of Sect. 1, Town. 47, R. 25. The rock-bluffs on the roadside exhibit a well denuded section across a synclinal trough of the formation, which is already described in former Reports on the Upper Peninsula by Major Brooks and myself. I briefly repeat it here. Commencing the examination from the north side, we find at first a large succession of white quartzite beds exposed on the lower levels near the roadside ; their dip is south. Next south of them follows, with conformable dip, a large series of purplish gray-colored novaculitic and argillitic schistose and slaty layers, interstratified with seams of red quartzite and of cherty beds ; upward in this rock-belt calcareous bands begin to appear in the alternation of beds, and finally a thick belt of siliceous lime-stones terminates the succession. The limestones are considerably corrugated, which corrugation becomes very conspicuous on weathered faces of the rock, on which the siliceous seams parallel with the stratification stand out in high relief. Besides the general corrugation, the entire body of limestone ledges is bent into a central synclinal trough, to which all the other rock-beds adapt themselves, so that by going farther south all the previously described strata occur again in an inverted order, and dipping north. The large quartzite belt forming the southern margin of the synclinal arch composes the highest crest of the range. In a ravine on the south side of this quartzite belt, much-corrugated silky-shining hydro-micaceous quartz schists become exposed, which conformably underlie it ; but the opposite side of the ravine is formed of dioritic and chloritic schists inclosing belts of granite, which are in anticlinal position with the quartzites and hydro-micaceous quartz schists.

In the bottom of this ravine a dyke is seen to intersect the dio-ritic schists and the hydro-micaceous quartz schists transversally, which consists of a rather light green-colored, middling fine-grained crystalline diorite. Farther south all the rock exposures disappear under the drift. The described bluffs near the lake shore are the truncated end of a large mountain ridge extending for many miles westward. Near the shore its height is about 150 feet, but farther west its elevation increases to 700 feet ; its top part is divided into multiple parallel smaller crests and rows of knobs, of which many are perfectly denuded of soil and vegetation ; the folded condition of the beds, together with their imperfect denudation, is often a serious obstacle to the recognition of the true order of things.

For the first three quarters of a mile west of the shore, the dark purplish argillitic and lighter-colored novaculitic schists, and other rock-seams described as the second rock-belt in the above given section across the synclinal trough, compose the north slope of the ridge. These schists form rather compact rock-belts, and are not very fissile ; the interlaminated seams of quartzite, partly of red. partly of white color, are sometimes shattered into small angular fragments and recemented into a breccia by a dark red iron-colored quartzose substance ; narrower seams of very fissile hydro-micaceous schists and of siliceous limestone are particularly confined to the upper horizon of the exposed belt. North of this hill-slope, where the large quartzite belt with southern dip should be expected in the outcrops, the whole surface is deeply covered by drift deposits ; looking south, we see ridges of quartzite all along, which represent the south margin of the synclinal fold ; consequently their ledges dip north. Proceeding along the north margin of the range farther west, we have to descend into the ravine-like bed of a previously mentioned small creek entering the lake near the centre of Sect. 36. On the opposite side of the ravine we find no more of the schists. All the cluster of knobs before us consists of quartzite beds folded into bubble-like anticlinal hillocks and synclinal intermediate depressions ; wherefore almost every exposure exhibits a different local dip. Over the summit of the highest of these quartzite knobs, the west line of Sect. 1, Town. 47, R. 25, runs, and at the foot of the knob the north-west corner of the section is located in the bed of a western branch of the creek we had passed in the ravine a short time before. Turning here southward, following the section line between Sects. 1 and 2, we descend from the summit knobs to a level more than 100 feet lower than we had been, and come, near the quarter-post, to a wave-like transverse elevation trending along the hill-slope, which is composed of granite, inclosing irregularly wedged-in belts of chloritic schists, disrupted in their continuity ; besides, we see the granite intersected by two kinds of volcanic dyke-masses, one of dioritic,

5

the other of a doleritic rock character. In close contact with this granite, and scarcely distinguishable from it, we observe easily disintegrating rocks, composed of vitreous quartz-grains mingled with a smaller proportion of red feldspar crystals, cemented together by a semi-transparent, fatty-feeling, pale yellowish-colored fibroso-scaly hydro-mica, usually mistaken for talc, but not of magnesian composition. As an additional constituent of this rock, sometimes also chloritic scales occur in limited proportion. Here is the locality cited on a former occasion, to give an example of the transformation of sedimentary strata into a granite-like rock, by being exposed to the contact with eruptive granite masses, which is fairly illustrated by the mentioned natural section through the centre of a quartzite knob, composed of ledges raised into a large bubble-like arch, in the centre of which we see lowest the granite, and above it a series of gradations from the most altered granitoid condition to the ordinary white homogeneous layers which form the top of the arch. Among the upheaved lower ledges of the quartzite group, we recognize in this locality the hydro-micaceous quartz schists exposed in the bottom of the ravine near the lake shore, which from there up to this place can be traced all along the brow of the hill-range ; they differ from the altered granitoid rocks merely by a more laminated schistose structure, and by a greater proportion of hydro-mica in their composition. Other black slaty rock-beds are noticed in this association, which contain a large proportion of small magnetite crystals sufficient to give to some of the seams the character of an iron-ore, but I could not see enough of them to determine their practical value.

A row of other large quartzite knobs extends in a south-western direction from the presently described locality to the west line of the S.W. quarter of Sect. 2. They are adjoined on the south side by granites in connection with dioritic schists ; their north-western slope forms the circumvallation of a deep kettle-shaped depression, whose bottom is occupied by a small lake. The north side of this kettle valley is likewise formed by a barrier of quartzite hills in synclinal position with the south range ; the inside slope of this oval-shaped valley is composed of the upper slaty division, and of the siliceous limestones, succeeding above the quartzites, on which they lean in an almost vertical position on both sides. Like in the eastern exposures, this rock series is formed of compact, fine-grained, dark purplish-colored argillitic and partly novaculitic schists, variegated with light-colored streaky seams, or spotted by irregular blotches devoid of pigment, in alternation with quartz or chert seams, and in the upper part with thick belts of siliceous limestones of reddish color. The lake has its outlet northward; through a crevice in the rock-wall it sends a small stream, rushing with velocity over the hill-slope, down to the Carp River. Beneath the quartzite wall inclosing the little valley from the north side, the lower novaculitic schists come to the surface on the northern slope, forming a belt of considerable thickness; they are very fine-grained, of a wax-yellow color, and quite fissile, with even surfaces of a fatty lustre. I take occasion in this place to point out the great lithological similarity between some beds underlying the quartzites, and others above them which have the essential qualities of a novaculite. It is for this reason frequently difficult to determine the horizon to which they belong, if their relative position to the quartzite cannot be seen. Lower down the hillside, the little creek, after it has passed over the novaculite ledges and some intermediate quartzite seams, flows over dioritic rocks (partly schistose, partly massive and crystalline), while it crosses the north line of Sect. 2 not far from the quarter-post, and for some distance lower down; but the basal portion of the hill is deeply covered by drift deposits, and the creek carved its way to the river through them, high above the solid rock-ledges underneath.

The above-mentioned exposures of dioritic rocks in the creek-bed can be traced westward for the distance of half a mile to the bed of another creek in the N.E. quarter of the N.W. quarter of Sect. 2, where it embraces between its terminal furcation a knob of massive coarsely crystalline diorite, well denuded on the summit; it projects at the foot of steep quartzite bluffs, which form the higher part of the ridge. This is, to my knowledge, the only exposure of diorite in the main valley of Carp River for the distance of eight or nine miles west of the shore of Lake Superior. Returning to the little lake on top of the quartzite range, we can follow a belt of the slaty and calcareous rock series westward across the centre part of Sect. 3 and into Sect. 4. A high chain of quartzite hills towering above the south side of Carp River valley forms its border on the north side; on the south side the granite formation comes close up to the slaty or calcareous formation, sometimes directly adjoining it ; in other places a belt of quartz ite intervenes. The whole south half of Sect. 3 and the southern quarter of Sect. 2, Town. 47, R. 25, are formed of granitic rocks. Fine exposures of flesh-red fine-grained limestones can be seen a quarter of a mile west of the centre of Sect. 3 in the forks of a creek which flows into Carp River ; following the bed of this creek downward to the river, we find the rock-beds mostly covered by loose débris ; but occasional outcrops of siliceous schists and of iron-colored slate rocks, analogous to those connected with the limestone formation, seem to prove the extension of this rock-series through this gap in the range down to the Carp River. It unites there with the equivalent rock-beds covering the south slope of the Mount Mesnard quartzite range on the opposite side of the valley, in which from here upward, for a distance of three miles, only the beds belonging to this upper horizon of the quartz-ite series can be found in the outcrops which sometimes occur in the river channel, while generally all the bottom and sides of the valley are covered by drift. A quite extensive exposure of fer-ruginous slaty argillites in the embankments of the river is seen at the falls, situated a quarter of a mile south of the adjoining north corners of Sects. 4 and 5, which exposure continues for some dis-tance above and below the falls ; not far above them we find thick ledges of siliceous limestone interstratified with the ferruginous slates.

Desiring to describe the geological features of the country in a topographical order, I have to lead the reader back to the sum-mit of the hill-range, near the west line of Sect. 3, where I men-tioned the occurrence of limestone outcrops in the fork of a creek. Taking from there a due west course, we notice some distance ahead a high ridge trending from north to south through the east half of Sect. 4 into the north part of Sect. 9. As we ascend the slope of this ridge, the silico-calcareous strata we were on con-tinue to be the surface rock for a part of the way, but rising higher we find the summit formed of heavy ledges of white quartzite in almost vertical position ; and past the crest, on the opposite slant-ing side, incumbered with drift, the granite crops out in various places. The highest point of this quartzite ridge is formed by a knob situated on the south line of the S.E. quarter of the S.W.

quarter of Sect. 4. Going west from there along with the section line, we make a rapid descent over the cliffs of quartzite to an offset in the hill-slope, whose basal part is formed by still bolder vertical cliffs bordering a small lake, which are composed of a large eruptive mass of a crystalline dolerite. The opposite side of the lake is likewise lined with steep bluffs of the quartzite on the terrace-like top of which we find the S.W. corner of the section. The S.E. corner of Sect. 4 is located on granitic hills, which there come in close contact with the quartzite formation on the west side ; south of this corner the line between Sects. 9 and 10 passes over several parallel undulating ridges ere it intersects a lake which covers the whole east half of Sect. 9. These ridges are all composed of granitoid rocks, but the most southern one bordering the lake is not a true granite, and evidently represents sub-conglomeratic altered strata of the quartzite formation, resembling by their hydro-micaceous composition a protogine. A swampy valley connects the large lake in Sect. 9 with the smaller one near the S.W. corner of Sect. 4, which receives the surplus water of the other and gives rise to a creek flowing into Carp River through a ravine-like valley carved into the drift-covered hill-slope, at times deep enough to denude the upper schistose ledges of the quartzite formation, of which the whole surrounding country seems to be composed. We pass over such silico-ferruginous slaty rock-beds with intercalated limestone belts, if we follow the section line northward from the S.W. corner of Sect. 4 to its intersection with the Carp River at the falls ; the line west of the corner leads over almost inaccessible limestone bluffs, across two high knobs composed of this rock-series, and thence down to the bed of Carp River, where slaty members of the same group are locally exposed ; finally, examining the line between Sects. 8 and 9 from the corner southward, we pass 200 steps from the corner over a small creek running east into the little lake, ascend then a high quartzite hill, descend into a depression, declining west, toward Carp River valley, and ascend again over the steep side of a granite hill, on whose brow we find the quarter-post located ; thence we step over undulating drift-covered plateau lands a quarter of a mile wide, and stand on the edge of the south slope of the hill-range, which is very steep, full of granitic cliffs and intermediate ravines ; climbing down over them, we find, about 300 feet below, at the foot of the slope, the south corners of the two adjoining sections located on a small hillock of granite ; farther to the south, as far as the eye can reach, all is one large sand-covered plain, overgrown with pine, or in places totally deprived of trees by former devastations of fire. This range of granite, fully a half mile in width, is not much over a mile long ; it commences near the centre of Sect. 9 on the west side of the lake in the east half of the section, and terminates in the west half of Sect. 8 by sloping down to lower levels, covered by drift, or formed of the upper calcareous and slaty division of the quartzite formation, which I will call, for brevity's sake, *marble series.*

On examination of the western Sects. 7 and 12 and 13 of the adjoining Town. 47, R. 26, we find the marble series to be their only surface rock, with exception of very few spots in which the lower quartzite beds are exposed, as, for instance, on the hill-tops crossed by the north line of Sect. 7, and at the base of the rock-bluffs in the south part of Sect. 13, or in the hills occupying the N.W. corner of Sect. 12. The south-east quarter of Sect. 11 of Town. 47, R. 26, has likewise the marble series for its principal surface-rock, with good exposures near the quarter-post on the west line of the section. The rockspur projecting into Goose Lake, at the S.E. corner of Sect. 14, is the most westerly exposure of marble-beds in this district ; four miles north of it are the marble hills of Morgan furnace. The abrupt termination of this group of rock-beds, which in all the eastern exposures conformably succeeded the quartzite formation, is very strange, as we notice here at once, and in close proximity with the other outcrops, a totally different sort of rocks conformably resting on the same identical quartzite formation, without a sign of an existing gradation from one into the other kind of the incumbent layers. The calcareo-siliceous rock-series, exposed in conformable superposition on the quartzites, amounts at the south-east end of Goose Lake to from 200 to 300 feet, while we see at the N.W. end of the lake a still larger succession of rock-beds resting on the quartzite in apparent conformity ; but its composition and general aspect are in striking contrast with the first, and no one will consider the two sorts of sediments for a moment as equivalents. The latter silico-ferruginous strata, which have a large surface extent in Carp River valley, north of Goose Lake, are considered as a separate subdivision, as Group V., and shall be more explicitly described in one of the following chapters. I continue therefore the description of the quartzite group, as it presents itself in the territory west and south-west of Goose Lake, and in some other localities not yet described, situated on the north and on the east side of the lake. In the N.E. quarter of Sect. 24, Town. 47, R. 26, a cluster of low quartzite knobs projects from the sand-plains through which the Escanaba River flows after its outlet from Goose Lake. The plains generally seem to be underlaid by granitic rocks, which come to the surface in some hillocks close to the Escanaba Railroad, in the centre of the south line of the above-named quarter-section, while the quartzite hills are intersected by the north line of it. The latter are noteworthy on account of the interlamination of ferruginous hematitic schists, and of tolerably fair seams of a schistose specular iron-ore with the quartzite beds, but the amount of good ore is too small to pay for its being mined. A short distance north of these hills, at the foot of a higher hill-range, the quartzites, overlaid by siliceous limestone beds, are extensively exposed. On the north side of Goose Lake, a quarter of a mile east of the N.W. corner of Sect. 14, a row of quartzite hills occupying the whole west half of the S.W. quarter of Sect. 11, strikes the shore in a north and south direction ; the beds are nearly vertical, or dip west-south-west. A broad swamp valley surrounds them from the east and north side ; north-east of the hill-range a string of lower hills, all surrounded by the swamp, occupies the north half of the S.W. quarter of Sect. 11, which is found to be composed of the upper limestone formation. West of the quartzite hills is a depression which separates them from a much higher hill-range trending parallel with them from north to south through the centre part of Sect. 10 ; its summit and main body are composed of dioritic rocks, but both sides of its base are formed of the silico-ferruginous rock-beds of the fifth group previously mentioned, which beds also fill out the whole interval between the two ridges, and lean directly on the west side of the quartzite range. North of the swamp valley a still larger body of quartzite hills covers the entire north half of Sect. 11 ; the strata of this range dip north under a high angle, and are on the north side overlaid conformably with the beds of the fifth group.

A large body of hills west and south-west of Goose·Lake is exclusively formed by the quartzite formation and its subordinate layers, of which the entire surface of the Sects. 21, 22, and 23, Town. 47, R. 26, is formed, besides a large portion of the adjoining sections on the north and south side. This mountain body is cut up by ravines and valleys into countless knobs and smaller ridges, which in a general way are arranged in parallel rows, trending east and west. Usually the strata are found in an almost vertical position, and exhibit such a variance in their dislocation, or are so imperfectly denuded, that even after a careful examination often much doubt remains about the order in their succession, and frequently one is obliged to determine in an outcrop what is above and what below in the series, more by inferences from the lithological quality of the rock than from its relative position to the other beds.

The basin of Goose Lake indicates evidently the spot of a great break in the continuity of the rock-beds and their faulted dislocation. On the north side of the narrow linguiform prolongation of the east end of the lake, near the S.E. corner of Sect. 14, we see the limestone beds in comparatively slow southward decline sink below the water level, and find on the south side of this lake arm, at a distance of 250 steps, different rock-beds, dipping in an opposite direction, under a very high angle at that spot, but the same ledges are, farther west at the coal-kilns, locally almost horizontal. If we follow the section line between Sects. 23 and 24 from the lake southward, we have to ascend almost inaccessible bluffs of dark gray slaty rock-beds in nearly upright position, and amounting to a great thickness. The substance of the slates is a finely granular or scaly crystalline aluminous silicate, easily cut with the knife and more or less fatty to the touch, and either of silky or waxy lustre, or in others more dull, novaculitic, or earthy in appearance ; their gray color is due to an abundance of minute magnetite crystals disseminated through the mass ; but seams occur which are entirely free of it, and are pale yellowish-white ; a seam of this kind is exposed near the water-house on the railroad track. The cleavage of all these beds is oblique to their sedimentary lamination. South of this belt of slate rock, which forms a terrace on the hill, a thick belt of white compact quartzites, about 100 feet wide, follows, projecting with vertically erected ledges in walls 40 or 50 feet in height, which form the summit of a front ridge of the large body of hills ; fissures in the quartzite, filled with large-leaved micaceous iron oxide, are here quite abundant. South of the quartzite is a depression, on the other side of which reddish quartzite layers in alternation with blackish gray compact argillitic, or novaculitic, delicately laminated rock-seams follow each other in a broad belt, which composes a second undulation of the hill-top. The dark color of the schistose rocks is due to the intermixture of a large proportion of minute granules of magnetite, or also martite in octahedric crystals, and their ground-mass is the same granular aluminous silicate of a talcy blandness which composes the schists on the north slope of the hill-range. Proceeding farther south, we come across another depression to a third undulation of the surface, edging the south slope of the mountain body, which is composed of another quartzite belt, differing in character from the former quartzites by the altered granitoid structure of its beds, composed of coarse vitreous opalescent quartz-grains in intermixture with flesh-red feldspar crystals, and cemented by the hydro-micaceous scaly or fibroso-granular mineral previously mentioned as a component of the altered lowest beds of the quartzite formation in other localities. Quartzite ledges of the ordinary compact and homogeneous kind are associated with the others, and are interlaminated with seams of schistose, specular, and hematitic iron-ore analogous to the ore-seams mentioned in the quartzite knobs of Sect. 24. In the same horizon occur also brightly shining mica schists, identical with the corrugated glistening schists exposed beneath the quartzites, near the shore of Lake Superior, in the bluffs north of Harvey's furnace. On the south side of these mica schists a large belt of black, thinly laminated but compact schists, similar to the dark schistose rocks composing the central ridge, but still more richly impregnated with magnetite than they are, forms abrupt walls and shorter cliffs along the hill-slope almost down to its base, where sandy pine-plains expand, on which the granite comes to the surface in isolated knobs, one of which is crossed by the section line we follow, some hundred steps before we arrive at the south corners of Sects. 23 and 24. All the strata of the described cross-cut through the range are nearly vertical, and it is difficult to determine whether the beds represent one continuous succession of more than two thousand feet in thickness, or whether plications exist, causing a repetition of the strata. Examining a cross-section through the centre of Sect. 23, parallel with the other, we find the rolling terrace land on which the coal-kilns are built formed of the same slate-rocks as in the first ; some drift-polished larger rock-exposures are particularly favorable for a detailed study of the different seams in the succession. South, on the slope of the higher hills, we find similar slate-rocks continued in association with curiously mottled dark purplish gray silky-shining schists, full of angular small dots like the decomposed earthy residue of former crystals, colored reddish brown by the higher oxidation of the magnetite crystals, which give color to the whole mass. This schist contains also small streaky seams of a pale waxy color, semi-transparent in thin splinters, of fine granular texture and almost talcy softness, which are evidently formed of the same material as the dark portions, colored by magnetite, but have in this form all the qualities of agalmatolite, and prove by chemical examination to be an aluminous silicate, and not a magnesian. Farther south the large quartzite belt of the previously described cross-section follows, and all the subsequent beds in the succession correspond with the former, not in all particulars, but in a general way. About in the centre of the section we have reached the summit undulation of the range, and commence the descent over the south slope. We find here micaceous quartzite beds crowded with small octahedric crystals of martite, and dark, much-corrugated, silky-shining schists, similar to those which we found on the north slope in the same cross-section, which indicates a plication and repetition of the strata ; lower down the hill the mica schists and compact dark schists, charged with octahedric iron oxide crystals, besides other flaggy ferruginous beds form the basal part of the slope, as they did a half mile farther east. At the base we find a swampy strip of land, beyond which, farther south, a rounded knoll rises, which is composed of quartzite beds of granular and well-laminated sand-rock structure, in alternation with flaggy arenaceo-ferruginous beds, and with seams of iron-ore partly in the coarsely crystalline form of granular specular ore, partly in the schistose form of slate-ore, all of very bright metallic lustre. In the lower part of this ore-bearing rock-series, in a nearly vertical position, with northern dip, the ore-seams are associated with dark green chloritic schists, inclosing crystals of iron garnets, which rock has much resemblance to the chloritic rock found with the ore deposits of the Michigamee mines. This is the location of the Gilmore mines, situated close to the south quarter-post of Sect. 23 ; they are not worked at present. South of the mines is the large swamp valley of a tributary of the Escanaba River ; a short distance east of them, the granite, with inclosed belts of schistose hornblende rock, is well exposed in a cluster of hillocks projecting over the sand-covered plains near the base of the high quartzite range. We have examined now two cross-sections of this range—one along the east line, another through the centre of Sect. 23 ; a general correspondence between them is obvious, and the same is found true if we examine the range a half mile farther west, along the west line of Sect. 23. We find the north-west corner of the section on the drift-covered slope of the same range, which has lowered here, and expands into a rolling high plateau. The large quartzite belt composing the brow of the summit farther to the east is here exposed in the ravine-like bed of a creek, and with it, interstratified beds of schistose, hematitic, and specular iron-ores similar to those connected with the quartzites near the south slope of the range on the east line of the section. Analogous ore-seams, interlaminated with the quartzites, occur a mile farther west in the N. E. quarter of Sect. 21, at which locality considerable work has been done by explorers, but with no success ; the ore in any of these places is too siliceous to be marketable. South of the quartzite exposures in the creek-bed, on top of the plateau, we find them succeeded by schistose, novaculitic, and argillitic beds, interlaminated and alternating with quartzose belts, part of which constitute a coarse breccia. Numerous small knobs projecting over the drift-covered, undulating level offer a chance to observe the denuded succession of these ledges, continued without a material change of character as far as to the quarter-post of the line, which is situated on the south slope of the range in a depression between high ridges formed of quartzites, partly in homogeneous, compact ledges, partly in a granitoid form, composed of a granular mixture of quartz and feldspar, cemented by interstitial seams of hydro-mica, as we have noticed it before in the more eastern exposures on the south slope. The high hill north-west of the quarter-post is partly formed of a coarse breccia of hard, steel-gray, ferruginous slate fragments, in intermixture with angular pieces of red and white quartz and of novaculite, partly of solid, unbroken ledges of quartzite and of slate-rock. South of this summit ridge are several parallel rows of rock-crests and knobs trending from south-east to north-west across the south half of Sect. 22, composed of a very coarse granite breccia inclosing blocks of large size several feet in diameter, cemented together by an arenaceous and chloritic interstitial mass of a laminated, evidently sedimentary structure, which exhibits itself plainly in some portions of the rock, in which the rock-fragments are more thinly scattered through the cementing ground-mass. In certain portions of these knobs the granite appears in solid masses, too large to be taken for fragments pertaining to the breccia, which fact induces me to suggest the nucleus of all these hills to be a solid granite mass, whose shattered surface portions are recemented on the spot by sedimentary débris washed into the interstices. A parallel ridge next south of these narrow, very abrupt ridges of the granite breccia is composed of hard, fine-grained steel-gray slate-rocks, partially with silky lustre, and of a large belt of quartzite, which forms the south side of the hill, both rock-belts adjoining each other in a nearly vertical position. A swampy interval separates this ridge from one farther south, composed of greenish-colored micaceo-chloritic sand-rock beds, partially compact, quartzite-like, partially porous, like ordinary sandstone ; seams of this very thick succession of beds are conglomeratic. The inclosed water-worn pebbles are in part granite, in part slate fragments. This ridge forms the edge of the hill-lands, and slopes down to the swamp plains and level pine-lands, through which the east branch of Escanaba River winds its way. The rock character of this last ridge does not differ much from the rock-series of the Gilmore mine, although no seams of ore are found in it so far ; but from one place to the other along the railroad track, almost uninterrupted outcrops of related rock-beds can be observed, of which some are intensely impregnated with hematitic iron oxide ; the dip of all these beds is northward, nearly perpendicular. As every locality exhibits different features of a formation, I will describe another cross-section from north to south along the west line of Sect. 22, Town. 47, R. 26. The north-west corner of this section is some distance below the summit on the north side of the western terminal hill of the same quartzite range, whose eastern end was the starting-point for our present examinations of the quartzite formation. The north slope of this hill is covered with drift, and has along the line north of the corner no outcrops, but farther west bulky quartzite ledges are exposed in the ravines.

South of the corner, 150 steps up-hill, gray conglomeratic quartzites project in low cliffs ; farther on, larger exposures of hard, dark gray slates, in alternation with quartzite belts, are met with. The summit is formed by heavy beds of white and red mottled quartzite inclosing bunches of micaceous iron oxide ; the strata dip north under an angle of 70°. A short distance west of the line are the previously mentioned test-pits, in which seams of schistose, hematitic, and specular ore, interstratified with the quartzite, are well uncovered. Descending the south slope, we notice slaty seams like the former, seams of novaculite and of quartzite alternately succeeding each other, and a short distance east of the line brecciated rock-masses are exposed in high perpendicular walls, which consist of intermingled slate and quartzite fragments ; another portion of these cliffs consists of compact reddish quartzite. Lower down, the slope is not so steep, and outcrops are less abundant, but we find the quarter-post situated on a belt of quartzite ledges, close to a small creek, on the south side of which rises a high ridge composed of dark, lead-colored, hard slate-rocks in a nearly vertical position. Another parallel ridge, separated from this one by a ravine, is found to be composed of the same slates, which inclose some interstratified belts of quartzite. Climbing across the hill, we come into the valley of a good-sized creek flowing from the west ; we cross it, ascend on the opposite side another very steep slate-hill, and find the southwestern section corner located on its summit. The slates of this last hill inclose conglomeratic seams, with water-worn granite pebbles ; they consist, like those on the other side of the creek, of a granular, quartzoso-feldspathic ground-mass, which in some more compact seams of the rock is full of pale green acicular hornblende crystals crossing each other in every direction. This large succession of slate-rocks, fully a quarter of a mile in width, without a material change in character, represents, in all probability, not one continuous series of sediments, but a repetition of the strata caused by their plication into one or several folds. We can follow these slate outcrops westward along the creek valley for nearly half a mile ; east, we find the hill over which the south line of Sect. 22 passes composed of a slaty conglomerate, and farther east the summit is formed of fine-grained, steel-gray slates interlaminated with quartzite seams. South of this slate knob, separated from it by a ravine, a high quartzite ridge rises, extending in a continuous body westward a little distance beyond the quarter-post on the north line of Sect. 28, and after an interruption by a valley, continuing in an equally high range of quartzite hills trending across the centre part of the N.W. quarter of Sect. 28 and of the N.E. quarter of Sect. 29. The south side of these hills is lined with vertical rock-walls of quartzite, or ascends in stair-like, cliffy offsets. The quartzite beds, of very massive character and raised into a nearly vertical position, dip northward ; part of them is red, colored by iron oxide, and incloses, besides, small crystals of martite, more or less copiously disseminated ; other seams are lighter-colored whitish ; often shattered rock-seams occur, recemented into a breccia. Interlaminated with the quartzites are schistose strata, partly light-colored, novaculites and argillites, partly dark, steel-gray, hard slates of hydro-micaceous composition of silky lustre ; some of them are fine-grained homogeneous ; other seams have a bird's-eye structure by glassy quartz-grains disseminated through the mass ; their gray color is due to the abundant intermixture of minutely granular martite. These dark slaty seams occupy the lower horizon of the series, and form generally the basal part of the rock-bluffs all along the range ; frequently we see them considerably corrugated or completely shattered, and recemented into a breccia by a sandy, hydro-micaceous, schistose material. South of the high range we find a detached lower quartzite ridge in the N.E. quarter of the S.W. quarter of Sect. 28. The beds dip north under an angle of 50° or 60° ; uppermost are compact, whitish, thick-bedded quartzite layers ; the lower beds of the series are conglomeratic, and consist principally of flinty quartzite pebbles imbedded into a ferrugino-micaceous or chloritic sand-rock mass of compact quartzitic structure. The south side of this ridge is lined with low cliffs of this conglomerate, at the base of which follow, in conformable succession, dark reddish brown silico-ferruginous beds, interlaminated with flaggy seams of more or less pure granular iron-ore ; other rock-seams are banded jaspers, like those of the Negaunee hematitic mines. A narrow swamp intervenes then, and on the high ground south of it the same iron-bearing strata come again to the surface, and compose nearly all the surface on the south side of the valley, where the Home mines, Gribben mines, and a number of others have been opened. At the Home mines and the Gribben mines we find the ore-bearing beds not directly overlaid by the conglomerate of quartzite, but a dark blackish-green chloritic schist, of obscurely brecciated structure, more visible on the bleached, weather-worn surfaces, intervenes, in a belt of 60 or 70 feet in thickness. A small knob in the swamp, about 150 steps west of the first-mentioned outcrops of the ore-formation, consists of the same brecciated chlorite schist.

The just-mentioned mines, and several others adjoining them, were abandoned, some time ago, as the ore is too siliceous. The ore-formation in these localities may amount to an aggregate thickness of 500 or 600 feet, and consists principally of thin-bedded, flaggy layers of siliceous, low-graded ores interstratified with richer seams of sub-specular flag-ore, and of jasper-banded mixed ore-beds, very similar to the jasper-banded rock of the Negaunee hematite mines. There are also white and red mottled argillitic belts similar to the so-called soapstone of the Jackson mines, interlaminated with the series, which leans in steep inclination with northern dip, on the north slope of a high granite range trending along the north line of Sects. 32, 33, and 34, from west to east.

Above the ore-bearing rock-beds, in some places the before-mentioned chloritic schist is deposited ; but most generally we find a very coarse quartzite conglomerate to be the hanging wall of the formation, which conglomerate may locally have the quality of an ordinary coarse-grained ferruginous quartzite. The foot-wall of the formation is a series of micaceo-chloritic, quartzose, or feldspathic and calcareous schists, mingled with novaculitic seams, with quartz-belts, and with irregular lenticular masses of a granular siliceous limestone. Frequently these rock-beds are found in a shattered condition, recemented into a breccia ; they seem to underlie the ore-formation conformably, and repose on the south side directly on the granite ; their thickness is in these localities not much over 250 or 300 feet. A large hill, with truncated plateau-like top occupying all the south half of Sect. 27, and detached from the granite range, is totally formed of the ore-formation ; but the numerous test-pits opened on it have never uncovered anything better than jasper-banded mixed ores, which are on the south side of the hill naturally exposed in high bluffs ; the dip of the strata is to the north.

The largest and most valuable deposits of iron-ore are found farther west, in the south half of Sect. 29, and in the north half of Sect. 31 ; and there the relative position of the ore-bearing series to the quartzite formation is so well exhibited by natural and artificial exposures that I consider these localities as the most instructive with regard to the geological structure of this part of the country. In the north half of the S.E. quarter of Sect. 29, Town. 47, R. 26, an insular low ridge, not over 80 feet elevated above the swamp lands encircling it from all sides, is composed of the iron-ore formation conformably overlaid by thick ledges of a coarse-grained red quartzite, locally changing into a coarse conglomerate rock, composed partly of rounded water-worn pebbles, partly of angular fragments of flinty quartzite, of red-banded ferruginous jasper of novaculitic or argillitic schist and other kinds of rock. The strata dip under an angle of 60° northward. The large body of the ore-formation is formed of red jasper-banded mixed ores, entirely corresponding with the red jasper-banded mixed ore-belts of the Jackson mine or Cleveland mine ; and in these mines, various larger and smaller belts of a pure hard specular ore are found interlaminated, and are successfully mined. On the south side of the valley the slope of the high hill-range is formed of the same succession of rock-beds, which there exhibit considerable variations in character of the same ledges within a very small distance. Also the dip of the strata is locally changing from an angle of 70° to an inclination of not more than 25°. Red jasper-banded siliceous ore-beds succeed one and another in great uniformity, folded and twisted, as if once they had been in a perfectly soft, flexible condition, and amounting to a thickness of perhaps more than a thousand feet. Interlaminated with them are belts of high-graded specular ore, partly of granular structure, partly in the form of slate-ore. On this series lie, at the opening of the Cascade mine, dark iron-colored, compact quartzite beds, of a middling fine granular structure, which, a short distance farther east on the hill, are in their turn overlaid by a conglomerate rock, having partly the structure of a very coarse sandstone with a micaceo-ferruginous cement being partly formed of an agglomeration of large pebbles and angular fragments, some of which have the size of a man's head, which are all firmly cemented together by a micaceo-chloritic sandy interstitial mass, often disseminated with granules of martite. The pebbles are glassy or flinty quartzite, jasper-banded siliceous iron-ores, novaculitic, and argillaceous slate fragments, and dioritic rocks. These conglomerates have the thickness of from 50 to 60 feet, and can be followed in one continuous sheet all the way east to the Gribben mines, whose ore differs considerably from the Cascade mine ores by its lower-graded, flaggy quality, although they represent exactly the same geological horizon. The foot-wall of the Cascade mine is not well exposed, but on the intervening space between the jasper-banded ores and the granite which forms the hill row in the south half of the N.W. quarter of Sect. 32, hydro-micaceous and novaculitic beds, in connection with dioritic and chloritic schists, are occasionally denuded. A large doleritic belt transversally intersects the ore-belt of the Cascade mine ; it is well exposed in the south part of the S.E. quarter of the S.W. quarter of Sect. 29, and again in the bluffs at the saw-mill in the S.W. corner of the N.W. quarter of Sect. 32, not 50 steps from the granitic outcrops at the large bend of the creek, which a short distance below unites with the east branch of the Escanaba River. The drift-covered plateau on the west side of the creek, which occupies the north half of Sect. 31, and is on the north side bordered by high granite hills, while along its south border, formed by the Escanaba River, the granite only comes to the surface in low knobs, is in its central part underlaid by the iron-bearing rock-series. The Palmer mine, opened in this locality, is the only mine of the Cascade range which was constantly kept in operation, while all the other mines had to suspend work ; it furnishes a good quality of granular specular ore and of slate-ore. The ore-bearing rock-belt, consisting, as in the Cascade mines, of red jasper-banded mixed lean ores, with interposed richer seams, amounts to a great thickness ; it dips north under an angle of about 45°. Next below one of the productive seams is a series of light-colored hydro-micaceous schists, interspersed with large leaflets of white mica, and in the same pit these beds and the ore-seam are transversally intersected by a doleritic dyke, part of which is in a decomposing condition, friable with the fingers into

6

a sand-mass ; west of the pit the continuation of the same dyke crops out in a row of cliffs in which the rock-mass is fresh and extremely hard. The hanging rock of the mines is a very coarse-grained quartzite, composed of glassy opalescent quartz-grains as large as peas, and some larger, in intermixture with red feldspar crystals, cemented by a fine scaly, micaceous, and somewhat ferruginous interstitial mass. Going from Palmer mine north-eastward, aiming for the high, conspicuous rock-bluffs in the centre of the north half of Sect. 30, we have to cross two rows of low granite hills, which are terminal spurs of the high granite hills west of there ; the low ground between these granitic rock-ridges is covered with a very coarse boulder-drift, full of large quartzite blocks of identical nature with those forming the hanging wall in the Palmer mines, and abounding in masses of float-ore of very fine specular quality, and in blocks of the red jasper-banded mixed ore. Beyond these granite hills, after passing across the creek draining Lake Palmer, we find in the centre of Sect. 30 a row of low rock-knobs in our way, formed of the same quartzite as the before-mentioned drift-boulders. The well-denuded, drift-polished rock-ledges dip under a high angle to the north, and seams of the generally very coarse-grained rock are full of larger, partly angular pebbles, of glassy or flinty quartz in different colors, of banded jaspery rocks, partly free of iron, partly formed of an alternation of specular ore-seams, with red jasper, besides fragments of chloritic schist, etc. A deep ravine on the north side of these quartzite knobs separates them from the much higher rock-ridge, which was the guiding landmark for us in our course. It faces the south with vertical walls consisting of stratified silico-ferruginous rocks of reddish brown color at the breast of the cliffs, which exhibit the same northern dip as the quartzites on the opposite side of the ravine. The more northern summit-part of the rock-walls is formed of a peculiar granite-like massive rock, intimately connected with the stratified portions of the cliffs by gradations. It is a fancifully red-spotted rock, composed of a fibrose scaly, hydro-micaceous, and sometimes chloritic ground-mass, serving as a cement for densely crowded quartz-grains, with intermixture of a granular feldspathic mass ; the red dots of the rock, at first sight taken for blood-red feldspar crystals, are actually produced by a seamy impregnation of the rock-substance in this place by hematitic pigment. The intimate relationship of this rock with the conglomeratic quartzites of the hills south of this range is obvious ; it follows the latter in regular succession, and is in its composition perfectly analogous with the altered protogine-like quartzites, which we found in nearly all the exposures in which the quartzite formation came in contact with the granite formation. On the north side of the presently considered granitoid rock, a belt of a very coarse conglomerate rock follows in conformable superposition ; its cement is dark green, colored by intermixture of chlorite scales. On this belt reposes a large succession of dark greenish-colored quartzites, of granular arenaceous structure, composed of glassy grains of quartz cemented by a hydro-micaceo-chloritic interstitial mass ; these hard compact beds inclose sometimes distantly dispersed quartz-pebbles. Some of the rock-beds exposed in association with iron-ore seams at the Gilmore mine, and those seen in the outcrops all along the railroad for a mile west of the mine, are so similar to the last-described chloritic quartzite that hand-specimens of them, laid side by side, cannot be distinguished from each other. Examining the hills farther north in this direction, we find this quartzite rock overlaid by arenaceo-ferruginous flagstones, which represent the group above the quartzite formation. Similar chloritic quartzite beds and arenaceo-ferruginous flagstones succeed above the white compact quartzites, which form the hills in Sects. 20 and 21, north of the Cascade mines. Two miles west of the Cascade mines an outcrop of the lower beds of the quartzite formation occurs under rather peculiar circumstances, and totally isolated from the eastern exposures of this rock-series. If we follow the centre line of Sect. 26, Town. 47, R. 27, from the south quarter-post of the section to the quarter-post on the north line, we find all the surface rock to be granite until we come to the centre of the section, where, on top of a terrace-like projection of the slope of a higher range, we step at once from well-denuded characteristic granites unto a coarse-grained sub-schistose light-colored reddish and yellowish tinged quartzite, consisting of grains of vitreous quartz imbedded into a silky-shining hydro-micaceous cement-mass. These well-stratified beds of about 30 feet thickness dip under high angle northward, and are regularly succeeded by another rock-belt of 25 feet thickness, very similar in composition with the former, but dark lead-colored,

with sub-metallic lustre, which color is due to a large proportion of
martite granules mingled with the mass. Next above this rock
another belt of a finer grained and lighter colored reddish quartzite
follows, equalling the former in thickness, and then a high bluff of
dark green chlorito-hydro-micaceous schists inclosing irregular
concretionary seams of a siliceous lime-rock, ascends closely
adjoining the quartzite beds, and, as it appears, conformably
superimposed on them. It forms the south part of the summit
elevation, which is formed of a large granite belt adjoining the
schists, and occupying the centre and the north slope of this ridge.
The thickness of the chloritic schistose belt amounts to about 70
feet. The next following hill is formed of chloritic and dioritic
schists, which have a northern dip ; farther on, the line descends
to a somewhat lower level, and passes over several knobs of crystalline diorite ; but arrived at the quarter-post of the north line
we find the flaggy beds of the iron formation beneath our feet.
A very short distance east or south-east of this spot are the so-
called old Tilden mines, and north-west of the place we find the
Foster mines ; both of them are at present abandoned. The
above-described exposure of the quartzite formation, wedged in
between two granite belts and overlaid by schists, which, according
to their lithological character, belong to a lower horizon, must present the ledges in an overturned position. We should expect, according to the structural arrangement in the Gribben mines, to see
the iron formation represented in this exposure between the upper
ledges of the quartzite and the chloritic schists inclosing calcareous
bands, which latter are very similar to the schists forming the
foot-wall of the ore-formation in the Gribben mines, but I could
not discover a sign of its being there ; and north of this locality,
where the iron-formation is very extensively exposed, directly reposing on rock-beds similar to the chloritic schists of the bluff, we
cannot find a trace of the quartzite formation incumbent on the
ores. Farther west, no more quartzite is seen within the examined
district, which could with propriety be considered as a continuation of this large body of rocks, followed without interruption
from the shore of Lake Superior, near Harvey's furnace, to the
western town-line of R. 26, Town. 47.

CHAPTER IV.

IRON GROUP.

BEFORE I entered the special description of the different groups into which I subdivided the Huronian rock-series, I made the remark that, owing to the circumstance that I confined myself to the next environs of Marquette when I began my investigations, I was led into a misconception of the true order of sequence between the beds by the local conditions existing there, but that subsequent examination of the more western districts convinced me of being in error when I considered the quartzite formation as older than the iron formation.

The first reposes near Marquette, and also in the Teal Lake range, in apparent conformity on the dioritic rock-series, without intervention of any deposits which could be taken as an analogon or equivalent of the iron-ore group, developed a very short distance south of the Teal Lake range in so great a thickness that one can hardly imagine how so large a succession of beds should at once be eliminated from the succession in the series in a locality so near to the other. This fact, supported by several rock-exposures, in which the ore-bearing beds seem to be actually incumbent on the Teal Lake quartzites, if the conformable dip of the strata is taken as a proof of their regular succession, induced me to consider the ore-formation of the Negaunee mines as much younger than the Teal Lake quartzites, and, as a matter of course, the quartzites visibly reposing on the ore-beds in all the different mines of the district, I then thought to be still younger deposits totally different from the other quartzites, in accordance with the opinions of my predecessor in the examination of this district, Major T. B. Brooks.

According to the information subsequently acquired by me,

during the study of other localities, I had to change my views; and I hope to prove in the following pages their correctness—that is to say, I will demonstrate the identity of the so-called upper and lower quartzite formations, and the older age of the ore-bearing rock-series than these deposits have.

The conformable superposition of the quartzite formation on the iron-bearing rock-belt of the Cascade range, and the deposition of the latter on schistose beds analogous with those of the dioritic group, which on their part rest on the granite formation, is sufficiently described in the previous chapter, and needs only to be remembered here.

Major Brooks could not help making the same observation; but prepossessed by the idea that the ore-belt of the Negaunee mines was a much later deposit than the quartzite formation of the Teal Lake range, and at the same time acknowledging the identity of these quartzites with the quartzites overlying the Cascade ores, he solved the dilemma by the assumption of two ore-bearing horizons, one below, the other above the quartzite, although he found it strange to see the Cascade ore-belt not represented on the north side of the Teal Lake range, where it should be expected, according to the synclinal arrangement of the rock-crust.

The surface rock of the environs of Negaunee and Ishpeming is almost exclusively formed of the iron-bearing rock-series, but much of it is covered by drift deposits.

The strata are in an extremely disturbed condition, folded and distorted in every possible way, usually without causing a rupture of the beds; but in some other instances the laminated banded seams composing the thicker ledges have ruptured, and the ends often came in a faulted position to each other, and were so re-cemented by the siliceous ground-mass, or else the cracks of the shattered rock were filled out with hydrated oxide of iron in various form, from the compact aphanitic porcelain-like condition, to the coarsely crystalline, or the fibrous structure of grape-ore, or in porous ochraceous masses. These disturbed beds lie, in every instance, directly, but very often inconformably on chlorito-hydro-micaceous schists, or on crystalline dioritic masses, which are constant associates of these chloritic schists, or sometimes dioritic schists, as hornblende and chlorite substitute each other, or are both components of them.

Overlooking the extremely plicated and corrugated condition of the strata, they form, considered in their totality, a synclinal basin hemmed in between dioritic ridges. A northern ridge of diorite hills commences north of the last houses of Negaunee village, in the centre of the N.W. quarter of Sect. 6, Town. 47, R. 26, and extends in due western direction to the west line of Sect. 2, Town. 47, R. 27 ; the summit of this narrow ridge is cut up into rounded knobs, severed from each other by drift-covered intervals.

The diorite hills forming the south border of the synclinal, much higher than the northern, are not connected into one continuous ridge ; they are parts of a large dioritic mountain mass, covering over 8 square miles of surface on the south side of Negaunee and Ishpeming, and cut up by deep valleys and ravines into a large number of smaller sub-parallel ridges and knobs, which trend from east-south-east to west-north-west, and many isolated diorite knobs, found dispersed over the inner part of the synclinal trough, actually are parts of this large southern body of diorite.

The structure of the ore-formation in the vicinity of Negaunee is well exhibited by the Jackson mine, which principally opens the upper part of the formation, while the lower beds, occupying the slope of the high diorite hills on the south side, are the mining ground for a large number of other companies, which have riddled the surface with hundreds of test-pits, besides the numerous larger excavations from which the ore is taken. The Jackson mines are situated on the north side of a short isolated ridge of from 100 to 150 feet elevation, which extends from east to west across the eastern two thirds of the north part of the south half of Sect. 1, Town. 47, R. 27. This ridge is completely formed of thick ledges of a banded, very compact rock of quartzoso-ferruginous composition. The banded appearance of the rock is produced by an alternation of narrow, inseparably united seams, of which one kind consists of a jaspery quartz-mass, generally bright red colored by iron oxide ; the other likewise quartzose seams of the rock are dark blackish, or else of a metallic steel color, by impregnation with a large proportion of granules of martite, or with scaly micaceous ore particles of metallic lustre. Oftentimes these ferruginous seams have the quality of a rich ore-mass, with very little siliceous matter in it. Interlaminated with these mixed rock-ledges are belts of pure iron-ore, in compact granular masses, or in the schistose form of the so-called specular slate-ore, amounting to greater thickness, available for the miner, but found to be quite irregular in their extension, widening locally into large pockets, twenty, thirty, and more feet wide, or wedging out in another place to almost total disappearance, and some distance farther on perhaps expanding again into a seam of valuable thickness. Associated with these ore-seams are usually belts of argillitic schists called soapstone by the miner for its talcy lubricity ; and the occurrence of these schists in a test-pit is considered by him as a sure indication of an ore-deposit somewhere near by. They consist of a fine scaly or granular soft aluminous silicate, readily cut with a knife, which, colorless in itself, is tinged by red oxide of iron, either uniformly and in various degrees of intensity, or the pale yellowish ground-mass is dotted with irregular large streaky blotches of red, or other beds of red color are found regularly speckled by white dots of the size of a lentil, which I cannot better describe than by comparing their aspect with the dotted plumage of a Guinea-hen. Such peculiarly speckled schists are met with in many other mines besides the Jackson. Other schists of similar argillitic and partly hydro-micaceous composition, of a gray sub-metallic color, are more or less densely disseminated with small octahedric crystals of martite, which, however, are also not missing in the red-colored layers. The ore of the Jackson mines is taken from different belts, of which nearly every one furnishes a different kind of ore, but the chaotically plicated and dislocated condition of the rock-beds rarely allows recognition of the exact relative position which one belt holds to the other ; the miner pursuing a belt often finds it wedging out or abruptly cut off, and has to take his chances by drifting ahead in some direction to meet the other end again, or to find another different seam.

A very rich seam of ore is almost invariably found on top of this jasper - banded rock-series, immediately beneath the quartzites which form the terminal strata in all these exposures. This upper ore-belt is almost regularly brecciated in its upper part, and the same is true of the lower quartzite beds, which often are a mixture of ore-fragments with quartzite pieces held together by an arenaceous cement. As this is the case in nearly all the mines of the district, we must suggest that great disturbances, of not only a local extent, must have occurred at the end of this era of iron sediments. At the Jackson mine these quartzites, terminating the succession of rock-beds, are only represented by a small series of dark iron-colored ledges. The general dip of the formation is northward, and the south side of the described ridge is formed of vertical rock-walls exhibiting the edges of the steeply inclined beds. Near the west end of the Jackson mines several small knobs of diorite, associated with schists belonging to this rock-group, project, closely surrounded by the jasper-banded rock-beds in a vertical position, and evidently corrugated by the intrusion of these masses. In the valley south of the bluffs of Jackson mine hill, and on the slope of the high diorite ridge on the south side of it, exposures of more thinly laminated ferruginous siliceous rock-beds follow, amounting to a belt of at least a thousand feet in thickness. The largest portion of this rock-series is made up of regularly alternating bands, from a quarter of an inch to one inch in thickness, of a paler or darker drab-colored jasper, and of similar seams of ferruginous matter in different degrees of purity, and of different molecular structure. Sometimes these seams, intimately coherent with the jasper-seams, are an almost pure granular martite of metallic lustre, but usually a dull blackish red impure siliceous iron-ore with a sandy fracture composes them, or else they are formed of a bluish black aphanitic oxide, hard, but quite brittle, breaking with very smooth conchoidal fracture.

Another part of this series, interstratified with the jasper-banded beds, consists of argillitic rock-seams, all impregnated with considerable proportions of red oxide of iron ; but there are also rich ore-seams intercalated at different horizons of this large succession of beds, which make it one of the most productive fields for the miner. These ore-deposits are not regular sedimentary layers, originally formed of iron oxide in this state of purity, but are evidently the product of decomposition of the impurer mixed ferruginous ledges by percolating water, leaching out the siliceous matter, and replacing it by deposition of oxide of iron held in solution ; the ore-seams are therefore very irregular, narrow in one place and widening in another into large pockets 40 and 50 feet in diameter, or even larger. They consist generally of a crummy, porous, dark brown or blackish mass of dull earthy aspect, readily dug out with the pickaxe and shovel, composed partly of not-hydrated, partly of hydrated oxide. Within these seams are more compact concretionary masses, partly of small nodular size, partly in large bulky seams, so-called hog-backs, consisting almost exclusively of hydrated oxide of the radiated fibrous structure of grape-ore, or in the granular crystalline form of goethite, or in an amorphous compact condition. In other parts of the mines the ore is a yellowish-brown earthy ochraceous mass. All those ores contain a certain variable percentage of manganese, and a part of the concretionary masses consists of pure pyrolusite in brightly shining fibrous crystal clusters ; more rare is the occurrence of concretions of the pale rose-colored sparry carbonate of manganese and lime. Associated with these concretionary hydrated ores are seams of milk-white glassy quartz, and nests of fine crystals of heavy-spar ; occasionally occur also cubical pseudo-morphous crystals of hydrated iron oxide an inch and more in diameter ; but particularly interesting is the abundant intermixture of snow-white nodular masses of a soft, very lubricous, minutely scaly aluminous silicate, termed by the miner *magnesia,* and mentioned in Major Brooks' Report under the name kaolinite ; it is somewhat surprising how such concretions, totally inclosed within the intensely-colored ore-masses, could form without the least contamination with oxide of iron. The material of the so-called soapstone of the mines is chemically the same as that of the kaolinite, only in a harder, more compact, granular, instead of scaly condition. This lower thin-bedded series is, like the beds of the Jackson mine, bent into numerous sharp folds, many of which curvatures are splendidly exposed in the mining-pits ; we can observe in the same places the contiguity of these rock-beds with dioritic rock-masses, which squarely broke through such arches of ledges, and pushed their severed ends in faulted positions to each other on the two sides. The discordance existing between the dioritic and the iron-bearing rock-groups is obvious in the majority of natural or artificial exposures, although it often occurs that they adjoin each other in parallelism.

On the higher part of the hill-slope south of the Jackson mine ridge, very close to the south line of Sect. 1, and not far from the margins of the ore-formation where it abuts against the dioritic summit part of the hill, a large doleritic dyke 70 or 80 feet wide intersects it in a direction from east to west. The external portions of the dyke-mass, in contiguity with the ferruginous beds, are in a rotten, friable condition ; the central parts of it are very hard and compact ; the grain of the rock is coarse enough to distinguish with the naked eye its composition of greenish-brown augite crystals, and of glassy white feldspar in about an equal proportion. The feldspar, in the weathered, decomposing portions of the rock, is milky white, and some of it totally transformed into kaolin.

The above-described section across the ore-formation, from the Jackson mine southward, comprises Groups XII., XIII., and XIV. of Major Brooks' subdivisions. The quartzites constituting Group XIV. are, according to my views, analogous to the Teal Lake quartzites, which are in Major Brooks' arrangement placed with his Group V. These strata are in the Jackson mining location only poorly represented ; we find them much better developed in the mines farther west. All the ore-bearing rock-beds of the Negaunee district I left together in one group ; they form an uninterrupted succession, and are composed of similar material ; moreover, these lower beds, constituting Group XII., are restricted to the vicinity of Negaunee and Ishpeming, while in the western mines no equivalent for them is found. I consider them as a locally developed series of deposits, not deserving to be ranked as a separate formation. The beds of hydrated ores are not peculiar to the lower strata alone ; similar seams of hydrated oxides in the shape of grape-ore and non-crystalline earthy masses occur in the Jackson mines, closely adjoining the belts of specular-ore. In one of such seams of the Jackson mine, cellulose earthy hydrated ores occur, whose cavities are filled with a soft, bright green mealy mineral, which, on chemical examination, proves to be silicate of chromoxide.

All other parts of the hill-side situated north of the pits of the Jackson mine, and north of the Houghton and Ontonagon Railroad track, are formed of the same red jasper-banded ferruginous rocks as those composing the higher part of the ridge ; they likewise inclose valuable belts of specular ore, which is mined on the west side of the slope. In the adjoining valley, and on the slope of the diorite range on its opposite side, the rock-beds are deeply buried under drift-deposits, with exception of a patch on the hill-slope, about 150 or 200 steps in width, where the red jasper banded lean ores are seen to repose with southern dip directly on the diorite. The ledges exposed amount to a belt of 75 or 80 feet in thickness, and the ferruginous bands of the rock are rich in bright ore particles, but no ore-seam of any value has been found, although explorers have left vestiges of their work at this spot. East of the Jackson mine the ore-bearing beds soon disappear under the drift. About 300 steps from the most eastern pit, close to the Houghton and Ontonagon Railroad depot, a productive belt of soft hydrated iron-ores has been discovered by sinking a shaft ; but farther east, across the creek passing Negaunee village, the ore-formation disappears beneath the dark-colored sandy flag-stones of the fifth group. Some test-pits near the base of the knobs east of the Negaunee iron-furnace have uncovered red-colored siliceous flags of a ferruginous character, which are the last exposure of the ore-formation seen in this direction. The course of the above-mentioned creek, a tributary of the Escanaba, forms near Negaunee a natural line of demarcation for the different rock-formations. All the hill-slopes on the west side. of the valley are formed of the lower, thinly-laminated part of the ore-bearing rock-series, and all on the east side, leaving drift deposits out of consideration, are found to be arenaceous and slaty rock-beds representing Group V. of the subdivisions adopted by me for the Huronian rock-series.

The description of the lower part of the iron formation south of the Jackson mines applies also to the more eastern exposures on the south side of the creek. The McOmber mine, in the N.W. quarter of the N.W. quarter of Sect. 7, Town. 47, R. 26, next adjoining the Jackson mine property, is one of the most productive mines of soft hydrated and generally more or less manganiferous ores, which the miner, ignoring their partially hydrated condition, calls hematite ores. East of the McOmber mine is Schade's mine, still richer in manganese ores than the former. It is situated in the N.E. quarter of the N.W. quarter of Sect. 7, high up on the hill, in a depression between two ridges formed on the summit of diorite and dioritic schists, but surrounded completely by the ore-bearing beds, which in their extremely folded condition dip in every direction, sometimes toward the diorite, other times falling away from it. Lower down on the slope of the northern ridge several other large mining-pits are opened in the S.E. quarter of the S.W. quarter of Sect. 6, and recently rich deposits of hematite ore have been discovered in the S.E. quarter of the N.W. quarter of Sect. 7.

Many other mines in the same rock-belt are found scattered along the east slope of the hills in the S.E. quarter of Sect. 7, and in the N.E. quarter of Sect. 18. In the latter localities the dip of the ore-bearing beds is generally directed toward the hill, and on a higher level we find in some of these localities a series of dark blackish-colored ferrugino-arenaceous flagstones, or thicker quartzose ledges incumbent on them, which often contain large proportions of granules of magnetite. Good exposures of these quartzose magnetic strata can be seen near the S.E. corner of Sect. 7, where they lie on the side of a diorite hill near its summit, dipping toward it, while at the base the hematitic rock-beds crop out, dipping in the same direction as the black magnetic rock-ledges. The last mining-pit on this eastern slope of the range has been opened near the quarter-post on the east line of Sect. 18, but no merchantable ore was found ; farther south, the above-mentioned arenaceo-ferruginous flagstones form the surface-rock, which I consider as representatives of the fifth subdivision of the Huronian series. Very extensive exposures of the lower iron-bearing rock-beds are in the N.W. quarter of Sect. 8, and in the adjoining parts of Sect. 7, where they surround an isolated short ridge of diorite, partly leaning on its sides, partly dipping toward it ; they inclose valuable seams of the so-called hematite ores. In direct continuity with these outcrops is a cut of the Escanaba Railroad, made across

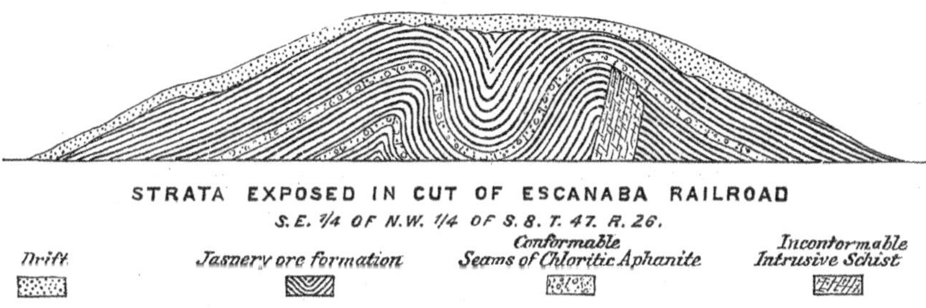

a bubble-like hillock of this formation, which forms a basal spur of a higher hill-range composed of massive quartzites and of slaty and flaggy arenaceo-ferruginous rock-beds. The strata in the cut form two successive anticlinal arches, which are in two places transversally intersected by wedge-like masses of chloritic schists intruded from below. The upper portion of the ledges is formed of the banded alternating beds of pale brownish jasper, and of siliceous ore-seams like the jasper-banded rocks of the McOmber mines ; beneath them are intensely red-colored argillite strata, in alternation with a few thick seams of dark green chloritic rock of very fine, almost aphanitic grain, and with siliceous flagstones richly impregnated with specular ore particles. The quartzites composing the higher part of the hill are not seen in direct contact with the ore-bearing beds, on account of heavy drift-deposits on the place, but from the general position of the ledges, and from the circumstance that masses of schist analogous with the schists of the dioritic group have been forced into the ore-belt from below, I infer that this could not be, if the very massive quartzites closely adjoining were the underlying rock ; they should have first been pushed to the surface and been wedged into the ore-beds. In the mining-pits, not 50 steps from the place, several other such anticlinal bubbles of iron-rock, intersected by chloritic schists, can be seen denuded ; and, moreover, we observe in these pits the direct superposition of the ore-beds on the diorite. I believe, therefore, that the quartzites forming the higher part of the hill are the incumbent, and not the underlying rock in this exposure. The absence of the upper ore-bearing, red jasper-banded rock-series, with inclosed seams of hard specular ore, and of the quartzites incumbent on it, from the exposures of the lower part of this group on the east side of Negaunee, is remarkable, because younger strata, which elsewhere have their place above these eliminated beds, directly succeed the others. These younger rock-beds cover most of the surface east of this place for many square miles, and no more of the iron-formation can be discovered in that direction. West of Negaunee and of the Jackson mines we find the ore-formation expanding over a large portion of the surface for a distance of three miles ; much of it is covered up with drift ; but the miner, diligently searching over all this space by sinking shafts and with the diamond drill, has demonstrated its uninterrupted extension beneath these drift-masses as a fact. Scattered over this area are numerous insular hills of dioritic rock, which pierces the incumbent ore-bearing layers, and stands out in high precipitous cliffs, or in lower hillocks rounded off by drift action. Mines are opened in the red-banded jaspery lean ores in the S. E. corner of Sect. 2, Town. 48, R. 27, close to the base of vertical bluffs of diorite, which furnish principally soft hematite ores. Farther west, some hillocks in Sect. 11, south of the Houghton and Ontonagon Railroad track, are composed of a dioritic nucleus incased within a girdle of the jaspery lean ores, and next ahead of them a large knob, over which the west line of Sect. 11 runs, is totally composed of an anticlinal arch of these beds, with inclosed valuable seams of specular ore. In a western prolongation of this knob the Cleveland Mining Company has worked some of these seams ; on the south side of the knob are the Marquette mines. North of this hill are the main openings of the Cleveland Company and the New York mines, which work the same body of ore-deposits. North and east of the mines are large diorite hills, on which the ore-bearing strata lean with southern dip, in direct contact with the schistose beds of this rock-group.

The ore-bearing rock-beds, after falling away from the diorites under a steep angle, bend up and down again to form several more shallow successive folds, which in places have been totally undermined, and the synclinal troughs excavated in that way, with a heavy hanging wall suspended over them by frail distant pillars, look very dangerous, and will sooner or later break down, as has already happened in some parts of the mines.

The quartzites covering the ore-bearing ledges are compact, dark-colored by hematitic pigment, and by intermingled granules of martite ; the inferior strata are almost regularly brecciated and intermingled with ore-fragments. In the pits of the Cleveland mine, south of the Houghton and Ontonagon Railroad, these brecciated quartzites are immediately underlaid by a fine seam of specular ore, which itself is on its surface of brecciated structure. This ore-bed is underlaid by a series of light greenish or grayish-colored silky-shining hydro-micaceous schists, impregnated with small martite crystals, which on their part repose on the red jasper-banded lean ores, with inclosed seams of granular and of slaty specular ore. In the pits north of the railroad the quartzite is generally underlaid by chloritic schists inclosing locally quite large octahedrons of martite ; below them usually follows a valuable seam of specular ore, schistose chloritic beds again, and then mixed jasper-banded lean ores, with other interstratified seams of ore, partly in the granular form, partly as a slate-ore ; lowest, resting on dioritic schists, are, in the New York mines, fine-grained silky-shining dark gray-colored argillites, charged with minute granules of martite more or less abundantly. The lower beds analogous to the strata of the McOmber mines are not found here.

Outcrops of the iron formation continue all along the hill-side from the Marquette mine west to the Lake Superior mine, situated on the north slope of an isolated diorite hill, which forms the terminal western spur of the range of diorite hills commencing south of Negaunee. By boring with the diamond drill it has been ascertained that the whole swamp valley on which Ishpeming is located is underlaid by the iron formation.

The ore-bearing beds in the Lake Superior mine lie in steep inclination, with northern dip directly on the diorite, or on schistose beds belonging to this group, but in other parts of the mine the strata are seen to be bent and folded repetitiously, and to dip in the most irregular way—much more so than in the Cleveland and New York mines. Uppermost in the succession we find heavy compact beds of a light-colored whitish or reddish quartzite, which are particularly well exposed in the pits of the Barnum mine, which naturally forms an integrant part of the Lake Superior mine, although owned by different parties. Beneath the quartzite succeeds a series of hydro-micaceous and argillitic schists, inter-laminated with seams of quartzite. The variety in the aspect of the schists is quite manifold, but closer examination shows them all to be composed of a fine scaly hydro-micaceous, or of a more granular crystalline argillitic ground-mass, modified by the admixture of different proportions of hematite or chlorite, or of martite in smaller or larger octahedric crystals, or in the form of micaceous iron oxide, which latter kind of schists is by gradations in the proportion of the micaceous iron particles directly allied with the specular slate-ores which occur in this upper horizon. These schists are underlaid by a fine-grained chloritic rock-seam, which overlies a seam of rich specular ore, and lower, a large succession of red jasper-banded mixed ores follows, which incloses other valuable ore-seams. In the old pits, mined out, we see large belts of the so-called soapstone interstratified with the jasper-banded lean ores, and adjoined sometimes by dioritic schists, protruding from beneath, and, as it appears, wedged in between the ore-bearing belt during the uplift and dislocation of the strata. On the east side of the hill, and south of the jasper-banded specular lean ores, soft hydrated iron-ores similar to the Negaunee hematites are mined by the same company ; the deposits visibly underlie the jaspery massive rock-ledges, and repose in a much-corrugated and shattered condition on the schists of the diorite group. These lower beds extend southward along the hill-slope, and are in all probability in direct connection with the soft ore-beds of the Lake Angeline mine. The Lake Angeline mines, situated in the north part of the N.W. quarter of Sect. 15, close to the shore of the west end of Lake Angeline and at the foot of a steep-sided ridge of diorite, principally work the lower hematitic ore-belt, which closely adjoins in an almost vertical position the dioritic rock-walls. Some distance farther east on the slope the higher red jasper-banded ledges, with inclosed belts of hard specular ore, are found developed, and some mining work is done in these hard ore-seams. On the south side of these same diorite hills are the Salisbury mines, in which locality only the lower strata of the ore-formation are represented. A large portion of the ledges exposed there are siliceous flag-ores which are not rich enough to be mined ; the main product are hydrated ores, similar to those of the Negaunee hematite mines. In the Salisbury mines a large quantity of waste rock is hoisted and used as a bedding for the railroad track, not only there, but also on the road-bed of the North-Western Railroad, where it runs through the swamp lands near Ishpeming. The peculiar structure of the rock excites particular interest. It is a siliceous rock, richly impregnated with hydrated oxide of iron of a brownish, and to a great extent of a bright yellow ochraceous color. A part of it is compact, but most of it has a very open, cellulose, and to a certain extent laminated structure. The compact portions are comparable to an accumulation of layers of branching fucoidal stems, with club-shaped ends, which were imbedded in a solid siliceous ground-mass, which siliceous skeleton, after destruction of the material of the stems, had the remaining cylindrical branching and anastomosing cavities replenished with a porous silico-ochraceous substance. In the rock of cellulose structure, which seems to be a partially decomposed form of the first-mentioned compact rock, the compact interstitial siliceous skeleton seems to be removed by being leached out, and the porous, stem-like parts are the preserved portion.

7

Other portions of the rock of porous or cellulose structure consist of a succession of delicate laminæ, with a hollow interval between each of the layers, which are connected and support each other by their regular wavelike curvation, causing their alternate approximation and anchylosis, and the subsequent divergence of the laminæ. These last-mentioned rocks have a striking resemblance to the so-called eozoon, but I have not the least idea of considering either them or the eozoon as of organic origin, although I made the comparison, which was done simply to point out the occurrence of such resemblance to organic forms by a *lusus naturæ*, as it may be termed, because I am not prepared to give an explanation of the mode in which such singularly shaped rocks were formed.

A half mile south-east of the Salisbury mine a rich belt of specular ore has been discovered on the south side of a diorite knob in the N.W. quarter of the S.E. quarter of Sect. 16 ; the strata dip north toward the diorite, and were there covered deeply with drift-masses. Lower down the slope of this hill-side the strata come to the surface in natural outcrops at the location of the Parsons mine. On the N.W. side of the mining pits is a cluster of small rocky knobs, of which the largest, most western, consists of thick-bedded massive quartzite ledges in a succession amounting to about 200 feet. The highest of the strata, which dip under an angle of 45° west-north-west, are of a light whitish color ; they exhibit on their side faces a striation of sedimentary deposition in discordant layers, which is so often noticeable in the sandstone deposits of Silurian age, and in all the more recent formations. Below the light-colored quartzites follow similar very compact ledges of dark purplish color, and of a rather coarse sandy grain, but a vitreous fracture ; the dark color of the rock is due to abundant intermixture of martite granules with the mass. The lower strata of this dark quartzite are of brecciated structure, and inclose fragments of siliceous iron-ore. Underneath this rock-series, which composes the western of the knobs, follows a heavy belt of a breccia, composed almost exclusively of specular ore fragments cemented by siliceous matter, which rock-belt forms for itself the second row of lower knobs bordering the narrow valley of a small creek, beyond which, at a distance of a very few steps from the bluffs of the ore breccia, the diorite rises in steep walls at the base of a high ridge composed of this rock. By artificial exposure in mining, the ore breccia is found to be underlaid by a thick belt of solid specular ore of a rich quality, and beneath it a large succession of red jasper-banded mixed ores follows, which inclose several other valuable ore-seams. Fissures in the ore-belt of the Parsons mine are sometimes lined with heavy spar crystals of exquisite beauty in hexagonal tabular form, with sharpened edges, some of brilliant lustre and translucid, others dull opaque. Associated with the spar occur crystals of quartz, large bunches of micaceous iron, and a soft, nacreous, scaly, white kaolinite.

South of the Parsons mines a high ridge trends westward across the centre of the N.W. quarter of Sect. 21. On its north slope the naturally and partly artificially denuded red jasper-banded ore-beds are conspicuous from a distance. The strata dip north under an angle of 60° or 70°, and are overlaid by the quartzite formation which composes the lower undulating hills farther north. The south side of these hills of ore-bearing beds is mostly covered by drift, but in the western part, opposite the New England mines, good exposures are found in which the ledges of the jaspery lean ores are brecciated and inclose seams of a rich specular slate-ore, besides more siliceous beds of slaty structure. These are in descending order conformably succeeded by a large series of thin-bedded ferruginous ledges, corresponding with the Negaunee hematite ore-belt, which contain rich seams of soft hydrated ore, mined on the New England location, where the strata lay on the north side of large diorite bluffs, in close, but, as it appears, discordant contact with them. Also the rich hematite ores of the Winthrop and Shenango mines are mined from the eastern continuation of the same rock-belt in the N.W. quarter of the S.E. quarter of Sect. 21, which is there in similar contiguity with the dioritic knobs bordering it on the south side.

From the New England mines the ore-formation trends west and little north, and can be traced by outcrops and in test-pits to connect directly with the ore-belt of the Saginaw mines and Goodrich mines, everywhere overlaid on the north side by the quartzite formation, and on the south side in contact with dioritic rocks.

South of the diorite knobs, at the Shenango mine, is another large drift-covered hill, composed of jasper-banded ferruginous ledges, but it contains, as far as known, no valuable ore-seams.

East of it, on the opposite side of the swampy valley of a tributary of the Escanaba River, commences a high hill-range, trending eastward, regularly followed by the south section line of Sects. 22 and 23, which is totally composed of siliceous flag-ores, generally not rich enough to be valuable. The strata dip under a high angle northward, reposing on dioritic rocks, which form a chain of lower hills on the south side of this ridge, which is on its north side likewise followed by a parallel row of diorite hills severed from it by the valley of a creek. The Tilden mines and Foster mines are located on the eastern part of this ridge of lean ores, both near the south quarter-post of Sect. 23—the first south of it, the second north-west of it.

In the abandoned pits of the old Tilden mine, and in several neighboring natural exposures, the ore-formation is found to repose on the diorite or on the schists belonging to this group, but as it seems always in discordance. It consists of a large succession of thin-bedded arenaceo-ferruginous layers, dark brownish red on the surface, and blackish gray with some metallic lustre on fractured faces. All the rock contains martite granules and amorphous hematitic oxide as constituents, but a good portion of the layers is so richly impregnated with these oxides as to constitute ores of from 45 to 50 per cent metal assay. These richer beds of flag-ore were mined once, but did not prove to be salable in the market. In the Foster mines, on the north side of the hill-range, the ore-formation is not altogether formed of flaggy ledges, but a great part of the very thick rock-series is formed of thicker seams, resembling the jasper-banded ores of the Ishpeming mines or Negaunee mines. The productive ore-belt of the Foster mine is not composed of flag-ores, as in the Tilden mine ; it is a secondary accumulation of hydrated oxides in the form of a brecciated, very open cellulose, partly soft earthy, partly harder compact rock-mass ; the cavities of the amorphous cellulose harder oxidic rock are incrusted with a thin minutely warty coating of grape-ore, and often with brilliant small quartz crystals, and in addition the porous ores contain frequently a brightly cinnabar red oxide of iron in pulverulent masses. The percentage of these ores in iron is about 50 ; the mines have long been abandoned, and most of the ore taken out of them lies there unused.

On the slope of the high plateau, a quarter mile south-east of the old Tilden mine, is an exposure of a very large succession of ferruginous beds, dipping north under a high angle, which likewise resemble more the red jasper-banded rock-belt of the northern mines than the flaggy ore-bearing beds of the neighboring Tilden mines. At the base of the slope we find the granite at the surface.

The large succession of ore-bearing rock-beds surrounding the base of the diorite hills in the S.W. corner of Sect. 13, and the adjoining exposures in the S.E. quarter of Sect. 14, which were formerly mined by several companies, but are abandoned now, are perfectly analogous deposits with those of the old Tilden and of the Foster mine, and the same is the case with another outcrop on the north side of Lake Hall, in the N.E. quarter of the N.W. quarter of Sect. 14, which almost connects with the ore-deposits of the Lake Angeline mine.

Every one of these localities differs somewhat from the other in the character of its layers, but the unity of all these deposits as co-ordinate members of one formation is plainly obvious. The iron range on which the Tilden and Foster mines are located, and the deposits in Sects. 13 and 14, unquestionably represent the lower horizons of the ore-bearing series, but it is a remarkable fact that in the case of superposition of other strata on these beds we do not find them to be the quartzites next in the order of succession, but arenaceo-ferruginous beds identifiable with the younger group overlying the quartzite formation, which same observation I made before, when describing the exposures of the lower ore-bearing strata on the south-east side of Negaunee. A glance on the accompanying geological map will show a direct continuity existing between the beds incumbent on the ore-formation in the two mentioned places, and also the intercalation of the quartzite formation between these beds and the ore-bearing rock-belt of the Cascade mines will be noticed by looking more southward on the map.

Before I proceed to describe the ore-formation, as exhibited in the more western mining districts, I have yet to consider very interesting parts of the Negaunee and Ishpeming iron-bearing rock-belt on the north side of these villages. North-west of the Jackson mine we see the chain of diorite hills previously described interrupted by a depression through which a side-track of the North-Western Railroad Company is laid, which leads to the so-called

Teal Lake mines, situated on the north side of the aforesaid diorite range, and south of the west part of Teal Lake. The surface of this depression is covered with drift, but by examining the numerous test-pits opened on this space one can readily convince himself of the uninterrupted continuation of the iron-bearing rock-series across this gap from one side of the diorite range to the other. We found, as previously stated, a patch of the upper red jasper-banded beds of the iron formation leaning with southern dip on this diorite ridge, a few hundred steps east of this gap, but here we find the lower thin-bedded flaggy series, dipping likewise southward, on one side of the range as well as on the other ; therefore, while on the south side the strata lie on the diorite, they seem to dip under it on the north side. The flaggy layers are rich in granular martite ; some of them contain as much as 65 per cent of the oxide, and have been mined in the S.W. quarter of Sect. 36, Town. 48, R. 27, but the mines are now abandoned. Farther west, in the S.E. quarter of Sect. 35, other mines are opened in the brown jasper-banded layers, similar to those of the McOmber mine, which contain a rich belt of the soft hydrated ores, the belt is traced from there to the south-west corner of the section, south of which, in Sect. 2, Town. 47, R. 27, this soft ore-belt has a very great width and is of excellent quality. The soft ore in that locality, lying right under the surface, is taken out with the shovel like gravel, but as the excavations become deeper and the loose rock-masses cannot be timbered up, these mines are rather dangerous places to work in. The lower series of the ore-formation in the Teal Lake mines has a very great thickness, which cannot accurately be estimated, as the strata are much folded, but they amount at all events to six or eight hundred feet in thickness. By the excavations, various bubble-like dioritic masses have been uncovered, which by their intrusion into the stratified series have caused considerable corrugation of the adjoining rock-ledges.

This locality has caused me much perplexity with regard to the recognition of the true order in which the different groups of strata succeed each other. The ore-formation dips in this place, as previously stated, south, toward high cliffs of diorite, and is on its north side in close contact with slaty argillites, interstratified with sand-rock belts ; still farther north follows a series of banded ferrugino-siliceous beds, charged in certain seams with consider-able magnetite, all of which strata dip south in apparent conform-ity with the ore-formation ; then comes the bed of Teal Lake, and on its other side, the quartzite formation rises with its ledges from the water into high slanting bluffs, which likewise dip to the south. When I first saw this I felt great satisfaction, and con-sidered this place as one of the rare examples in which the succes-sion of the rock-formations could be plainly observed, and for a long time afterward I took it as an established fact that the ore-formation is the youngest of the three succeeding different rock-belts, and the quartzite-formation the oldest ; but after a while I came across a good many other exposures, which did not har-monize with this supposed order in the succession, and finally, by inference from a multitude of facts observed, I became convinced that the seeming conformity of these beds is not a proof of their actual order of succession, and that their present relative position is the result of an overturn of the strata.

I must confess to have not yet clearly conceived the exact mode of dislocation which would bring the beds in their present overturned position ; and I find it strange to see this ore-bearing series not at all developed on the north side of the quartzite range, where one naturally would expect it ; but con-sidering the other side of the question, I find a slaty and arena-ceous rock-belt identical with the one adjoining the ore-formation of the Teal Lake mines on the north side, largely developed on the south side of the quartzite range east of Negaunee, which leans with southern dip on the quartzite, just as in the other place, but a mile south of the range, this rock-belt is reverted into a northern dip, and the ore-bearing strata, exposed on its south side, appear to underlie it conformably.

The previously described cut of the Escanaba Railroad, near the centre of Sect. 8, Town. 47, R. 26, offers another example of the superposition of this arenaceous slate formation on the iron-ore group. The most forcible argument, however, for the lower position of the ore-formation is the circumstance that we find it in all the mining locations of the Negaunee district, never underlaid by quartzites or slaty rock-beds of the above-mentioned class, but always resting on the dioritic formation, and in several localities a large belt of quartzite reposes on the ore-group, which, by its light whitish color and great compactness, is so similar to the Teal Lake quartzite that hand-specimens cannot be distinguished. A quartzite of this description is naturally exposed in the village of Ishpeming on the railroad track a short distance west of the North-Western Railroad depot ; the heavy strata dip south under a high angle. A drill-hole was sunk two years ago through this quartzite to the depth of 400 feet, when a valuable seam of specular ore was struck, after the drill had gone for most of its length through quartzite, and then through a breccia of quartz and ore fragments. Several other holes were drilled west of this place, on the high ground south of Lake Bancroft, all with the success of striking an ore-belt about 400 feet below the surface. The Barnum Mining Company is at present engaged in sinking a shaft in one of the spots explored by the drill. One of the most instructive exposures of the ore-formation, and of the incumbent and succumbent rocks, is found west of Lake Bancroft, on the other side of Carp River, in the S.W. quarter of Sect. 4. The red jasper-banded mixed ores are on the top of a terrace-like extension of the hills, in several places well denuded from the drift-masses which cover the greatest part of the surface ; according to the distribution of the exposures they must amount to a belt of considerable thickness. North of this red-banded jasper rock follows a series of brownish jasper-banded ferruginous beds, which project in a row of low cliffs on the north edge of the terrace land. On its south side, and several hundred steps west of its exposures, a large belt of light-colored heavy quartzite beds crops out in low cliffs ; the almost vertical strata dip south like the jasper ores, on which they lean conformably. On the slope directly south of the quartzites, which amount to about 200 feet in thickness, is another undulation formed by an alternating series of dark-colored slates with sand-rock seams which dip south, in conformity with the quartzite belt ; they correspond in position and lithological character to the slate and sand-rock belt north of the Teal Lake mines, but are here indubitably deposited above the ore-formation. In this locality the superintendent of the Barnum mines, Mr. Sedgwick, sunk a hole with the diamond drill to the depth of 476 feet, and had the kindness to give me a complete set of cores in the order as the boring went on. The boring commenced in the quartzite. At a depth of 150 feet, sunk through quartzite, a 50-feet-wide seam of hydro-micaceous schists, interspersed with an abundance of martite crystals, was pierced ; then came again quartzites, part of them light-colored, others dark, highly ferruginous, and in a degree chloritic, to the depth of 320 feet from the surface ; at 324 feet a seam of a very coarse breccia of quartz and ore fragments, only one foot wide, was bored through ; then came an 18-feet seam of micaceous argillites, rich in martite granules ; and again 5 feet of a brecciated ore ; argillites 2 feet, same as before ; brecciated ore, 35 feet ; from 383 feet below the surface to 414 feet occur hydro-micaceo-chloritic schists, crowded with blackish octahedric crystals of martite ; and the last specimen received from the drill-hole, at a depth of 476 feet, is again a brecciated siliceous iron-ore.

North-west of these exposures of quartzite, on the west line of Sect. 4, rises, at a distance of a few hundred steps, a steep crest of dioritic composition. The dioritic nucleus is surrounded with schistose beds dipping almost upright in position to the south ; the beds next to the diorite are dark green, colored by chlorite, and consist of a granular feldspathic ground-mass in intermixture with considerable sparry carbonate of lime ; the higher schistose strata are hydro-micaceous, richly disseminated with good-sized octahedric crystals of martite, and perfectly correspond with the rock found in the drill-hole at a depth of 400 feet. West of this diorite hill, a row of other, likewise dioritic, hills is seen to trend across the centre of the south half of Sect. 5. We find on their south slope a large belt of the just-mentioned hydro-mica schists, and on them follows a seam of brecciated specular iron-ore, more or less contaminated with quartzose matter, which does not naturally crop out, but is artificially denuded on the location of the Excelsior mine, situated on the west line of Sect. 5, 500 steps north of the south-west corner.

In the mine, which is on the west side of the diorite hills, at the base of a rounded drift-covered slope of the highlands, the belt of brecciated ore is overlaid by a compact, fine-grained sub-crystalline argillitic rock, which exhibits a banded sedimentary structure oblique to its imperfect schistose cleavage ; a part of it is paler grayish green, with sedimentary stripes of a copper color imparted to it by ferruginous, silky-shining scales, which I consider to be an altered chlorite, by higher oxidation of its iron component, as the green color of the rock is due to chlorite and insensibly merges into the red streaks. Other portions of the rock are dark green, and agree with the chloritic rock, which forms the hanging wall of the ore in the Lake Superior mine ; it is in this form richly impregnated with octahedric crystals of martite. With the brecciated ore, which is always somewhat siliceous, a seam of a very pure coarsely crystalline ore occurs, which resembles the coarse-grained magnetite of the Champion mine, but is not at all magnetic. Next above the chloritic argillites, which amount to about 25 feet in thickness, follow light-colored, white and reddish quartzites, completely similar to the Teal Lake quartzite, in a thick belt, which is for about 50 feet uncovered, but south of there disappears under the drift.

The higher hills, ascending about 300 steps north of the ore-pits, are superficially covered with drift, but by natural outcrops and by numerous test-pits they are known to consist of a large succession of ferruginous sandy flagstones or jaspery mixed ores, erected into an almost vertical position, while the strata in the mine dip under an angle of only 45° to the south. Farther north argillitic slaty strata and seams of quartzite are found in the test-pits, also angular fragments and larger blocks of slate-rock are scattered abundantly over the surface ; these slates have likewise a southern dip. The large series of banded lean ores are equivalent with the hematite ore-belt of the Negaunee mines ; the slates and quartzites found north of the ore-formation are not underlying but younger deposits, which constitute the fifth group of Huronian deposits.

On the high lands west of the Excelsior mine the ore-bearing jaspery rock-series is across the centre part of Sect. 6, often seen in natural outcrops, and found at no great depth under the surface by test-pits, in which very fair seams of specular ore have lately been discovered, but they are not large enough to be profitably mined. The strata dip south. South of the exposures is a small knob of quartzite, situated a few hundred steps north of the south quarter-post of Sect. 6.

On the west line of the section, along its south half, are several knobs composed of the jasper-banded beds of the iron-formation ; west of them is the swampy valley of the head-waters of Carp River, and no more is seen of this group in that direction for more than a mile ; but recent explorations have led to the discovery of a very valuable ore-belt in the S.W. quarter of Sect. 32, Town. 48, R. 28, which is the location of the newly-opened Boston mine. Intermediate between this mine and the before-mentioned exposures on the west line of Sect. 6, Town. 47, R. 27, the quartzite is seen in outcrops near the quarter-post on the line between Sects. 3 and 4, Town. 47, R. 28, and in the north half of the N.E. quarter of Sect. 5, and the ore-bearing jaspery rock-series is found on the north side of the quartzite outcrops in every one of these localities well exposed.

The Boston mine is opened on the north side of a hillock situated in the midst of a swamp ; across the swamp, 500 steps northward of the mine, are high granite bluffs ; south of the swamp are high drift-covered hills underlaid by slaty rocks of a blackish color, which belong to the upper horizon of the Huronian series subsequently to be described. The ore-belt of the mine is from 5 to 10 feet wide, stands nearly vertical, and is, without the intervention of many other rock ledges, conformably overlaid by a thick belt of light-colored compact quartzites, which have a dip to the south. The foot-wall of the ore is formed by a large succession of the red jasper-banded mixed ores, which inclose seams of fine-grained subcrystalline argillitic schists analogous to the soapstones of the Ishpeming mines. The ore itself is a fine-grained, very compact laminated specular ore of a bluish gray color, with dull metallic lustre, but also seams of brightly shining slate-ore are found in the mine associated with the other kind.

The ore-formation has been traced for some distance west of the Boston mines, but I have not personally examined that district.

Returning to the south side of the synclinal trough of ore-bearing deposits, I have yet to describe the Saginaw and Goodrich mining locations, which, as we learned by previous remarks, are in direct continuity with the deposits of the New England mines.

The north slope of the hills, on top of which these mines are located, is largely covered with drift deposits ; but in various places the higher arenaceous and slaty strata of the fifth group come to the surface, and in the swamp at the base of the hill, a little more than a quarter of a mile east of the Saginaw Railroad depot, a knoll of diorite protrudes. Next north of the mines we find the quartzite formation in a belt of great thickness ; the upper strata are light-colored compact ledges, the lower beds are con-glomeratic and brecciated, full of ore fragments ; and next to the productive ore-belt these brecciated very massive layers are almost totally composed of pure ore and of red jasper-banded mixed ore fragments. The productive ore-belt of the mine is interstratified between jasper-banded ledges, which amount to a great thick-ness, and consist partly of a bright metallic granular specular ore, partly of slate-ore, and in association with it are argillitic and hydro-micaceous schists in all shades of color, from white to red, yellow, brown, green, or gray, by impregnation with hematitic or ochraceous iron oxide ; or with chlorite, and with granular martite. some have an earthy aspect, others are silky-shining. We find also among these the peculiarly white and red dotted argillites, whose color I previously compared with the dotted plumage of a Guinea-hen. The strata dip all to the north. South of the mines is a high rocky knob in close proximity, which consists of a large succession of banded, thinly-laminated arenaceous beds, richly im-pregnated with iron oxide and in part with magnetite ; frequently also the sandy rock-seams alternate with seams of actinolite, or the fibrous crystals of this mineral are scattered through the whole mass. The position of these beds is almost vertical, they suc-ceed the ore-formation conformably, but the surface is too much incumbered with drift to allow us to see the junction between the contiguous rock-belts. Drift-deposits cover also, south of this knob for quite a distance, all the surface, with exception of limited exposures of granite, on the lower levels, a half mile distant from the knob, or, to indicate their position exactly, they are found in the S. W. quarter of the S. E. quarter of Sect. 19, Town. 47, R. 27. West of the Goodrich mines, located in the N. W. quarter of the N. W. quarter of Sect. 19, next adjoining to the Saginaw mines, the ore-formation disappears under the drift, and is not seen again for a distance of six miles, where it is uncovered by test-pits opened in the S. W. quarter of the S. W. quarter of Sect. 7, Town. 47, R. 28, adjoined on the north side by the quartzite formation and by a large series of higher arenaceo-chloritic rock-beds, all dipping conformably with the ore-belt to the south. The ore found there is partly a granular non-magnetic specular ore, partly a specular slate-ore, and is associated with gray hydro-mica schists, disseminated with an abundance of small martite crystals.

On the south side of the ore-belt we find the higher part of the ridge composed of banded arenaceo-ferruginous actinolitic rock-masses, similar to the strata composing the knob south of the Saginaw mines ; the dip of these rock-beds is likewise southward, all these different strata must therefore be in an overturned position. A mile north-west of this locality we find in a continuation of this same hill-range the Washington mines and the Edwards mine. These mines surround in a semicircle the slope of a ridge isolated from the main body of the range by ravines. The new Washington mine and the Edwards mine occupy the north slope ; the old Washington mine and the pits of the abandoned Hungerford mine are on the north-west and west side of the ridge.

North of them is the swampy valley of the Escanaba River. The rock-beds dip under a high angle to the north in the eastern pits, and curve into a western dip in the western ; but considerable local deviations from this rule occur, as the strata are much folded. Quartzites of various character form the top layers of the formation ; uppermost are light-colored, compact, thick-bedded ledges, which are well exposed near the railroad depot, a short distance up the hill-side ; and still better exposures are half a mile farther west, on the north side of the railroad track to the Republic mines, above the cut it makes through the lower conglomeratic hydro-mica schist. The lower portion also of these quartzite ledges constitutes a coarse conglomerate of rounded pebbles of quartzite of different color, of siliceous ore-fragments and of schistose pieces of the ore-bearing series. Next under them follows in the latter locality the just-mentioned conglomeratic hydro-mica schist, which amounts to considerable thickness. The quartz pebbles in it are sometimes much crowded, at other times only distantly scattered through the silky-shining schist, gray-colored by minute scales of micaceous specular iron oxide. South of these conglomeratic schists, which compose a separate undulation of the surface, are other quartzose hydro-mica schists of very bright metallic lustre from intermingled scaly ore particles, and inclosed within these a large seam of excellent slate-ore occurs, which is merely a modification of the schists by total replacement of the hydro-mica by micaceous iron oxide ; all gradations of the transition from the leanest schist to the rich ore can be seen in the mining-pits opened lately on the south side of the railroad cut, and it requires some experience to make the distinction between the valuable ore and the less rich waste rock. Farther south the surface is covered by drift-masses, but not far off from the schist massive blackish crystalline rocks with brightly glistening fracture come to the surface, which consist of an intimate intermixture of white feldspar with black hornblende in thin-bladed, somewhat fibrous crystals. This rock, in composition a diorite, has an entirely different aspect from the ordinary diorites associated with the ore-formation in the eastern mines. In the Hungerford pits, south-west of the western part of the old Washington, the slate-ore is much more compact and harder than in the adjoining before-mentioned pits. East of the rock-belt inclosing the slate-ore occurs in the Hungerford location a peculiar kind of hard siliceous hematitic ore, which forms a part of the actinolite schist series which composes the higher part of the ridge. In the Franklin pit, on the west side of the Edwards mine, the following section through the ore-formation is observable. Uppermost of the strata exposed is a banded rock-belt of considerable thickness, composed of alternating thin seams of white granular quartzite interspersed with magnetite granules, and of other seams intensely impregnated with magnetite, so as to constitute a more or less siliceous ore-mass. Under it follows a pale yellowish-colored silky-shining hydro-mica schist in a seam of eight or ten feet in thickness ; then comes a belt of siliceous specular slate-ore several feet wide, and again another seam of hydro-mica schist similar to the former. Next below are again banded quartzose magnetite ores like the upper rock-belt, which inclose a 15-feet wide seam of a high-graded pure magnetic ore.

Associated with this ore-belt is a dark blackish-colored glistening schist of micaceo-chloritic composition. Lowest in the mine follow actinolitic and quartzose schists, richly impregnated with granular magnetite, and in certain seams abundantly interspersed with brownish small garnet crystals. On the south side of these ore-bearing beds, all of which dip under an angle of about 70° to the north, a massive belt of a dark dioritic rock follows, and then the higher main body of the ridge is found to be composed of an actinolitic quartzoso-ferruginous banded rock-belt of immense thickness, which dips the same way and incloses chloritic seams full of brown garnets, and is from time to time interrupted by parallel dioritic belts, of which it is uncertain whether they are intrusive or not, but I think they are. All these diorites, next to the ore-belt and the others farther south, are very similar to each other, but differ as before mentioned from the diorites in contact with the ore-belts of the eastern mines.

In the eastern pits of the Washington mines a good opportunity is offered for the study of the beds incumbent on the ore-belt by a long tunnel driven into the hill-side. The quartzite formation has in that locality a great thickness. Its upper beds are light-colored ; the lower ones are dark, by intermingled ore granules and hematitic pigment, or by intermixture of chlorite. Interstratified with the quartzites occur chloritic seams and larger belts of micaceous quartz schists ; next under the quartzose rock-series succeeds a dark blackish-green colored massive crystalline rock, in connection with other distinctly stratified sedimentary beds of similar mineral composition, which by gradation into the crystalline rock show its origin from such sediments, greatly altered by metamorphic agents. The massive part of the rock-belt resembles a dark, very coarsely crystalline diorite ; it consists of black, rather hard, large tabular crystals, with a brightly shining micaceous cleavage, which I identify with ottrelite, and of a lighter-colored minutely granular feldspathic, or other times hydro-micaceous interstital mass, serving as a scanty cement, or prevailing over the crystal blades, which finally entirely disappear in the sub-schistose laminated layers of the same rock-belt. Generally these rocks contain considerable proportions of minutely granular magnetite equally distributed through the mass, besides coarser octahedric magnetite crystals in clusters, or disseminated singly. Portions of this belt have an amygdaloid structure, by segregation of nodular rounded lumps of light greenish-colored earthy substance within the rock-mass, which by exposure of the rock readily becomes washed out, and leaves the exposed surface portions full of small cavities, from the size of a pin's head to that of a pea. Immediately beneath this rock series is a rich belt of magnetic ore, of a thickness from 15 to 25 feet, which is associated with narrow seams of hydro-micaceous and chloritic schist. The ore-belt reposes on a large succession of quartz-banded mixed magnetic ore-seams too low in percentage of the metal to be of value for the miner. In the presently considered eastern mining-pits of this location, the strata of the ore-bearing group are seen to be transversally intersected by a doleritic dyke of about ten feet in width in one place, and much narrower in another ; it divides into several branch seams. South of the mixed magnetic lean ore belt, which forms the foot-wall of the mine, an immense body of well-laminated, banded, but firmly coherent rock-strata succeeds in apparent conformity, but a direct superposition of the ore-belt on them is not observable. This large rock-belt, a quarter of a mile wide, consists of an endless alternation of thin laminar seams of arenaceous character, with seams of actinolite and with ferruginous, or jaspery, or chloritic bands, all united into clumsy masses like a crystalline non-stratified rock, and exhibiting great distortion and corrugation.

The actinolite forms partly seams exclusively composed of the stellate fibres of this mineral in longer asbestine crystals, or as a magma of minute needles, which are generally interspersed with magnetite granules and with small cinnamon-colored garnets ; but also the other arenaceous, ferruginous, or jaspery seams of the rock are very often full of actinolite needles mingled with their substance. In the same way garnets are to be found in nearly all of the seams ; but in the chloritic seams, which usually are larger than the others, the garnets are most abundant, and form clusters of sometimes quite large crystals of brown color, and not translucid. Narrow seams of this rock-belt are almost completely formed of magnetite ; some others are composed of hematitic ore of a more or less siliceous character ; the before-mentioned ore-seams, uncovered in the old pits of the Hungerford mine, belong to this class of sediments.

Four miles west of the Washington mines are the Keystone mines, and west of them the Champion mines. North of the Keystone, near the railroad track leading to the Champion mines, are exposures of a large belt of schistose arenaceo-chloritic and micaceous strata, interlaminated with coarsely conglomeratic seams, containing pebbles of granite, diorite, quartzite, banded jaspery rock-fragments, besides pieces of schists and slate-rocks. The not-conglomeratic seams are well-laminated striped rocks by alternation of lighter and darker colored layers in the composition of the strata. Certain seams rich in chlorite or black mica contain garnet crystals in abundance, and are disseminated with clusters of actinolite crystals. The dip of this rock-belt is northward under a high angle ; south of it, separated by a ravine, follows conformably another large rock-belt of light-colored quartzite, partly in heavy compact ledges, partly in more thinly stratified beds ; the lower portion of the series has a schistose structure from copious intermixture of white mica scales with the quartzose mass, and a still lower succession of beds, amounting to 12 or 15 feet, is formed of fine-grained silky-shining mica schists, full of decomposed brownish earthy garnet crystals. These repose on a granular quartzite, intensely impregnated with magnetic granules, so as to impart to it the quality of a low-graded siliceous ore ; it incloses, not far from its upper limits, a four-feet-wide belt of a pure rich granular magnetic ore, and in association with it chlorito-micaceous schists occur, densely crowded with dark reddish garnet crystals of the size of a pea and larger. The mixed siliceous lean ores continue on the south side of the productive ore-seam, and form a quite large belt, which is partially denuded in the mining-pits. South of the pits rise abrupt rock-walls, composed of the banded actinolite rock in compact masses, which form the crest part of the hill-range, and continue southward for about 800 feet, where a belt of diorite and then granite succeed.

Very similar is the succession of rock-beds in the Champion mines. Their dip is likewise northward. The schistose conglomeratic rock-belt, succeeded upward by black slate-rocks, and above them by siliceous and ferrugino-argillitic beds, compose the north slope of the hill-side, which layers are well exposed on the side of the road leading from the mines to the railroad depot. The underlying quartzite belt is well denuded in the mining-pits ; its upper ledges are light-colored, thick, and compact ; the lower are thinner and micaceous, like those of the Keystone mine, alternating with light-colored, argillitic, and hydro-micaceous, silky-shining schists. Beneath them follows a series of chloritic beds, interlaminated with quartzose seams, all of which are more or less intensely impregnated with magnetite granules. The chloritic rock is partly fine-grained, almost aphanitic, partly very coarsely scaly and glistening ; it incloses an abundance of large-leaved black mica, and often white mica, which appears black from chloritic substance deposited between its laminæ, besides large crystals of iron garnet, some of which have a diameter of three

8

inches, and all are complete ; with them usually occur also octahedric magnetite crystals larger than a mustard-seed, and not rarely radiated bunches of long needle-shaped crystals of black turmaline and cubes of iron pyrites are seen imbedded within the chloritic mass. The chloritic rock-belt forms the hanging wall of a large seam of granular magnetic ore, which is associated with silky-shining hydro-micaceous schists ; some of them are even-bedded, dark gray colored by copious intermixture of granules of magnetite ; others have a very rough brecciated structure from chloritic rock-fragments, inclosed by the much-corrugated hydro-micaceous ground-mass, or else large-leaved micaceous blades of black color copiously mingled with the whitish fatty schistose sub-stance, compose these peculiar schistose beds. In some of the pits of the Champion mine a band of specular slate-ore occurs, which seems to have its position not far apart from the magnetic ore-belt. The foot-wall of the productive ore-seam is formed of a thick series of banded quartzite ledges, charged with large propor-tions of granular magnetite, unequally distributed in the mass in seams, with the magnetite prevailing over the quartz, and in others more sparingly dispersed. This ferruginous quartz-rock is on its south side in contact with a parallel belt of dioritic rock of partially schistose, partially massive crystalline structure ; south of it are no more rock-beds exposed, for a distance of about 400 steps, which space is occupied by a swampy depression, on the other side of which granite, with inclosed hornblendic and micaceo-chloritic seams, comes to the surface and projects in a row of cliffs. In the eastern part of the mining location the granite disappears under drift deposits, and in its line of strike a diorite hill projects, which on its south side is in contiguity with actinolitic schists in irregular, nearly vertical position, much corrugated and twisted in some places, in others not. A broad strip of the sur-face is underlaid by a continued succession of these actinolitic beds ; and high rock-knobs situated some distance farther south are found to consist of the same actinolite rock ; still farther south are granite hills.

Eight miles south of the Champion mines we find the Republic mines, located on the S.E. side of Smith's Bay, a lake-like dilata-tion of Michigamee River. The iron formation surrounds this bay in a horseshoe-like arch, dipping with steeply erected beds from

all sides toward it. The inner circle of rock-beds is formed of
compact, reddish-colored, in part brecciated quartzites, with a
micaceo-schistose cement. Under the quartzite follows a seam of
magnetic ore about 10 feet wide, inclosed within a series of
quartzose beds impregnated with ore particles. Next below comes
a narrow belt of silky-shining hydro-mica schists, some of which
layers are charged with scales of brightly metallic, specular iron
oxide, and beneath these occurs a thick seam of granular, coarse-
grained, specular ore of great lustre. This ore-seam is succeeded
by a large series of red jasper-banded mixed ores, which incloses
other valuable ore-seams in connection with schistose bands of
micaceo-argillitic character. The jasper-banded mixed ores exposed on the south-west side of Smith's Bay contain large seams
of quartzose slate-ores of high percentage in iron, which are not
regarded as being worth mining ; but recently valuable specular
ore has been discovered there in connection with the leaner beds.
Above the jasper-banded strata of that locality are conglomeratic
and brecciated layers, composed of larger and smaller pebbles and
fragments of quartz of red and of white color, cemented by a
siliceous mass of specular ore. The outer circumference of this
jaspery rock-belt, which amounts to about 300 feet, is in contact
with a large body of diorite of blackish color, similar to the diorite
beneath the ore-belt of the Washington mine, but unlike the
diorites of the Negaunee district. Portions of this diorite are
much richer in feldspar than others, and from the red color of the
spar I infer its being, in part at least, orthoclas. On the other
side of this diorite belt adjoin it dark-colored, blackish ferruginous
flaggy rock-beds, banded with lighter-colored narrow linear siliceous seams, in a nearly vertical position, which are succeeded by
dark blackish-green colored micaceous and chloritic schists, full of
good-sized brown garnet crystals ; they are much corrugated and
folded. South of them the whole slope of the hill-side is composed
of an endless succession of banded ferrugino-siliceous actinolite
schists, united into bulky compact masses, which are here and
there interrupted by intrusive diorite belts of short local extension, and not, as represented by Major Brooks, in regular continuous bands encircling the whole side of the mountain. All these
rock-beds dip under a high angle toward the hill-side, in apparent
conformity with the direction of the ore-bearing rock-beds. At

the base of the slope, south of the actinolitic rock, a separate undulation of the surface is formed of a fine-grained quartzite of sand-rock structure, partly white, partly brownish-colored by admixture of small garnet crystals. I consider this quartzite merely as a local modification of the actinolite schists. A few steps farther, across a narrow strip of swamp, another hill chain rises, which is composed of gneissoid laminated rocks and of massive granite, both very rich in glistening white and blackish mica scales; the gneissoid ledges dip irregularly. In another locality farther east, the actinolite schists are in close contact with the granite, and dykes of it intersect them. At the Kloman location, north-west of the Republic mine, on the other side of Michigamee River, the quartzite formation and the ore-bearing rock-beds have a vertical position, and are seen in immediate contact with a dioritic rock-belt in a similar upright position, which is, on its other side, adjoined by ferrugino-quartzose banded rock-ledges, identical with those adjoining the same diorite belt on the south side at the Republic mine.

North-west of the Kloman mine are several other mines, close to Michigamee River—the Chippewa, Cannon, and Magnetic iron mines—which I have not examined, to my great regret, as the ore deposits in these localities, represented to be lower than those of the Republic mine, are not far off from the great body of staurolitiferous mica-schists, which form the youngest strata of the Huronian series, and quite probably important facts regarding the succession of rock-beds could be observed in the surrounding country.*

Two other mines on the north side of Lake Michigamee—the Spurr and Michigamee mines—are yet to be described, not only for their economical importance, but as being of the highest scientific interest by the regularity and completeness of the geological sections offered there to the observer. The two mines are situated on the south slope of high diorite hills, which form a separate range in front of a large body of granite hills on their north side. The strata of the ore-formation, directly incumbent on the dioritic rocks, dip south under angles from 50° to 60°. These so-called diorites differ from the ordinary dioritic rocks by an abundance of

---

* While these pages were going through the press I had occasion to examine all these mines carefully, but it was too late to insert the results of my examinations.

quartz in their composition, and by the comparative scarcity of feld-spar. Chlorite is one of the principal constituents of the rock-mass in intermixture with granular quartz, and usually with some proportion of carbonate of lime, which is readily discovered by the lively effervescence of the rock when put in muriatic acid. Within this chloritic ground-mass are dark-colored, somewhat fibrous actinolite-like hornblende crystals, more or less copiously dispersed, often without any visible admixture of feldspar ; in other cases, crystals of this mineral can be distinguished. The generally massive non-stratified rock exhibits sometimes obscure traces of former stratification. Immediately on the diorite leans, in steep inclination, a large succession of banded ferruginous strata, which consist of an alternation of seams of a red-colored granular sand-rock-like quartz, with brightly metallic-shining seams of scaly specular ore ; frequently these alternate seams are irreg-ular, and represented by interrupted lenticular bands, wedging out on both ends. These are, in the Michigamee mines, succeeded by an equally large succession of banded quartzose beds of sand-rock structure, which differ from the former by the white color of the quartzose bands, and by the magnetic quality of the interlam-inated alternating ore-seams, which have a more dull, blackish color, and are sometimes a soft friable mass. The ledges of this ore-bearing sand-rock belt are often brecciated, or else intersected by a dense network of shrinkage cracks, which are filled with ore particles. In the Spurr mines we find, between this and the lower red-banded series of ore-bearing beds, a belt of garnetiferous chlorite rock in-tercalated, which is associated with a massive crystalline diorite of somewhat different character from the other dioritic rocks at the base of the formation, as this one contains a good proportion of feldspar crystals, or else a granular feldspathic interstitial ground-mass. Above the quartzose rock-belt, banded with seams of mag-netic ore, follow some layers of chloritic schist interstratified with quartzose seams, on which the productive magnetic ore-beds, from 20 to 40 feet in thickness, are deposited, and above them succeed other chloritic strata containing large crystals of well-formed iron garnets, and smaller octahedric crystals of magnetite, needles of actinolite, or larger stellate clusters of it in connection with smaller seams of magnetic ore, intermingled with larger masses of actino-lite and with seams of quartzite. On top of them lies a thick belt of heavy compact quartzite ledges, green-colored by chloritic scales, or light gray-colored. Part of these layers is conglomeratic, and incloses larger fragmental masses of the lower red-banded specular mixed ore-belt. This quartzite formation is overlaid by several hundred feet of chloritic and actinolitic quartz schists, which are succeeded by a very large succession of ferrugino-arenaceous banded actinolite schists, in appearance almost identical with the actinolite schists south of the Washington, Champion, and Republic mines.

Certain chloritic seams of the actinolitic rock-series are permeated with leaf-like agglomerations of crystal blades of margarite, which on the weather-worn surfaces of the rock project in high relief with a nacreous splendor ; the same beds contain also black turmaline crystals. Some of the actinolite seams contain a large percentage of magnetite, and in all of them small brown garnet crystals abound. Directly on the actinolitic series follow other banded, more slaty, and micaceous beds, dark green-colored by chlorite, or blackish by magnetite granules, which in some of the seams are also crowded with small garnet crystals ; they are well exposed on the north side of the railroad track between the Michigamee and Spurr mines, and correspond to all appearances with the strata north of the quartzite belt of the Keystone mines ; they are also intimately allied with the mica schist formation on the south-side of Lake Michigamee, opposite Michigamee village, which are doubtless the next succeeding deposits of the Huronian group.

The iron formation is traceable without interruption for six miles west of Michigamee to the vicinity of the three lakes ; but I have only superficially examined these localities, and am not prepared to give a description. The ore-deposits of the L'Anse district I had not the time to examine.

Note.—These localities have been examined since, but I have to desist from their description at present as the printing of this report has advanced too far.

CHAPTER V.

ARENACEOUS SLATE GROUP.

I HAVE designated this large series of deposits with the name prefixed as a heading, because a large proportion of them consists of sandy siliceous layers in alternation with slaty argillitic rock-beds ; but if we compare the strata representing this group in different localities, remote from each other, we will often find them to differ considerably. It is therefore impossible to select a name which would give a definite conception of the nature of all these multitudinous kinds of sediments. We find them incumbent on the quartzite formation, but sometimes also resting on the ore-bearing rock-group, and quite often in direct contact with the dioritic series.

The most eastern exposures of rocks identifiable with this group are found near the centre of the S.E. quarter of Sect. 6, Town. 47, R. 25. A thick belt of black, fine-grained slaty rock-beds, interlaminated with siliceous sandy seams, forms there with its vertically erected ledges the bed of Carp River, and its southern embankments ; next south of the slates are high walls of massive light-colored quartzites in direct conformable contact with them, and also on the north side, at some distance from the river-bed, are large hills composed of the quartzite formation. In all the outcrops south or east of this place the quartzite formation is found to be overlaid with rocks representing the Huronian limestone formation, as we know from the previously given descriptions. Following from here the course of the river up stream, in a north-western direction, we find at intervals similar dark blackish-colored slates and lighter-colored arenaceo-ferruginous banded rock-ledges, exposed in the embankment and on the adjoining hill-slopes, but most of the surface is covered deeply with drift. Near the N.E. corner of Sect. 1, Town. 47, R. 26, on the north side of the river, commences a conspicuous row of drift-hills, trending north-west, which terminates in the south part of Sect. 35, a half mile east of Eagle mills. The central nucleus of these hills is very probably formed of the banded silico-ferruginous layers of this group, as plenty of angular fragments of such rock are mingled with the drift-masses, and in one place an actual outcrop of the ledges is observable. A half mile north of the drift-hills are the limestone knobs of the Morgan furnace location ; but as all the interval is covered with drift, we cannot inform ourselves of the relative position of the two rock-groups to each other. South of the drift-ridge is the swampy valley of Carp River, bordered on the south side of the river channel by highlands, slowly rising in several successive undulations until they culminate about a mile from the river in a row of knobs, formed of thick compact ledges of a light-colored quartzite, which dip under a high angle northward. The undulating, and to a great extent drift-covered north-slope is composed of a large succession of thin-bedded arenaceo-ferruginous flagstones, of slaty argillitic layers and of banded fine-grained siliceous ledges, interstratified with several larger belts of a granular sand-rock-like quartzite of whitish color, while the other rock-beds have a dark brownish or dirty greenish tint. This series has in part a conformable northern dip with the quartzites, but frequently also a southern dip is observed ; the direct contact of the two formations is nowhere visible, on account of the covering drift-masses. The ferrugino-arenaceous schists, in considerably contorted corrugated condition, and dipping to the south, are well exposed in a rounded knob, a little distance north of the S. E. corner of Sect. 3, Town. 47, R. 26. A short distance west of this knob are other knobs composed of diorite, which are on their north side in close contact with the ferruginous flagstones and the associated beds. Examining the south slope of the most eastern of the before-mentioned quartzite knobs, over which the west line of Sect. 12 runs, we find it very brisk, full of cliffs ; at the base is a swampy creek-bed running south-west, and across it, just at the quarter-post, rises another much lower rocky hill, formed of limestone. Taking from here a due west course, we pass over several low knobs of quartzite, which make part of the high ridge farther north ; in the centre of Sect. 11 we descend into a broad swamp valley, in which we remain until we come to the quarter-post on the west side of Sect. 11, close to the bed of a creek. Very few steps farther west we are at the base of a high ridge, the summit of which is composed of diorite ; it extends from the west end of Goose Lake northward through the centre of Sect. 10, and terminates at the north end of the section. The slope of this diorite range is in all its circumference formed of the banded silico-ferruginous flagstones of the fifth group. We find them particularly well exposed at the south end of the ridge, near the west end of Goose Lake ; the layers are in close contiguity with the diorite, and surround the base of high vertical walls of the diorite.

In the same locality the intersection of the diorite by a doleritic dyke is observable. A low hill, in front of the dioritic bluffs, which faces the Escanaba River near its entrance into Goose Lake with high vertical walls, exhibits a fine section through more than 200 feet of strata identical with those in contact with the diorite, and on the south side of the river channel an equally fine section, through the same banded silico-ferruginous beds, is seen in a cut of the Escanaba Railroad. The strata dip west, or north of west, under a moderate angle ; east of these exposures the road-bed is cut through a large succession of lighter or darker gray-colored clay slates, with interstratified arenaceous seams which dip in the same direction, but under a much steeper angle than the former ; and these are succeeded downward by a large belt of massive beds of light-colored compact quartzites, which form a high knob bordering the west side of Goose Lake, and are well laid open in a quarry close to the railroad. The upper, banded, flaggy rock-series amounts here to considerable thickness, as south of the railroad cut for a quarter of a mile all the surface is underlaid by rocks of this kind, somewhat differing from the others by lighter, more variegated colors, and representing another horizon of the series. Going from the exposures on the railroad westward on the track, we see the strata rapidly sink under the surface of marsh-lands adjoining the river channel on the west side. Farther on, after crossing the river a second time, the road passes for nearly two miles along the valley of this stream, which suddenly widens into marshy plains, bordered on the north side by a range of high hills composed of sand-rock and slate-beds analogous to the rock-belt exposed in the cut near Goose Lake, although they have not as much similarity with each other as to allow an identification by the rock-character alone. South of the valley we observe an isolated knob of diorite at the place where it begins to widen, about 400 steps south of the N.W. corner of Sect. 15 ; west of it is a drift-covered ridge separated from the high quartzite range on its south side by a swampy depression ; the slope of the quartzite range is deeply covered with drift. Farther west, beyond Partridge Creek, the valley is bordered by a high ridge of diorite ; the west line of Sect. 16 runs over its highest summit knob. The slopes of this ridge, in its whole circumference, are composed of the banded arenaceo-ferruginous flags of the fifth group, but a large portion of the surface is covered with drift.

Near the west end of the ridge the lower hematitic rock-beds of the iron-formation come close to its base, but the contact between them and the flagstones of the fifth group is not seen. The high undulating plateau-lands on the south side of the ridge are underlaid by the arenaceous slate-group, which extends from there southward in a belt, hemmed in on the west side by dioritic rock-crests, on the east side leaning at the base of quartzite hills. "In the centre part of Sect. 20 this rock-belt bends and is continued in a western direction, covering all the surface of Sect. 19 and the eastern diagonal half of Sect. 24 in the adjoining township, where it runs out into a point at the south-west corner of this section, close to the old Tilden mines. It reposes there on the ore-bearing rock-belt, as I infer from the relative position of the outcrops, although I have not observed the direct contact of the two rock-groups. The largest part of the rock-beds, representing the fifth group in the presently considered localities, consists of sandy, somewhat micaceous flagstones, or of finer-grained banded siliceous rock-beds, all more or less impregnated with protoxide of iron as a coloring matter, and with granules of magnetite. Some of the layers are almost rich enough to be used as iron-ores ; such richer beds, dark blackish-colored by magnetite, are well exposed on the side of the railroad track near the N.E. corner of Sect. 24. The strata lie on the side of a diorite hill, dipping under a low angle toward it in a northern direction, and a few hundred steps farther east another body of these ledges lies in a slanting position on the diorite. Identical beds are observable near the N.E. corner of Sect. 18, Town. 47, R. 26 ; likewise in contact with diorite and dipping toward it. In this latter locality they are conformably underlaid by a compact dark greenish colored rock, which by weathering turns rusty brown, and becomes full of small cavities ; it effervesces with muriatic acid, which dissolves the small crystals of sparry carbonate of iron abundantly disseminated through the mass ; the green color is due to chloritic scales. By boiling the rock with muriatic acid, it decolorizes, and a glistening cavernous white mass of micaceo-feldspathic composition remains. Good outcrops of this rock are observable a short distance south of the mentioned locality, in which its contiguity with the magnetic lean ores is not so well exposed ; near the centre of the S.E. quarter of Sect. 17, a similar rock is found in connection with the flag-stones of the fifth group.

In the above-mentioned exposures, near the N.E. corner of Sect. 18, we find, on a lower level of the hill-slope, the hematitic flags of the ore-formation uncovered in test-pits, which likewise dip toward the hill in conformity with the black magnetic ledges on the higher part of the slope. The just-described rock-series representing the fifth group, is, in the south part of Sect. 19, underlaid by a large body of massive layers of a granular, partly conglomeratic quartz-rock, with a chloritic cement ; and therefore dark blackish-green colored, and from a distance is easily misapprehended for a dioritic rock ; it is most favorably exposed for observation in the N.E. quarter of Sect. 30, Town. 47, R. 26, and is seen there to repose in apparent conformity on the altered granite-like quartzites, which compose the previously described rock-bluffs in the centre of Sect. 30. Equivalent, but less altered conglomeratic quartzites form a half mile farther south the hanging wall of the ore-belt in the Palmer mines.

Returning from here to the north margin of the examined belt of the fifth group, we find deposits of this kind to extend northward along the narrow valley of a creek which takes its head-waters from the S.W. quarter of Sect. 7, and passes near the south quarter-post of Sect. 18. The exposures in the S.W. quarter of Sect. 7 are particularly fine ; the siliceous flags richly impregnated with magnetite, and amounting to a belt of considerable thickness, lean with western dip in steep inclination on the side of bubble-shaped hillocks of diorite. We are here on the top of a high plateau crowned with numerous dioritic ridges in parallel rows trend·

ing from south-east to north-west ; and in every valley intervening between these ridges we meet again with these ferruginous flag-stones. Exposures of this kind are found in the N.E. quarter of the S.W. quarter of Sect. 7, which continue into the S.W. quarter of the N.W. quarter of the same section, and into the S.E. quarter of the N.E. quarter of Sect. 12 in the next adjoining township, from whence the strata can be traced almost without an interruption to the N.W. quarter of the N.W. quarter of this section into close proximity with outcrops of the lower hematitic beds of the iron-ore group.

Other large deposits of this group are found in an adjoining parallel valley, which sends a creek westward into the small lake at the quarter-post of the west line of Sect. 12. The strata lean on the north side of the valley, steeply inclined on the hill-slope, in apparent conformity with the underlying dioritic rocks which compose the body of the ridge. On the south side, which is likewise bordered by a dioritic ridge, the strata, retaining the same direction as on the north side, dip toward the hill whose slope they form. Going across this ridge, we find its south slope again surrounded by a belt of these ferruginous flagstones. They are well exposed near the N.E. corner of Sect. 14, on the side of a wagon-road leading to the Ogden and Tilden mines, and farther east in the N.W. quarter of Sect. 13, up on the higher part of the hill-slope, and down near the shore of Lake Miller. As we pass along on this road to the south end of Lake Ogden we leave the area invested with deposits of the fifth group, and descend unto the older sediments of the iron-ore group, which are here well exposed in the now abandoned pits of the Ogden, Tilden, and Iron Mountain mines, of which I have spoken in the previous chapter.

We have followed in the preceding exposition the exposures of the fifth group southward and westward, after we left the track of the Escanaba Railroad, which was the starting-point, but we find the much larger display of this formation on the north side of the road. It covers, in Town. 47, R. 26, in one continuous body, almost the entire surface of Sects. 2, 3, 4, 5, and 9, besides the east halves of Sects. 6 and 8, and in the adjoining northern Town. 48, R. 26, the south halves of Sects. 31, 32, 33, and 34 have the same rock-series as a surface rock.

A large portion of the deposits in this northern part of the formation consists of clay slates with interstratified larger belts of light-colored quartzites of a granular sand-rock structure, sometimes quite compact, of a vitreous fracture, other times porous ; but the silico-ferruginous banded rock-beds and flagstones seen in the before-described localities are also represented in this part.

The chain of hills which commences at the previously mentioned cut of the Escanaba Railroad through a bubble of the lower beds of the ore-formation, and trends from there eastward across the north part of Sects. 8 and 9, is formed of a belt of white quartzite in association with clay slates of a more or less arenaceous character. In some of the outcrops the quartzite is rather porous, and incloses an abundance of angular slate fragments ; its ledges are much corrugated. In other exposures we find the rock intermingled with martite granules, and in blotches tinted red by hematitic pigment, again in other places the rock is compact and has a glassy fracture. The hill north of this ridge, close to the north line of Sect. 8, consists of siliceous sandy flagstones, blackish colored by an abundance of magnetite granules ; a few hillocks farther north, in the S.W. quarter of the S.E. quarter of Sect. 5, are composed of clay slates in a nearly vertical position. By crossing over this large body of hills, which on its north side is bordered by a broad belt of swamp, we see a constant alternation of rock-beds of the described kind, without any observable regularity in the succession, a large portion of the surface is covered with drift, and in all probability numerous plications cause a repetition of the strata, which I infer from the much-corrugated condition of the rock-beds in many of the exposures. A short distance north of the quarter-post on the east line of Sect. 5, the section line crosses a narrow rock-ridge about 60 feet high, which is isolated from the other hill-lands in all its circumference by a strip of swamp. It consists of nearly vertical ledges of sand-rock and clay slate, with some intermingled ferruginous seams. East of it are other good exposures of light-colored massive quartzite beds in alternation with clay slates ; the strata there dip north. The north half of the S.E. quarter of Sect. 4 is occupied by an insular cluster of high diorite hills, surrounded on all sides by the arenaceous beds of the fifth group ; on the north side of these hills, which are quite steep, we find the sandy flagstones dipping north under a high angle. At the coaling kilns, situated on the east line of Sect. 4, the arenaceous flags are dark blackish-colored and contain a large proportion of magnetite ; a part of the beds is more argillitic, and merges with the clay slates which occur in association with the flags.

The nature of the eastern continuation of this rock-series in Sects. 3 and 2 has been described in a previous page of this chapter. I proceed, therefore, from the coal-kilns northward across a strip of swamp, and find on the north line of the N.E. quarter of Sect. 4, on the summit of an insular body of high land, three small knobs of a coarsely crystalline diorite, surrounded on all sides by the sand and slate rock-ledges of the fifth group, and in close contiguity with them. The old State road to Marquette passes close by the knobs, and the nearly upright sandstone and slate beds dipping north, are well exposed in the road-bed, and in some knobby protrusions north of the road. The greatest part of the hill-side sloping down toward the bed of Carp River is covered with drift, but on the opposite side of the river-bed the sand-rock and clay slate beds come again to the surface, and form an isolated chain of hills completely surrounded by marsh-lands ; the strata have likewise a northern dip under a high angle. The west line of Sect. 34 runs over the highest part of this ridge, and the quarter-post is at the base of the north side of the hills, not many steps from the Houghton and Ontonagon Railroad, which leads through the marsh-lands. Following the railroad westward, we find, near the quarter-post of the west line of Sect. 33, another isolated knob in the marsh, consisting of the same sandstone and slate beds as the ridge east of it, and dipping north as they do. A few hundred steps north of this knob rises the high quartzite range which extends westward to the north side of Teal Lake, and has been described in a previous chapter ; its rock-ledges have a southern dip, as will be remembered. Along the south side of this ridge extends, from this point westward, a broad belt of drift-covered undulating plateau-lands, from which in various places the underlying rock-beds of the fifth group project in low crests and knobs over the surface. In the exposures next to the quartzite ridge the strata have a southern dip conformable with it, but between the outcrops of the two rock-groups is always an interval several hundred feet in width, covered with soil and loose material, and their contact is not seen. The very large belt

of this younger rock-series consists, in the proximity of the quartzite range, of an alternation of clay slates with belts of sand-rock,
which often has a density and compactness little inferior to the
glassy quartzites of the high ridge on their north side ; the clay
slates are in part light gray-colored, others are dark blackish or
lighter and darker sedimentary streaks alternate with each other
in the slaty layers, whose cleavage is always contrary to this sedimentary striation ; some of the slaty layers contain an abundance
of small mica scales. Very good exposures of the clay slates are
observable along the railroad where it intersects the west part of
Sect. 32 ; others are found south of the centre of Sect. 31, near
the wagon-road leading across the hill-range to Carp River. On
the plateau we noticed, near the centre of the S.E. quarter of the
N.E. quarter of Sect. 6, an old test-shaft with a large pile of rock
thrown out of it, which consists in part of the ordinary clay slates,
in part of banded fine-grained silico-ferruginous rock-beds, impregnated with magnetite granules, and of other silico-argillaceous
rock-beds brightly red-colored by hematite, and also of dark
green-colored chloritic schists. I am informed by the parties
who dug this shaft that the strata had a northern dip, and that
the hematitic rocks and chloritic schits were the lowest. We have
here an instance of a direct superposition of the arenaceous slate-
group on beds which evidently represent the lower strata of the
iron-ore group, and the schistose chorlitic beds, on which they are
generally found to repose in the neighboring hematite mines on
the other side of the valley, and from this we also may infer a
considerable thinning out of the iron-bearing series, as the shaft,
which in all is not over 300 feet deep, went clear through it and
struck the usual foot-wall of the formation. South-west of the
test-shaft, near the edge of the plateau, are several knobs formed
of highly ferruginous, dark-colored siliceous flags, and of thicker
banded ledges, which are identified with the large series of rock-
beds intersected by the Escanaba Railroad near the west end of
Goose Lake. They dip under a high angle northward, and seem
to represent the upturned ends of the lowest beds in this rock-belt,
which do not appear at the surface near the foot of the quartzite
chain, and probably would be found to fill out the covered interval
which, as I stated before, always exists between the slate exposures
and the quartzites of the high ridge. The same strata are seen

exposed farther east, near the quarter-post on the west line of Sect. 5. West of the mentioned knobs, in the centre of Sect. 6, is an isolated rounded hillock composed of dioritic rocks, partly schistose, partly massive, crystalline, and about a quarter of a mile north-west of it, the previously mentioned ridge of diorite commences, which extends in a straight western direction to the west line of Sect. 2, 300 steps south of the north-west corner, near the Teal Lake hematite mines.

The occurrence of the slates and sand-rocks of the fifth group in that locality, and their contiguity with the hematitic strata of the iron-ore formation, is previously described. We find there the banded silico-ferruginous flaggy layers farthest north, close to the shore of the lake, and evidently holding a lower position than the slate and sand-rock layers. This rock-series extends in all probability across the south part of Sect. 34 to the north part of Sects. 4 and 5, but in Sect. 34 no outcrops of it are seen, on account of the heavy drift-deposits, while in 4 and 5 they occasionally are on the surface ; we find them exposed in the N.W. quarter of the N.W. quarter of Sect. 4, in the S.W. quarter of the N.E. quarter of Sect. 5, and in test-pits in the N.W. quarter of the N.W. quarter of Sect. 5. The sandy ferruginous flags which compose the hills north of the Excelsior mine, and those leaning on the north side of the diorite knobs in that locality, I consider members of this rock-group.

Before I follow these deposits farther westward, I have to return to some more eastern exposures which I had omitted to describe, in order to adhere to the adopted system of giving the descriptions by guiding the reader in a certain direction from place to place without deviations.

On the south side of the large cluster of diorite knobs, north of the New York mines, we see generally the ore-formation in direct contiguity with the diorite ; but on the higher part of one of the rock-bluffs another kind of stratified rock is found to repose on the diorite in seemingly discordant position. It is quite a large succession of well-laminated, banded, rather thin ledges of a dark rusty color, which consist of a radiated agglomeration of minute needles of actinolite, with intermixture of some proportion of granular magnetite ; the ledges are intersected by numerous narrow asbestine seams vertical to the lamination or more irregular, and are in some places of the outcrop considerably plicated and corrugated, or else shattered into irregular fragments. Portions of the exposed rock-faces are covered with a thin crust of malachite recently deposited there from decomposing nodules of copper pyrites inclosed within the rock-mass.

A mile west of this locality we find analogous beds on the slope of the diorite hills north of Lake Bancroft. Close to the north end of the lake are some lower hills formed of slate-rocks of dark blackish-brown color, very tough, of great specific gravity from a large proportion of magnetite disseminated through the mass. The cleavage of the beds is in discordance with the sedimentary lamination of the rock, which is well observable, as the slabs of slate are banded in that direction with streaks of different shades of color. The strata dip southward under an angle of about 60° ; they are intersected by seams of long-fibred asbestus in intermixture with quartz ; some of the asbestus is flexible, but most of it rigid, wood-like. Next under them follows a massive, very tough, dark greenish-gray rock of crystalline structure, which contains a large proportion of carbonate of lime in bladed, acicular crystals, which on weathered surfaces of the rock become washed out, and leave in their place linear slits, intersecting each other in every direction. This rock is inseparably allied with the dioritic rocks, of which the main body of the ridge is composed, and consists of a granular feldspathic ground-mass in intermixture with delicate, partly chloritic, partly micaceous scales, and with a fibrous hornblendic mineral, in which mass larger bladed crystals of feldspar are dispersed. Another undulation of the hill-side next north of the slate-hill is composed of banded ferruginous and actinolitic rockbeds, which cleave with very even surfaces in accordance with the sedimentary lamination, but parts of the ledges are bent and twisted into serpentine curves ; their dip is southward, like that of the slates, and the same massive diorite-like rocks underlie them. These actinolitic beds, richly impregnated with magnetite, I considered as analogous with the banded silico-ferruginous rock-beds exposed in the railroad cut near Goose Lake, and to those composing the knobs north-east of the furnace of Negaunee ; but later observations convinced me of a much greater analogy existing between them and the actinolite schists below the ore-formation of the Saginaw, Washington, and Republic mines ; still as actinolite

9

also occurs sometimes in the strata of the fifth group, I am not positive whether they represent these upper or the lower schists.

South of the exposures of ferruginous slates and actinolitic flag-stones on Lake Bancroft, are knobs of diorite on both sides of the lake, which are not incumbered with these ledges; not far from their base the ore-formation is struck by test-pits and by the diamond drill. The diorite forming the nucleus of the knob on the west side of the lake is coarsely crystalline, and consists, besides the hornblende and feldspar, of a good proportion of epidote; with the massive rock occurs a large body of schistose beds of chloritic and hydro-micaceous character, some of which are crowded with red feldpsar crystals dispersed through the mass, with a copious intermixture of granular octahedric crystals of martite. The knobs on the east side of the lake are composed of a different sort of crystalline rock, which consists of red feldspar crystals imbedded within a chloritic cement mass abundantly interspersed with granules of iron pyrites, which causes its rapid decomposition and disintegration on exposure; in intimate connection with the crystalline masses are well-laminated chloritic schistose strata.

Proceeding with the examination westward, we find the fifth group as a surface rock of a very extensive area, but frequently so much covered with drift-masses that the accurate relative position of certain rock-belts of the series can rarely be ascertained for want of connected exposures.

The occurrence of arenaceous and slaty deposits representing this group in the S.W. corner of Sect. 4 is mentioned; analogous beds underlie the drift-covered hills west of the Lake Superior mines, in the S.W. quarter of Sect. 9, and cover all the surface of Sects. 7, 8, 17, 18, and the west half of Sect. 16 in Town. 47, R. 27. If we start from the Parsons mines and follow the railroad which connects the mines with the main road, we pass the quartzite knobs west of the mine, and through a swampy valley densely strewn with large angular blocks of the same quartzite, we come to a crossing with the wagon-road to the Saginaw mines, and then take that road. Ascending the hill we soon see outcrops of thick ledges of white quartzite, which dip in a north-western direction; above them follows a large series of flaggy, ferruginous, and micaceous sand-rock ledges, which occupy the whole hill-side westward, and are particularly well exposed in a cut of the railroad to the Saginaw mines, near the quarter-post on the west line of Sect. 16, where the strata have an almost southern dip, and are likewise seen to repose on a thick belt of a white compact quartzite. As we approach on the wagon-road the summit of the hill, we see it diagonally intersected by a thick belt of a bluish gray, dark-colored, banded siliceous rock similar to the banded siliceous beds of the fifth group in exposures of other localities. Farther on the strata disappear under the drift, and are not seen again until we come to the first houses on the Saginaw mining location, where the quartzite formation is well exposed on the roadside in massive compact ledges. The actinolitic silico-ferruginous rock-beds composing the knob on the south side of the Saginaw mines, considering their great lithological affinity with the sediments of the fifth group, I at first erroneously identified with this group, but I am fully convinced at present of their conformable succession below the ore-formation.

In the north part of the above-indicated area, over which the fifth group extends, I could not find any outcrops within the limits of Sect. 8 ; the drift-masses contain there an abundance of large boulders of brecciated specular ore, similar to the ore of the Excelsior mines. In Sect. 7 the larger portion of the surface is covered with drift, but we find exposures in various parts of it.

An outcrop of fine-grained black slates, which dip under a high angle southward, is observable on the south line of the section a quarter mile west of the east corner ; other quite extensive exposures of dark blackish, siliceous, even-bedded flagstones, which carry a large proportion of magnetite, are seen farther on toward the west corner of the section, near which locality a large belt of a dark-colored, compact quartzite has been denuded in test-pits in association with the magnetic flagstones ; the dip of the nearly vertical rock-beds is also here southward. In the north part of the S. W. quarter is a row of hills composed of these black magnetic flags interlaminated with slaty and arenaceous seams, which present themselves well denuded in cliffs. West of them is another rocky hillock, in the N. E. quarter of the N. E. quarter of Sect. 12, of the adjoining town, range 28, which consists of lighter greenish-gray colored, somewhat variegated, and much-corrugated seams of micaceo-argillitic, ferruginous, and arenaceous character, all firmly united into a bulky banded rock-mass.

A chain of hills continues along the section line from the S.W. corner of Sect. 7 to the S.W. corner of Sect. 12, which consists of an alternation of dark slaty seams with thick belts of compact granular quartzites of various darker or lighter shades of color ; with them occur also brecciated layers composed of slate and quartzite fragments. The strata dip south, but are nearly vertical. I have to mention yet a chain of rock-exposures along the north line of Sect. 7, which consists of peculiar schists and other more massive beds, some of which have an amygdaloid structure ; within a dark gray or greenish-colored chlorito-argillitic or feldspathic ground-mass are flattened nodules of the size of a lentil, or somewhat larger, copiously imbedded, which in part consist of calcspar or sparry carbonate of iron ; others are a granular white quartz, and still others are filled with radiated blades and fibres of a soft talcy, green-colored mineral. In the not-amygdaloidal beds the carbonates of lime and of iron are found abundantly disseminated through the mass in small crystals. The amygdaloid beds are best observable in the hills south of the Excelsior mine, in the N.E. corner of the section ; farther west, near the quarter-post of the north line, the outcrops are much larger, but the amygdaloid structure of the rock is not so well developed. The dip of the strata is south ; a short distance north of the quarter-post is a small quartzite knob, with ledges dipping in the same direction, and north of the knob succeed the jaspery beds of the iron-formation which have been mentioned in the previous chapter. From this relative position of the different rock-seams I infer the age of the schist to be the younger, and the other arenaceous and ferruginous strata in the south part of the section seem to follow them conformably in the ascending order ; but south of these, in the north part of Sect. 18, and of Sect. 13 next to it, we meet again with a very large body of rocks resting in apparent conformity on the others, which, although not exactly identical with the amygdaloidic schists, resemble them so much that I consider them as analogous. The amygdaloid rocks in these exposures have a more perfect crystalline structure, and contain more mica in their composition ; intimately associated with them are massive rocks of brecciated structure, composed of a similar dark-colored chlorito-feldspathic mass, intermingled with calcspar or carbonate of iron, and not rarely with small crystals of black turmaline ; the brecciated rock is not always formed of intermingled fragments of different kinds of rock, but often consists only of an agglomeration of nodular lumps of the shattered rock, recemented by the same substance. Rocks of this description form the large bluffs north of the Saginaw Railroad depot, across the bed of Carp River. Half a mile farther west the analogous beds exposed close to the railroad track inclose an abundance of foreign rock-fragments, of slaty argillites, or of banded siliceous ledges, united with the mass in a mode which suggests to me its semi-fluid condition from the effects of heat, at the time the rock-fragments became imbedded in it ; but the very plain sedimentary striation exhibited by the conglomeratic bluffs is, on the other hand, a positive proof of the origin of these sub-crystalline, much-altered rock-masses from sedimentary deposits.

On the line between Sects. 13 and 18, if we follow it from the railroad northward, we find, after ascending the front part of the hill-side, which is formed of the dark-colored, diorite-like, massive brecciated rocks, a second undulation of the range, formed of lighter-colored, more distinctly stratified beds, which are almost rich enough in sparry carbonate of iron and lime to pass for a siliceous limestone ; the decomposed rock forms bright orange-colored, ochraceous, cellulose masses of soft friable condition. These rocks, of the conglomeratic and amygdaloid kind, are in the N. W. quarter of Sect. 13 in immediate contact with black-colored, very even-bedded flaggy layers in a vertical position, which form a small knob, partially intersected by the railroad. South and west of this knob only crystalline diorites are found in the exposures. On the north side of the railroad, near the last western bridge across the river, are fine exposures of the conglomeratic rocks, partly in massive, bulky form, partly schistose and rich in micaceous scales. The hills composed of them are on the west side closely adjoined by other hills, composed of dioritic schists and of massive coarsely crystalline diorites, which two sorts of rock are denuded in almost uninterrupted continuity on the south slope of this row of hills, and perfectly merge into each other, evincing in this case the original deposition of these altered sediments on the diorite, and not a merely accidental contiguity resulting from the dislocation of the strata, although they are in neighboring localities, to all appearances, reposing on the quartzites above the iron formation. In Sect. 11, Town. 47, R. 28, the south-east corner is located on the terminal knob of the quartzite ridge, which follows the south line of Sect. 12. About 500 steps north of this knob, across the bed of Carp River, emerges an isolated knob above the drift-covered rolling lands, composed of black slates in an upright position, which are at least 300 feet in thickness ; the south-west corner of this section, near the Greenwood furnace, is situated on a hill composed of the same black slate interstratified with quartzose seams ; north of it, for three quarters of a mile, no outcrops occur, but in the north half of the N.W. quarter of Sect. 11 the black slates are again largely exposed in a row of hills bordering the north side of the wagon-road leading to the Greenwood and Clarksburg furnaces. The slates dip south under a high angle. North of the slates rises another higher hillock, consisting of banded ferrugino-arenaceous rock-seams firmly united into a bulky solid rock-mass, which exhibits an extreme degree of corrugation and torsion, made very conspicuous by the banded variegated structure of the rock. The iron formation must pass not a great distance north of this hill in its western extension toward the Boston mine, but there are no outcrops.

At the Clarksburg station the railroad passes a knob, composed of the altered sub-crystalline and occasionally amygdaloid rocks, encountered before on the side of the railroad in Sects. 18 and 13 ; they are here not conglomeratic, quite compact, partly of fine homogeneous grain, partly of coarser, crystalline structure. The carbonates of lime and iron are regular constituents of the rock, largely composed of a feldspathic ground-mass, with micaceous and chloritic scales dispersed through it ; and in some of the collected specimens clusters of actinolite fibres are interspersed. Opposite this knob, toward the furnace buildings, the banded arenaceo-ferruginous beds, in a much corrugated condition, can be seen in close contact with the just-mentioned rocks. The hills north of the station are formed of a large succession of sandy flags and schistose, more or less chloritic and ferruginous rock-beds, representing the fifth group ; they dip northward. Farther north a broad belt of surface is occupied by black slates, but the denudations are very imperfect. North of them, separated by a swamp, is the Boston mine. On the south side of Clarksburg are likewise the slaty and banded siliceous rock-strata of the fifth group—the general surface rock ; they dip north, and beneath them the ore-formation is found, as previously stated; but on the higher part of the hill-range the same strata dip south, and above them succeeds a large belt of quartzite; next above it is a belt of specular iron ore partly granular, partly of slaty structure, in connection with hydro-mica schists, more or less impregnated with magnetite granules.

The summit of the ridge and its south slope are composed of an immensely thick series of banded but very tough and compact actinolite schists which on their part come in direct contact with diorite hills farther south.

All the described succession of rock-beds dips south, and as it represents the regular succession observed in other localities, but in inverted order, we have here before us a large overturn of the formations exhibited.

From Clarksburg to the Washington mines the rock-beds of the fifth group occupy both sides of the valley, presenting continued large exposures of this remarkably great succession of strata. The finer-grained schistose sediments prevail here over the coarser quartzite rock-belts, which, east of the Greenwood furnace, and generally in the eastern exposures of this formation, compose the greater bulk of it. At the Washington mine no rocks of this kind are visible in the hill-slope, but in the east half of Sect. 1 the outcrops of a large succession of micaceo-chloritic schists, dipping under a high angle southward, commence near the bed of the Escanaba River, and the strata continue to be exposed in a number of undulating hillocks south of there, without much change in their character ; nearer the high hill-range where the dip of the strata is reverted into a northern, fine-grained arenaceous beds, with some magnetite granules and mica scales disseminated through the mass, begin to alternate with the schistose seams, and arriving at the base of the highest part of the hill-range, we find a large body of very even-bedded banded granular quartzose beds richly impregnated with granules of magnetite, leaning with steeply inclined beds on the side of the ridge, whose summit is formed of a diorite similar to, if not identical with, the diorite cropping out on the south side of the Franklin pits of the old Washington mine.   This hill is separated from the hill of the Washington mine by a deep ravine ; close to the ravine a tunnel is driven on the mining property into the hill across a thick succession of micaceous quartz schists and of quartzite layers ; no trace of these, or of the ore-formation, is observable on the east side of the ravine.   Major Brooks considers, therefore, the chloritic schists and the banded ferruginous beds above mentioned as older than the iron-ore group ; but the direct connection of these schists with the schists on the north side of the Escanaba valley, which are indubitably higher than the quartzite and the ore-formation, and their lithological resemblance with rock-beds of the fifth group in other localities, are sufficient proof for me to take them as such.   The hills on the north side of Escanaba River, north-east of the Washington mines, are a direct continuation of those near Clarksburg station, and consist, like these, partly of schistose micaceo-argillitic beds, partly of the harder sub-crystalline and frequently conglomeratic rocks, of chlorito-feldspathic composition, with a good proportion of the carbonates of lime and iron.   On the rolling drift-covered lands, north of the first-encountered rock-bluffs near the river, which are formed of the just-mentioned kind of rock-beds, dipping south under a high angle, we find numerous limited exposures of slaty micaceous and chloritic argillites and of banded siliceous rock-beds, most all of which inclose some granules of magnetite.   These beds, amounting to a great thickness, are often considerably corrugated or bent into larger serpentine curves.   Farther north succeeds a very large belt of fine-grained black slates, colored by carbonaceous matter, but only the general local distribution of all these deposits is observable, and about their order in the succession, their thickness and dip, nothing definite can be determined in this part of the country, where drift hides the rock ledges almost completely. West of the Washington mines we find, by following the railroad toward the Champion mines, the hills on both sides of the valley consisting of the same kind of rocks which compose the rock-ridges north of the railroad, between Clarksburg and the Washington mines ; the black carbonaceous slates are in several places denuded on the road track.   Near the Keystone mines the superposition of a schistose conglomeratic rock-belt, on the quartzites above the ore-formation, is observable in the most unequivocal distinctness. These outcrops, in connection with the ore-bearing rock-series of this locality, have already been described. The identity of this conglomerate rock with the conglomeratic rocks encountered all along on our westward course, and first met with in the bluffs north of the railroad depot of Saginaw station, is not only indicated by a great similarity of the structure and of the material of these strata, but an almost direct continuity in the extension of this group of deposits can be traced.

In this locality we find for the first time, in this particular horizon of the rock-series, actinolite and garnets as constituents, which minerals are very abundant farther west, not only in the layers identifiable with these, but they are found to be equally common throughout the whole series of the ore-formation of the Spurr and Michigamee mines. In the higher strata of the mica schist group, garnets are likewise characteristic, and actinolite enters into the composition of some of the rock-seams. For this reason I suggest that at one time within the concerned area local conditions existed which were favorable for the formation of such minerals from the sedimentary material, while in other localities the same sediments were not altered in this way.

The large series of actinolitic rock-beds found south of the Washington mines, the Keystone, Champion, and Republic mines, in a position which evinces their older age than the ore-formation, has been previously described in connection with the ore-formation of these localities. In consideration of the total absence of such rock-beds beneath the ore-formation in the Michigamee and Spurr mines, and in most of the other mining localities, and of the occurrence of a rock-belt almost identical with these strata, resting in conformity on the ore-formation and on the quartzites in the Michigamee mine. I for a time believed in the equivalency of these similar deposits, and placed them all above the ore and quartzite formation, which position is unquestionably held by the actinolite beds of the Michigamee mine ; but I have fully satisfied myself by subsequent careful examinations that the actinolite schists form two different belts, one above the ore-formation and another below it.

It remains yet for me to say that the schistose rock-ledges, analogous with those composing the north slope of the hills at the

Keystone mine, form also the opposite-hill slope near the Champion furnace, and continue westward to the north side of Lake Michigamee, where they are for a while interrupted by older rock-beds coming up to the shore ; but they appear again on the west side of the Michigamee mines, and hold there a position next above the upper actinolitic rock-belt. The next succeeding strata, exposed on the south shore of the lake, will be described in another chapter as a separate group.

The Dead River, while it flows within the limits of Sect. 14, Town. 48, R. 26, has a narrow, ravine-like valley, bordered on the north side by a high ridge of granite, on the south side by steep drift-bluffs which form the edge of a high plateau. At its exit from the eastern limits of the section it rushes in small cascades and rapids over granitic rocks, which at this place form a narrow gorge with vertical rock-walls on both sides. Higher up stream the granitic rock-bluffs recede some distance from the channel on the north side, and are on the south side replaced by the mentioned drift-bluffs. Near the middle of the section the granite bluffs recede still farther north, and the river channel is, to the west end of the section, bordered by lower hills, which form a belt on the slope of the granitic summits. These hills are composed of quartzites and arenaceous flagstones, interstratified with argillaceous slaty rock-beds, which dip north toward the granite. The quartzites, of a purplish color, are partly thick-bedded, compact, with glossy fracture, but have a distinctly granular structure ; other beds are more thinly laminated, finer-grained, and more porous, with a scaly micaceous or chloritic cement, or are more of an argillitic nature and merge into a slate-rock, with a cleavage discordant with the sedimentary stratification ; these slaty and thin-bedded arenaceous beds have a dark gray color.

Farther up the river, in Sect. 15, we find in its embankment, and on the slope of the drift-covered terrace-lands, intervening between the river-bed and the granitic summit part of the hills, exposures of a large succession of black carbonaceous rather hard slate-rocks, interlaminated with more massive fine-grained silico-ferruginous layers of a banded structure, which is particularly obvious on weathered surfaces of the rock, as the darker and lighter-colored alternating seams contrast more than on fresh fractures. The strata dip north. We can follow from here for two miles up the stream continued outcrops of similar black slates and banded siliceous ledges in the steep bluffs which border the river on both sides. Near the S.W. corner of Sect. 9 we arrive at the base of a cascade, in which the river leaps down over walls 90 feet high, formed of these dark carbonaceous slate-rocks, lifted up in all degrees of inclination, and bent into serpentine curves. This excessively disturbed condition is caused by a large doleritic dyke 42 feet wide, which here intersects the rock-ledges transversally. The outer part of the dyke is an amorphous black-colored homogeneous mass, which by degrees assumes a more and more perfect crystalline structure toward the centre of the rock-belt, consisting there of a magma of well-formed crystals of a white glassy feldspar and of a dark brown augite. The extensive exposures of slaty strata at the falls and in the hills south of the river give a conception of the great thickness of this rock-belt, but the folded condition of the strata allows no exact estimate of it ; we see local dips in any direction, but generally a northern dip is observed in the outcrops.

South of the falls the slates continue for the distance of half a mile to form the surface rock, until we approach, in the south half of Sect. 17, the north slope of a granite-range which intersects the centre of Town. 48, R. 26, from east to west ; here succeeds them conformably a series of arenaceous flagstones full of mica scales, brownish or reddish-colored by iron oxide ; under them follow thick-bedded compact quartzites, part of which is conglomeratic.

These beds form the slope of the granite ridge, on which they lean with northern dip. A similar succession of rock-beds is exposed in numerous places, if we follow the slope of this granite range westward. The lower thick-bedded quartzites are not always found, and in their absence the next higher micaceous sand-rock flags lie directly on the granite, or sometimes on the schists of the dioritic group, which, in a part of the range, cover the granitic nucleus. The black slates above the sandy flagstones have a very great surface extension ; they compose a broad belt of undulating hill-lands on the south side of Dead River, which extends from the falls without interruption to the west line of R. 26 of Town. 48, and spreads in the next Town., R. 27, still farther, occupying almost the whole north half of the township. We find them often interstratified with arenaceous rock-seams ; it must be remarked, however, that drift deposits are ignored in this consideration, or else the slaty rock-beds would have an inferior claim to the configuration of the surface.

A mile north of the falls of Dead River, in the S.E. corner of Sect. 5, Town. 48, R. 26, I found an isolated mass of banded silico-ferruginous rock-beds, consisting of lighter-colored jaspery seams, containing a small proportion of granules of magnetite, in alternation with darker-colored ones intensely impregnated with ore-particles, which are perfectly similar to the banded siliceous rock-beds of the fifth group in the environs of Negaunee. This succession of ledges, amounting to more than 40 or 50 feet in thickness, is wedged in between dioritic crystalline rock-masses, of which all the surrounding country is formed. It is, in all probability, a detached body of layers which, during the general upheaval, became inclosed within a fold of the dioritic rocks, and so escaped destruction during the drift period, or at any other time in which erosive forces acted on the surface. Another instance of the intercalation of still larger masses of ferrugino-siliceous banded rock-beds, inclosing narrow seams of magnetic flag-ore between the dioritic rock-series, occurs at the location of the Holyoke mines, in the N.W. quarter of Sect. 1, Town. 48, R. 27. They are found on the middle of the slope of a high ridge of dioritic rocks on the north side of Dead River, irregularly wedged in between the vertically erected beds of fine-grained dark-greenish gray schists, with a glossy surface and an almost perfect slaty cleavage, which are intimately connected with crystalline dioritic masses. A tunnel has been driven into the base of this hill-side through these schists, and the flaggy, ferruginous beds were there encountered. These were, however, not the object searched for by the miner. The dioritic rock-masses are here intersected by large veins of milk quartz, which carries some argentiferous galena, zincblende, copper and iron pyrites, in association with the sparry carbonates of iron and lime ; but the amount of valuable ore is not large enough to be profitably mined, and the location, on which at one time large sums of money have been expended to develop it, is now abandoned.

All the hill-lands south of the Dead River, near the mining location, are composed of the black slate-rock. A large tributary enters the river at this spot, which comes from the south-west ; on the east side of this valley is a very broken, densely-timbered country, which continually rises as it recedes from the river, until it culminates a little over a mile's distance in high knobs with very steep slopes, formed of highly inclined layers of black slates dipping northward, which amount to an enormous thickness. On the south side of these knobs, the largest of which is situated near the centre of Sect. 12, and others in the S.E. quarter of Sect. 11, the arenaceous flagstones underlying the slate-formation come to exposure. On the west side of the mentioned tributary river the surface is less broken, rising first slowly into a drift-covered, undulating terrace, sparingly covered with pine, and partly clear of all timber, and then a more brisk ascent brings us to the summit of this body of hill-land, which is found to be isolated in its whole circumference. East and north are the valleys of Dead River and of its tributary branch ; west and south a broad belt of marsh surrounds it. Nearly all the surface of this insular surface-elevation is covered with drift, but outcrops of the underlying slaty rock-beds are frequent enough in all parts of it to show the uniform structure of its nucleus of this kind of sediments. On the north-western slope of these highlands, in the N.E. quarter of Sect. 4, Town. 48, R. 27, are exposures of such slates with a fair-even cleavage, which induced the owners of this land to open various test-pits in search of a good quality of roofing slate, but, so far, they have not had success in finding any beds well qualified for this purpose, and as far as I examined the locality I can give no encouragement for continuing the explorations. West from here, on the other side of the broad marsh-belt surrounding this place, is another body of drift-covered hill-lands, which occupies the west half of Sect. 5, all of Sect. 6, the north half of Sect. 7, and the adjoining Sects. 1 and 12 of the next Town. R. 28. These are underlaid by identical slaty and arenaceous rock-beds, but outcrops are comparatively rare ; farther south, in the western part of Sects. 13 and 24, frequent exposures of the black slates, underlaid by ferruginous and somewhat micaceous sandy flagstones, are observable, and the superposition of the latter on thick-bedded compact quartzites, similar to the quartzites of the Teal Lake range, is seen in various localities ; as, for instance, near the N.W. corner of Sect. 24, which is located on the

ferrugino-arenaceous rock-belt, well exposed in this locality ; and
the higher part of the hills, situated in the adjoining Sects. 14 and
23, consists of quartzites of a coarse-grained structure, and partially in a brecciated form ; other strata of the quartzitic rock-belt
are sub-schistose by abundant intermixture of the granular quartz-
mass with pale yellowish, scaly, hydro-mica of a silky lustre.
Going from the N.W. corner of Sect. 24 southward on the section
line we find the ferrugino-arenaceous flags and slaty rock-beds
again well exposed near the quarter-post. Near the south-west
corner of the section dioritic schistose rocks come to the surface.
Taking from here an eastern course, we remain on diorite hills
until we come to the quarter-post on the south line, where the
quartzite formation crops out again in massive, partly conglomeratic ledges ; farther on, we pass, before we reach the south-east
corner, high vertical cliffs of quartzite, dipping with almost upright
beds to the north.   Ascending these cliffs and going north, we find
them overlaid by a large succession of arenaceous flagstones, which
continue northward until we reach the edge of the large marsh
surrounding the head-waters of several tributaries of Dead River.
A low undulation of the surface in the midst of the marsh, not
many steps west of the N.E. corner of Sect. 19, is composed of
steeply erected black slates interstratified with sand-rock seams ;
similar blackish slate and sandstone ledges underlie the drift-
covered highlands in the south part of the section and in the west
half of Sect. 20.   In the N.W. quarter of the S.W. quarter of the
latter section, a thick belt of massive conglomeratic quartzite
ledges, with a chloritic cement, is exposed on top of a small knob,
a short distance south of which the dioritic rocks are at the surface
near the south-west corner of the section.   In the N.E. part of
Sect. 20, along the east section line, is a row of high knobs,
with precipitous slopes rising above the marsh-lands, formed
of the black slates and of interlaminated sand-rock beds, which
dip north-west and are seen on the east side to repose directly on
the quartzite formation.   The drift-covered hills in the east part
of Sect. 17 and in the northern two thirds of Sect. 16 are all
formed of the black slates and connected quartzose seams ; they
are well-denuded in one of the parallel undulating ridges which intersects the central part of Sect. 16 in an east and west direction ;
their dip is always north, and on their south side follows another

parallel undulation formed of quartzite, in thick, light-colored, compact ledges. The same slaty rock-series, reposing on the south side, on the quartzite formation, composes the hills in the south half of Sect. 15, and in the S.W. quarter of Sect. 14. In the N.E. quarter of Sect. 15 is a row of hills composed of a peculiar variety of crystalline diorite, which extends into the N.W. quarter of Sect. 14, Town. 48, R. 27 ; all the surrounding country is formed of the slaty and arenaceous rock-beds of the fifth group ; their contact with the diorite is not observable. I have, in the previous description of the topographical extent and the lithological character of this northern belt of deposits, representing the fifth group, only attempted to give the general features, and refer the reader to the accompanying geological map for further details, in order to avoid a too frequent repetition of similar statements, which is necessarily involved with the description of a rock-formation, as it occurs in a number of different remote localities. In the third volume of the Reports of the Geological Survey of Michigan I gave a short description of a cursory tour into the slate district of L'Anse and of Huron Bay, on which occasion I fell into an error regarding the dip of the strata and the cleavage of the slates, which I intend to rectify. At the same time I remarked that my investigations were not far enough advanced to enable me to give an opinion of the relative age of the slates, compared with the other sediments of the Huronian rock-series. While I examined the sedimentary series representing the fifth subdivision of the Huronian group in the environs of Negaunee, and particularly during the examination of the more northern exposures in the valley of Dead River, the similarity of these deposits with the slate-formation of L'Anse and Huron Bay made me suggest the analogy of all these compared rock-beds in the different localities, and a subsequent visit of Huron Bay fully convinced me of the correctness of my supposition. As the visit was a short one, and I had made no preparations to extend my explorations to any great distance from the shore, I confined myself to the examination of the beds of several creeks entering the bay, which in their descent from the hill-sides have carved deep ravines into them, and laid open splendid sections across the upheaved strata, amounting to an immense thickness. Clay slates in all shades of color, from whitish-gray, yellow, red. brown, to the darkest black, and in all degrees of hardness, from the fragile, absorbent, earthy condition of a shale. to the hard and compact structure of a roofing slate, are to be seen here, in endless repetition, often for many hundred feet not interrupted by interposition of any other kind of rock-seam, other times in frequent alternation with arenaceous layers and with belts of compact granular quartzites. The cleavage of the slates, which in uniformly colored layers cannot be discriminated from a sedimentary lamination, is in other sedimentary belts composed of an alternation of differently colored seams, obviously distinct from it, and intersects these laminæ under a more or less acute angle, partly under a right angle. In the above-mentioned essay I had the uniformly colored roofing slates under consideration, and I stated then that their cleavage was coincident with the sedimentary lamination, which, as I now see, was an error. This discordance between cleavage plains and sedimentary lamination makes it often very difficult to recognize the actual position of such rock-seams with regard to others, and to determine the direction in which the strata dip, which contrariety in the dip of the sedimentary laminæ with the cleavage plains, caused me also in the above case to assert the observation of a southern dip of the beds in the slate quarries, which according to the sedimentary striation of the beds is northward. It requires more time than I have devoted to the examination of this very large succession of slaty and arenaceous sediments to recognize the existing order in the structure of this rock-belt, and to form an estimate of its thickness. The lighter colored variegated slates, which are so well exposed in the bed of Slate Creek and along the shore of L'Anse Bay, appear to be the upper strata ; the alternation of banded slaty beds with arenaceous seams, interstratified with larger compact quartzite belts of light color, and partly of dark blackish color, seem to represent the middle series, which in rock character corresponds most with the arenaceous slate-formation in the Negaunee district. These strata are best exposed in the bed of Silver Creek, near the bridge. The roofing slates form the lower horizon of the series ; they are intersected by volcanic dykes, and are nearest in position to the granitic rocks, which compose the higher mountains southward, but I have not seen the slates in close contiguity with these rocks.*

* At the time the proof-sheets passed through my hands, I had made further examinations of the horizon of the arenaceous slate group in the Marquette region, and found that large iron-ore deposits, partly recently discovered, partly known for a good while, form a part of this group, occupying a position above the black slates which in these iron districts are of a graphitic nature. Of this class are the ore deposits of the Taylor mine in the L'Anse district, of the Northampton and D'Alaby mines, north of the Champion mine ; likewise those of the S. C. Smith mine and of other localities not yet developed. At the same time I will mention that these deposits are contemporaneous and equivalent with the ore deposits of the Commonwealth mine in Wisconsin.

CHAPTER VI.

MICA SCHIST GROUP.

ON the west side of the Michigamee mines, near the railroad,
are outcrops of dark blackish gray rock-beds, partly of slate
structure, partly in well-laminated, banded, more compact seams,
which succession of beds follows immediately above the actinolitic
rock-series, dipping in conformity with that southward. These
rock-beds consist of a sub-porous ground-mass, formed of
very minute granules of white translucid quartz, in intermixture
with a large proportion of brightly glistening black mica scales,
and not rarely also with chlorite. In the softer, quite fissile
schistose or slaty beds, the mica overbalances the granular quartz,
and they have a silky lustre. In the compact banded ledges the
quartzose ground-mass prevails, and their aspect is dull. Certain
seams inclose an abundance of brown garnet crystals, from the
size of a mustard-seed to that of a pea. These beds I consider as
representatives of the upper horizon of the fifth group ; they correspond with the micaceous schists, inclosing garnets exposed near
the railroad track on the north side of the Keystone mines, which
in that locality are succeeded on the north side by black slates of
carbonaceous character, and by ferrugino-argillitic and siliceous
beds. At the Michigamee location no exposures analogous to
these are observable, as the hill slope on the north side of Michigamee Lake is deeply covered with boulder drift. On the south
shore of the lake, opposite Michigamee village, the rock-beds come
to the surface again near the water's edge ; we find there silvery-
shining gray-colored mica schists, some smooth, even-bedded,
others much corrugated, which essentially consist of the same minutely granular quartzose ground-mass intermingled with lighter-
colored mica scales, which composes the schists on the west side of

10

the Michigamee mines. This great similarity in the sedimentary material is an evidence of the close connection between this mica schist group and the arenaceous slate group, which proves the immediate succession of the first to the other more reliably than it is done by the southern dip of the strata, conformable with those of the Michigamee mine. These mica schists, interlaminated with large belts of a more compact, minutely granular, sub-porous quartz rock, not so rich in the micaceous constituent, but often mingled with a large proportion of hornblende in curved fibrous actinolite-like crystals of a dark green color, compose all the hills on the south side and west side of the shore of Michigamee Lake, and all the islands in the north part of it, as far as I examined them. The dip of the nearly vertical rock-beds is almost uniformly to the south, but the succession of beds is so immensely large that there must be suggested a frequent doubling up of the strata, which in a belt of several miles in width retain, from one end to the other, almost the same general rock character. We meet with a great many modifications of rock, differing in structure, or in the relative proportions of the constituents, or by admixture of accessory minerals, but the large bulk of all of them is formed of the same granular quartzose ground-mass mingled with mica scales. On Goat Island are very good exposures of this series, comprising there four or five hundred feet of strata. Some of the schists, composed of microscopically fine scales of a dark mica which loses its color by exposure to the weather, have a silvery-metallic lustre, made more conspicuous by the corrugated condition in which the schists frequently are found. Other schists are darker colored, less fissile, breaking crossways with a dull earthy fracture, but within the mass are scattered irregularly larger blades of a white mica, which on those dull fractured surfaces show with great brilliancy. Still others inclose quite abundantly small but very perfect translucid garnet crystals of the color of amethyst or ruby. The silvery variety of schists often contains a large number of good-sized twin crystals of staurolite dispersed through their substance, but usually the crystals are rough, with rounded angles, and always milky opaque. In the same kind of schists are irregularly digitated or cruciform clusters of nacreous margarite crystals associated with the staurolite.

Irregular fissure-seams in the schistose rocks are filled with milky quartz in association with agglomerated coarse blades of a pale whitish mica, which often appears to be dark green, from chloritic substance filling the interstices between the blades, and imbedded within these mica-masses occur not rarely large square columns of rose-colored andalusite, from one to two inches in diameter, besides well-formed green crystals of apatite, some of which polygonal columns, with squarely truncated ends, are often one inch in diameter. These fissure-seams observable on Goat Island are larger and richer in the named crystalline minerals on another island, a mile farther south, called Silver Island, very probably on account of the silvery lustre of the schists composing it, as no silver has ever been discovered there.

The thick belts of more massive ledges, interstratified with the schists of Goat Island, are, as above remarked, composed of the same porous granular quartzose ground-mass as the schists, but contain less mica. Their color is either uniformly darker or lighter gray, or minutely speckled ; a distinct sedimentary striation is observable in most of the beds. Other strata, in which hornblende is an additional component, have the fibrous actinolite-like green-colored crystals thinly disseminated within a white granular quartzose ground-mass, containing little or no mica, or the ground-mass is dark colored from intermingled mica. Elsewhere the bundles of curved, fibrous, actinolitic hornblende crystals compose almost exclusively the rock-mass, with very little of a dark micaceous cement in the interstices ; these blackish-green colored beds resemble a coarsely crystalline diorite, but they never occur in belts of any great thickness, and always exhibit some trace of their sedimentary origin. How far southward this rock-series, amounting to a surprising thickness, extends, and what kind of rock-beds come there in contact with this formation, I have not yet examined. We will, in the subsequent description of the Menomenee iron region, become acquainted with similar mica schists, believed to be identical with the just-considered group of sediments ; they may even be in direct continuity with these, as they occur in the lower part of the Michigamee River valley, about forty miles south of Michigamee Lake ; but this interval is not yet sufficiently examined to prove or disprove this suggestion.

CHAPTER VII.

SERPENTINE GROUP.

PRESQUE ISLE was for a long time the only locality in the Marquette district where serpentine and kindred magnesian rocks were known to occur.

During the summer of 1878, while engaged in the examination of the environs of Negaunee, Mr. Ropes, Postmaster of Ishpeming, informed me he had discovered large outcrops of marble and of serpentine some distance west of Deer Lake, in Sects. 29 and 30 of Town. 48, R. 27, and accompanied me to the indicated localities, where I saw his statements fully verified. Subsequently, when I came to extend my explorations over this district, I found the extent of the serpentine group much larger than it was previously supposed. A broad belt of such rocks, commencing with a narrow end in the centre of Sect. 27, Town. 48, R. 27, continues westward through Sects. 28, 29, and 30 ; thence, taking a southwestern direction, it intersects diagonally Sect. 31 and Sect. 36 of the next adjoining Town. R. 28. Farther west I have not examined. The distance between the outcrops of Presque Isle and those in the centre of Sect. 27 is 13 miles, on which intervening space not a trace of serpentine or other magnesian rocks could be discovered.

On inquiring which position the serpentine formation holds in relation to the other six groups, I find it difficult to give a satisfactory answer.

The outcrops of Presque Isle are completely surrounded by the granite formation, which comes close to the serpentine, but the contact between these rocks is not seen in that locality. The large western belt of serpentines is bordered on both sides by dioritic rocks, and is often seen in intimate contact with them.

In two localities the quartzite formation is found to repose on the serpentine, leaning on the two opposite slopes of a large body of serpentine hills, and dipping south on the southern slope, north on the northern. The quartzite on the south side is an isolated strip of the formation, about a mile long in an east and west direction, and in thickness representing about four or five hundred feet of strata, mostly in heavy compact beds of a white or reddish color ; their position is almost vertical. South of the quartzites rises another high serpentine ridge close by, so that this outlier of the formation is completely surrounded by the serpentine.

The intimate connection of the serpentines with the dioritic formation, and on the other hand the superposition of the quartz-ite formation on this rock-belt, might lead to the inference of its intermediate position between these two groups, as a link of the sedimentary series ; but if this was the case I could not well con-ceive how a rock-series of so large a bulk, and so different in com-position from the succumbent and incumbent layers, should be in some places sporadically developed, and in next adjoining localities be totally missing, in which the concerned strata, supposed to be above and below, are well represented and exposed. Another hypothesis, considering the serpentine formation to be the product of local metamorphic influences on the dioritic rock-series, is very improbable, as the lithological character of the two contiguous rock-species changes abruptly, which could not be if the differences depended upon a secondary transformation of the same, or at least a similar sort of sediments ; we would in this case doubtless observe intermediate stages of the transformation.

The rocks belonging to the serpentine formation occur generally in bulky non-stratified masses, which, if they ever originated from mechanical sedimentary deposits, are by chemical action so com-pletely transformed as to efface all traces of their former detrital structure. They resemble a volcanic eruptive rock, forced to the surface in a soft, plastic condition, and most likely heat was one of the prime agents in their formation, or else transformation, in combination with aqueous vapors, which is suggested by the hydrated composition of the serpentine.

The cliffs at the north-east end of Presque Isle are formed of a black, semi-crystalline massive rock, consisting of a dark greenish-brown amorphous ground-mass of serpentine, semi-transparent in thin splinters, in intimate intermixture with a crystalline foliated mineral of a brassy metallic lustre, which seems to me identical with the schillerspar of the Harz Mountains. In addition, the rock contains a large proportion of protoxide of iron as a coloring matter, and about 2 per cent of chrome iron in small octahedric crystals, readily attracted by the magnet.

Boiling muriatic acid dissolves about half the weight of the rock ; the solution contains a large proportion of iron and magnesia, besides small quantities of alumina and lime. The discolored white crystalline residue of pearly lustre, after its separation from the chrome iron by washing, is on analysis found to be composed of silicate of magnesia and alumina, with some lime ; it represents the discolored crystals of the schillerspar in the rock-mass.

Associated with the black serpentine are lighter-colored greenish or reddish or variegated rocks, intersected in all directions by seams of calcspar, or by asbestine or chrysotile bands of silky lustre with the parallel fibres transverse to the walls inclosing the bands. The material of these lighter-colored rocks is frequently identical with the black rock, but in a half-decomposed friable condition, with the protoxide of iron changed into hematitic oxide. In the more compact rocks of this seamy character often a system of capillary fibres pervades the rock in a rectangular position to these larger chrysotile seams, which are comparable to the capillary channels in a block of slowly melting ice ; they consist also of chrysotile, tinged sometimes with bright red hematitic pigment. There are also rocks, found in the same association of feldspathic composition, resembling a porphyry by intermixture of larger crystals of feldspar with the ground-mass. The principal bulk of the upper beds, which are much corrugated and folded, or shattered by the upheaval, is formed of dolomites in various modifications. Some beds are compact saccharoidal, white or reddish-colored, but the larger portion of the dolomitic rocks is a mixture of pale green milky serpentine, in concretionary nodular masses, with fine-grained dolomite. Fissures in the rock exhibiting a sliding dislocation of the walls are filled with long-fibred flexible asbestus, or with rigid wood-like masses of it, and druse cavities lined with brilliantly shining rhombic crystals of dolomite spar are quite common. The rock incloses also concretions of iron and copper pyrites, of zincblende, galena, etc., which have induced some min-ing experiments, but the quantity of these minerals is too small to be of practical value.

The inconformable superposition of Silurian sand-rock on the serpentine formation of Presque Isle is previously mentioned.

A rock identical with the black serpentine of Presque Isle com-poses an isolated knob near the centre of Sect. 27, Town. 48, R. 27, which is the first outcrop of the serpentine group observed west of Presque Isle. Next adjoining on the east side is another knob, consisting of a hard feldspathic rock of porphyritic structure by a copious intermixture of feldspar crystals with an almost aphanitic brown-colored ground-mass. Another portion of the rock is completely crystalline, granite-like ; it contains small hornblende crystals sparingly intermingled with the feldspar crys-tals. Adjoining outcrops on the south and west side of the ser-pentine knob are schistose dioritic strata, which show their affinity to the feldspar porphyry by insensible gradations into it. North. of the serpentine knob, on the opposite side of the marshy valley of a creek which intervenes, other outcrops of magnesian rocks occur in intimate association with diorites and dioritic schists. A part of these has a schistose structure, and consists of a dark green amorphous serpentine, intermingled with an abundance of pearly scales of talc, of which mineral, large bunches of beautifully greenish white color occur in the schists in association with the sparry car-bonates of lime, magnesia and iron. Another portion of the mag-nesian rocks is perfectly crystalline, and resembles the diorites of neighboring exposures, but by closer inspection they are found to be composed of pearly shining crystals of diallage, incorporated with an amorphous interstitial mass of dark green serpentine ; the rock is partially soluble in warm muriatic acid, which solution gives a strong reaction indicating magnesia and iron, besides small proportions of alumina and lime. The adjoining diorite is not acted upon by the acid, and decomposed by fusion with alkali, it is found to contain only 3 per cent of magnesia and 5 of lime ; the other constituents have not been determined by weight. All out-crops further north are formed of dioritic rocks. Westward, and yet within the limits of Sect. 27, we find a short ridge on the south side of Carp River, formed of bulky masses of a dark lead-colored steatite, which contains a good proportion of sparry carbonates (of lime, magnesia, and iron), besides an abundance of magnetite granules, and invariably some chrome iron. With the steatite occurs a belt of granular dolomite and sparry seams banded with streaky laminæ of pale green serpentine. South of this steatite ridge, and in close connection with it, are several other parallel undulating ridges, which consist of dioritic rocks of fine grain, cleaving into rhomboidal fragments.

On the north side of Carp River, opposite this place, we find the lower part of the slope of a high range of mountains deeply covered with drift ; higher up are cliffs of serpentine and dolomitic rock, and the crest part is again formed of diorite. Farther west, within Sect. 28, the entire body of the continuation of this range is composed of magnesian rocks belonging to the serpentine group, and a part of the same range, extending over the S.W. quarter of Sect. 21, and the S.E. quarter of Sect. 20. In the latter localities the whole mountain crest is formed of bold cliffs with vertical walls. In Sect. 21 is the before-mentioned locality in which the quartzites are seen to repose with a northern dip on the basal slope of this extremely broken body of serpentine hills. East from there, the novaculitic schists underlying the quartzite formation are observable in close proximity to the serpentine, and, further east, the dioritic schists come in contact with it. This large serpentine belt, over a half mile in width, exhibits a remarkable uniformity in its composition, although numberless varieties of rock occur, dependent upon differences in structure, color, or the admixture of accessory minerals to these specifically magnesian masses, which are partly silicates, partly carbonates, or an intermixture of both chemical combinations. The recognition of an order in the arrangement or succession of these rocks is scarcely possible, owing to their greatly disturbed upheaved position, and to their massive non-stratified structure. A large proportion of the rock material composing the presently considered group of hills consists of light grayish green and, in thin splinters, semitransparent serpentines, which usually have a granular, subcrystalline, glistening fracture, as the crystalline mineral *marmolite* is substituted for the amorphous serpentine, which amorphous form, with a waxy fracture, is however abundant enough, and forms masses of considerable bulk. Some of it is the so-called precious serpentine, of bright yellowish green color and semi-transparent ;

its adaptation for ornamental work is much impaired by nodular clusters of magnetite crystals, abundantly disseminated through the mass. The common serpentine has usually a much paler grayish green color, and is likewise full of magnetite granules, contains always some chrome iron, and not rarely, nikelglanz.

Other large masses of the rock, blackish green or dark lead-colored from copiously intermingled magnetite granules, and from a dark green-colored interstitial mass of amorphous serpentine, have a crystalline foliated or a stellato-fibrose structure, and are principally composed of crystal blades of marmolite, or, in the other case, of picrolite or chrysotile in intermixture with the above-mentioned cement mass. All these rocks exhibit on polished surfaces a peculiarly cellulose structure, from a network of capillary seams pervading them ; the magnetite in the darker rock is particularly concentrated into these seams. In other instances they are formed of picrolite fibres. Most all contain a certain proportion of carbonates, which make them effervesce by immersion in warm muriatic acid. The cellulose reticulated structure of the rock, caused by intersecting capillary seams mainly composed of magnetite granules, is particularly plain in rock-specimens collected on the north line of Sect. 28, a quarter mile east of the N.W. corner ; at right angles with these finer anastomosing filaments, the rock is banded by other larger seams of chrysotile or of asbestus in intermixture with calcspar, which usually are parallel with each other, or the bands composed of vertical fibres split into smaller seams, which occasionally may reunite and inclose lenticular segments of the rock-mass within the loops. It is difficult to give a plausible explanation of the mode in which such transverse fissures in the rock could form and fill up with these silky chrysotile and asbestus bands ; it could not be done by aqueous infiltration, as there is no indication of a successive deposition of the substance. It appears more as if it were an exudation from the capillary pores of the rock into these fissures, while it was in a plastic semi-fluid condition, which same process formed probably the bands of epidote in the diorites, which also consist of fibres transverse to the bands or the fissure walls.

Besides the serpentine and other magnesian silicates, magnesian limestones have an important share in the composition of these hills. Such limestones occur in the S.W. quarter of the S.E.

quarter of Sect. 20 on the south-west slope of the range. A part of the rock on the surface is in a decayed, soft, porous condition, and has a brown ochraceous color ; the not decayed, undecomposed rock is whitish, compact, of fine-grained crystalline structure. It contains, besides the carbonates of lime, magnesia, and iron, minute scales of talc, and is densely interwoven with fine seams of serpentine.

Still larger exposures of limestone occur in the N.E. quarter of the N.W. quarter of Sect. 29, on the south side of an isolated ridge surrounded by a swamp. The main mass composing this ridge is a dark-colored serpentine of subcrystalline marmolitic structure, which incloses seams of talc in intermixture with the sparry carbonates of lime and of iron ; other sparry seams contain long-fibred asbestus, permeating the spar in distant bundles, or its densely crowded fibres form the prevailing material of the rock-seam, and the spar fills out the narrow interstices between them. The talc of pale green color, partly in granular masses, partly in large-leaved micaceous form, is very curiously mingled with the spar, which forms parallel columnar stems of the thickness of a finger, down to that of a lead-pencil, more or less remote from each other, and the interstices between these columns are solidly filled out with the talc. I have observed this singular columnar structure of sparry rock seams associated with talc in several localities.

The limestone belt forming part of this ridge is best exposed on the south-east side of the slope ; it amounts to considerable bulk, and is partly composed of coarsely crystalline sparry masses of white color on fresh fractured surfaces, but rusty brown on exposed weathered surfaces, from oxidation of a certain proportion of carbonate of iron combined with the limy carbonate ; other portions of this limerock are gray-colored, fine-grained, with a conchoidal fracture. Both the fine and the coarser-grained limerocks are mingled with linear seams of talc and contain scattered columnar crystal blades of bright lustre which I have not chemically examined. South from there, on the other side of the swampy valley, rises a high mountain mass, cut up into numerous parallel summit ridges, which is formed of the serpentine group. We meet also here with calcareous rock-belts of a more impure mixed character. Some of these rocks, consisting of a reticulated intermixture of dark green amorphous serpentine with white spar-seams, take a good polish and are very ornamental. The serpentine, which forms the largest portion of the rock-mass of these hills, varies in color from dark blackish green to pale greenish gray ; most of it occurs in massive non-stratified belts ; sometimes an obscurely laminated schistose structure is observed.

On the east side of this hill-group, near the centre of Sect. 29, are large bluffs in which the various modifications of the magnesian rocks can be studied to advantage. We find there quite large veins of rigid asbestus resembling petrified wood.

By following these bluffs southward we come into the previously mentioned belt of quartzite which borders the south slope of the serpentine range, trending in south-western direction along the north side of the valley of a creek flowing to the Carp River.

The corner of Sect. 29 is on the other side of the creek, and south of the quartzite belt, at the base of another range of serpentine hills, in the north part of Sect. 31.

The high bluffs on the summit part of them are composed of a dark-colored steatite, which incloses seams of white calcspar, with cleavage plains large enough to split off rhombohedric blocks 8 inches in diameter. Associated with the spar occurs a pale green pure talc of pearly lustre, in bunches larger than a man's fist.

Passing over these hills next to the valley-westward, nearly all the before-described kinds of magnesian rocks are met with. The dark green-colored serpentines, intersected by a network of sparry seams, are locally well qualified to be cut and polished for ornamental trinkets, but not for larger-sized works of art. Light-colored serpentine is not so common as in some of the before-examined localities ; but dark lead-colored subcrystalline rocks, composed of pearly shining marmolite crystals imbedded in a green amorphous serpentine mass, and richly impregnated with magnetite granules, belong to the commonest in the exposures. Dolomite also occurs in fine-grained compact massive belts, dark blackish-colored by magnetite granules, and chrome iron is discovered in it by the blow-pipe. The serpentine formation composes all the hills on both sides of the creek from our starting point near the S.W. corner of Sect. 29 to the west line of Sect. 31. The quarter-post of the west line is situated on a hill of serpentine, but on the south side of this creek only the first row of hills adjoining the valley is formed of rocks representing the serpentine group ; the large body of hills south of there is all composed of dioritic rocks. On the north side of the creek the serpentine group covers not only all the surface of Sect. 31, which is on that side, but also the southern three quarters of the east half of Sect. 30 ; and in the S.W. quarter of the S.W. quarter of Sect. 30 are again several serpentine knobs, on one of which the corner of the section is located. North and west of the corner are only dioritic rocks, but south-west of it the serpentine continues diagonally across the N.E. quarter of Sect. 36, and forms the surface of the whole S.W. quarter of that section, entering into Sect. 35, but further the examination was not extended. In the S.W. quarter of Sect. 36 the exposures are very extensive and easily accessible, as the forest is cleared away from the greatest part of the section. A large portion of the outcrop is formed of crystalline marmolitic rocks of finer or coarser grain ; they have a dark gray color from intermingled granules of magnetite, which always is associated with small quantities of chrome iron. The bladed crystals of marmolite, imbedded in an amorphous ground-mass of serpentine, giving it a silvery glistening lustre, often occur in the rock-mass also red, copper-colored blades and scales, with the silvery ones. Polished specimens of this kind of rock are very beautiful on closer inspection, but disastrously for their value in the market, this same polished rock, seen from a greater distance, has a dull gray unpleasing color, because the eye cannot distinguish the small scaly molecules which constitute its beauty. Similar avanturine-like rocks of a brown color, with thickly disseminated copper-colored scales, are found in the S.E. quarter of the N.W. quarter of Sect. 29, Town. 48, R. 27, which polish well and look very fine held near enough to the eye, but their aspect from a distance is also not attractive. Occasionally narrow seams of precious semi-transparent serpentine are found disseminated with such scales of metallic lustre, these being polished are, also seen from a distance, very beautiful.

An industrious collector can gather a great variety of such specimens large enough to make paper-weights and other small ornamental trinkets ; but if I were asked for advice whether it would be a paying business to quarry these rocks, and send them to the market in sawed slabs and blocks, I would certainly warn one from this enterprise, because I know that not enough of the finest varieties could be found to make the success certain, and probably not enough to prevent a total failure and disappointment. In the S.W. quarter of Sect. 36 are good exposures of the contact between the serpentine and the dioritic rocks ; the serpentine leans with a southern dip on the diorite, both rocks being in an almost vertical position ; the diorite, in contiguity with the serpentine, is full of fissures filled with epidote, red feldspar, quartz, and chlorite ; but both kinds of rock are well defined, and no transition from one into the other is observable.

CHAPTER VIII.

E R U P T I V E   D Y K E S.

THE previously described series of rocks, representing the Huronian group, considered to be a succession of sedimentary deposits in a more or less altered condition, is frequently found intersected by rock-seams of a different kind, which must have come into the position held by them subsequent to the formation of the stratified sedimentary beds, and even subsequent to their transformation into rocks of crystalline structure and to their great dislocation. There are two essentially different sorts of these transverse rock-belts. One represents, evidently, fissures in the mother rock, replenished with various crystalline minerals, and partially with detrital fragments, by intervention of water as a transporting and solvent medium. These so-called fissure veins have nothing in common with the other kind of rock-seams formed of a homogeneous solid rock-mass, which evidently represents a cooled lava stream forced from the interior through the ruptured superficial crust of the globe ; this latter kind only shall be considered in this chapter.

Various lithologically different lava-masses can be distinguished, which represent different periods of volcanic action, as one kind is found to intersect the other whenever they come in contact, and the belt intersected must necessarily be the older of the two.

The oldest of the volcanic dyke-rocks in this district is a truly dioritic rock, consisting of a whitish or greenish anorthic feldspar and of hornblende. As accidental additional constituents, granules of iron pyrites and of magnetite are usually found sparingly intermingled with the mass ; less common is the intermixture of brightly yellowish green small clusters of epidote crystals. The color of the rock is lighter or darker greenish gray ; in the smaller dykes, which vary in width from less than a foot to 50 or 60 feet, or even more, the rock-mass is usually fine-grained, homogeneous for the naked eye, quite compact, with a smooth conchoidal fracture ; the wider dykes have generally a coarser crystalline grain, in which the component minerals can be recognized with the naked eye, or at least with a small magnifying power. The dyke-mass generally adheres firmly to the inclosing walls, but seems to have exerted little or no altering influence on them. Dykes are frequently seen to divide into numerous side-branches, which often are not wider than a few inches, and may extend in a geniculated course for quite a distance from the main belt. These thin seams are generally of a homogeneous aphanitic structure, owing to the rapid refrigeration of such narrow seams of molten substance.

Another younger kind of dyke rock, much darker than the other, and often intensely black-colored, has the composition of a dolerite ; it either forms a homogeneous basalt-like mass of aphanitic grain, or consists of a magma of crystals of dark brown augite, with translucid glassy crystals of colorless or yellowish anorthic feldspar ; nearly always a certain proportion of magnetite is mingled with the mass, which is often large enough to impart to the rock strong magnetic properties. These augitic dykes, if coming in contact with the dioritic kind of transverse rock-belts, invariably intersect them, and hereby prove their younger age.

Doleritic dykes frequently intersect the iron formation and higher Huronian rock-beds, while the dioritic dykes seem to be restricted to the lower horizons of the Huronian group, if we are not inclined to consider the larger belts of diorite which protrude in the central part of the synclinal rock-basin, from the midst of the upper Huronian strata, as analogous eruptive masses, coeval with the smaller transverse belts. The often perfect similarity of the dioritic rocks of the larger belts, parallel to the trend of the formations with these transverse, decidedly volcanic dyke-masses, proves, at all events, the transformation of the former sedimentary rock-ledges into a crystalline diorite, by the action of heat principally, or else the structure of these diorites could not be so absolutely similar with the dyke-rocks, whose igneous origin is unquestionable. Both kinds of dykes, the dioritic and the doleritic, are abundantly represented in the Marquette district. We can observe a dioritic dyke well exposed in the quarries at the Lighthouse Point of Marquette, while it intersects a large belt of nearly vertical well-stratified ledges of dioritic schists under an angle of 45°. This fine-grained crystalline transverse seam, about 12 feet in diameter, differs in its lithological character so little from the substance of the compact schistose ledges intersected by it, that it requires a careful observer to make a distinction in hand-specimens. In the same locality another larger dyke of doleritic composition is to be seen, which is parallel with the schists in its general course, but intersects the dioritic dyke. This doleritic rock-belt, of a coarsely crystalline structure and about 50 feet wide, extends into the Lighthouse Point, composing the knob on which the turret for the light is built. East of the building it divides into several branches, which inclose within their anastomosing loops, schistose masses, whose broken ends correspond with the ends of other segments of schist, inclosed within another adjoining loop in front of that one, and obviously the grain of these smaller branches of the dyke is finer, more homogeneous than that of the thick main belt, in which the crystals of augite and feldspar are plainly discernible. A third sort of dykes is disclosed in the Lighthouse quarries, smaller than the others, not over two feet in width, and sometimes only a few inches. It intersects the strata in an irregular geniculated course, and disappears for a while under the accumulations of lake-sand in this place, but reappears again in the subschistose dioritic bluffs on the road near the Marquette saw-mill. The dark olive green, perfectly amorphous, smooth-fracturing dyke-mass differs from any other I have observed in this district, but may perhaps be only a modification of the dioritic dykes; it does not intersect the other dykes in the place. The large augitic dyke of the Lighthouse Point appears to continue for three miles westward in one uninterrupted belt, parallel with the stratified rock-series. We meet with outcrops of the same rock in Michigan Street, east of Front Street, and again in the quarries at the west end of Arch Street, in which latter locality the broad main belt gives off several smaller side-arms which intersect the strata diagonally. Here it can be plainly observed how the more or less rapid cooling of the lava prevented the crystallization completely or partially. The narrowest side-seams and the outside of the larger belt in contact with the wall-rock, consist of a black, homogeneous, fine-grained mass, which toward the centre of the large belt gradually becomes a crystalline structure, and forms in the centre of the dyke a magma of well-formed crystals of white glassy feldspar with augite. Other narrower augitic dykes, intersecting a bulky crystalline diorite mass, are observable two blocks farther north in Vermont Street. West of the Marquette cemetery, not far from the south quarter-post on the north line of Sect. 22, the supposed continuation of this large doleritic dyke is found again largely denuded, and exhibits the homogeneous aphanitic condition of the rock, as well as the coarsely crystalline form, of a black and white speckled appearance, and of bright lustre on fractured faces. This dyke intersects in this vicinity, on Hudson's Hill, another dyke of dioritic composition, rather fine-grained, and copiously mingled with iron pyrites ; fissures in the mass are filled with epidote and quartz crystals.

Pursuing the doleritic dyke farther west, we find some low hillocks in the north-east corner of Sect. 21 composed of it, and a row of knobs already described in a previous chapter, trending along with the south line of Sect. 16 to its west end, is formed of the same augitic rock, which differs only from the eastern exposures, and the otherwise fully corresponding mass, by the admixture of a good proportion of flesh-red feldspar crystals. Farther west this rock-belt disappears under drift-accumulations.

It seems to me the most expedient way to describe the different kinds of eruptive dykes promiscuously as they occur in certain localities. I therefore lead the reader from the south line of Sect. 16 to a before-examined locality in the south-east quarter of this section, in which we have seen the repeated alternation of granite belts with the schists of the dioritic group. Here we see the schists and granites transversely intersected by various dioritic and doleritic dykes. One of the dioritic dykes in its main belt, about 25 to 30 feet wide, consists of a uniformly green-colored magma of hornblende crystals with feldspar, in which larger white feldspar crystals have segregated, which give the rock a spotted appearance ; narrower side-branches of this same dyke are a non-crystalline, homogeneous, compact mass of a pale green color. Iron pyrites is the hardly ever missing accessory constituent of all these dyke-rocks. Doleritic dykes of black color, in belts a few feet in width, are likewise seen here to intersect the granite and the schists. Another narrow dyke, only a few feet wide, and dividing into numerous narrower tortuous seams, is seen to intersect the dioritic schists of this locality ; it consists of a reddish

11

gray fine-grained ground-mass, principally formed of red feldspar, in which small dark green-colored blades of hornblende are distributed in a gneissoid laminated arrangement, which structure is, however, not in all parts of the dyke equally plain. A dyke of similar nature is found in the exposures at Stone's mills in the S.W. quarter of Sect. 7, Town. 48, R. 25, where it intersects the granite and associated schistose beds. Most likely also a dyke belongs to the same class, which intersects the granite in the N.W. quarter of the N.W. quarter of Sect. 17 ; though it contains a larger proportion of hornblende, and is of a coarser crystalline grain. In this association belongs probably also a dyke four or five feet wide, intersecting the dioritic rock-mass of the Picnic Islands, which I have previously mentioned in order to give an example of a laminated gneissoid structure, exhibited by an evidently eruptive rock-belt. Before leaving the S.E. quarter of Sect. 16, which is the same locality that offered us the natural section through the lower part of the dioritic series described in the second chapter, I must give a description of a most instructive exposure in the bed of the creek which follows the east line of Sec. 16. An augitic dyke, dividing in several branches and

loops, is seen here to intersect a large series of dioritic schist, interlaminated with several belts of granite, in the high vertical bluffs, which present a section through these ledges in steeply erected position. One arm of the dyke, about three feet wide, coming to the surface in the bed of the creek, cuts diagonally across the granite and schist ledges exposed in the rock-wall, causing a lateral dislocation of the disrupted corresponding ends of the beds, amounting to about eight inches. Another arm of the same dyke forced its way parallel with the bedding between two granite seams, and divides afterward into reuniting branches, which inclose within these loops fragmental portions of the granite belt. The above sketch shows the exposure.

North of here, in the granite hills intermediate between the valleys of Dead River and of Campo Creek, dykes are very abundant. I have mentioned the occurrence of a row of diorite hills, parallel to the trend of the formation, and on both sides surrounded by granitic rock, whose eruptive nature and relationship with the smaller transverse dioritic rock-seams is suggested on that occasion. Of the smaller dykes a great many occur in close vicinity to these larger eruptive masses ; they exhibit a good many minor variations in external aspect of the rock-mass in each dyke, but these depend only from a more or less perfect crystallization, and all of them can with propriety be arranged under the two classes, the dioritic and the doleritic. In the south half of Sects. 5 and 6, several dioritic dykes, from 30 to 50 feet in diameter, exhibiting all gradations of structure from the aphanitic to the coarsely crystalline, can be observed in the granite, and in a few places their intersection by doleritic dykes is seen. A large doleritic dyke in these localities, which sends out a number of smaller side-branches, exhibits the contrast of the quickly cooled aphanitic masses, with those slowly refrigerated, well-crystallized, and all the intermediate gradations, particularly well ; the narrowest seams and the wall portions of the larger are a homogeneous black mass of conchoidal fracture ; in other portions of the dyke the aphanitic black material is seen disseminated with scattered white, translucid feldspar crystals of good size, and the central part of the largest seams is formed of a magma of augite and feldspar crystals, without a trace of an amorphous interstitial ground-mass. Some of these augitic dyke-masses are strongly magnetic ; others, of exactly the same appearance, exert no influence on the compass needle. Partridge Island and the Gull Islands, east of Presque Isle, are other favorable localities for the observation of dykes of both kinds ; particularly the Gull Islands, perfectly denuded of soil, exhibit the intersection of the dioritic by the doleritic dykes most plainly. We notice there also the basalt-like, columnar cleavage of the dykes of doleritic nature, which is transverse, from wall to wall, of the fissures filled with the amorphous lava-mass.

Leaving the granitic districts, and examining the area of the dioritic rocks, the dykes occur not near as frequent, and there the doleritic dykes are much oftener seen than the dioritic, which may, however, in part be due to an oversight of the dioritic seams, which look so perfectly similar to the indigenous masses inclosing them, while the doleritic are at once discernible from them.

Still less common are dykes in the districts covered by Huronian rocks, younger than the dioritic series, and the doleritic kind is the only one observable. The intersection of the iron-formation by doleritic rock-seams on the north side of Negaunee, in the hematite mines on the Jackson mining property, at the Cascade mines in several of the different locations, and in the eastern pits of the Washington mine, has incidentally been mentioned in the previous pages. The intersection of the novaculitic rock-series beneath the quartzite formation by a doleritic dyke, is observable in the N. E. quarter of the S. W. quarter of Sect. 21, Town. 48, R. 27 ; this is the only locality in which I observed an appreciable altering influence of a dyke-mass on the inclosing walls, but it does not extend much over an inch sideways into the wall-rock.

The intersection of the black slates, representing the fifth group by a large doleritic dyke at the falls of Dead River, is previously mentioned, and in the surrounding country several other doleritic rock-seams can be observed cutting across the slate-rock.

The only instance of the intersection of the serpentine group by a doleritic dyke, occurred to me in the N.W. quarter of Sect. 31, Town. 48, R. 27. In the south part of the examined district, dioritic and doleritic dykes are equally common, as in the north part, within the area of granitic rock-exposures, but on the large space covered by the quartzite formation, and by the arenaceous slate-group, no dykes were observed, if we except the large insular protrusions of dioritic rocks which occur there.

A narrow branching dyke intersects the roofing slates in the quarries of Huron Bay, which in its rock character is unlike any of the before-described dyke-masses ; it consists of a compact amorphous light-gray colored ground-mass, sparingly disseminated with small pale green columnar hornblende crystals.

In connection with the volcanic dykes, I have to describe other narrow rock-seams of a partially schistose structure, which transversally intersect the granitic and dioritic rocks in the islands and on the shore of the main-land west of Presque Isle, and in several other localities more remote from there. The partially slaty structure of these transverse rock-seams induced me at first to consider them as sedimentary strata which became accidentally inclosed within a fold of the upheaved granitic masses, which case evidently happened sometimes. A slaty novaculitic rock-seam intersecting the quartzite formation near the east end of Teal

Lake is mentioned by Major Brooks under the name of a slate dyke, which belongs to this class ; but the above-mentioned transverse rock-belts have a different origin ; there is no rock-formation similar to them developed in these localities which could have been inclosed, except those narrow seams which in several instances are seen to intersect other dykes, of the dioritic and the doleritic kind, while it had to be expected that these lava-belts, erupted after the general large upheavals, should intersect them, if they are sedimentary layers wedged into a fold of the rock-masses. It is also impossible to suppose sedimentary deposits, holding a position as they do, could form subsequent to the eruption of the doleritic lava-streams. In fact, the laminated structure of the schists is totally unlike a sedimentary lamination, and is the result of sliding pressure on a semi-plastic mass ; moreover, the larger proportion of the substance of these rock-belts has a massive sub-crystalline structure closely similar to igneous eruptive rocks. The character of the rock-mass in dykes of this kind is not altogether alike ; a number of them occur in close vicinity in the N.E. part of Town. 48, R. 25, and almost every one of them varies some from the others. Some are richly impregnated with granular magnetite, and exert a powerful influence on the magnetic needle ; others of the dykes are not, or only faintly, magnetic.

On a naked granite island, situated near the imaginary north line of the N.W. quarter of Sect. 2, Town. 48, R. 25, a narrow dyke about five feet wide intersects the granite in a north and south direction. The exterior portions of the dyke-rock, intimately coherent with the granitic side-walls, have a laminated schistose structure ; the central portions are massive, not laminated. The schistose parts consist of a minutely granular pale greenish-colored feldspathic ground-mass, laminated by interrupted sub-parallel linear seams of dark green-colored fibrososcaly blades arranged in a similar mode as the micaceous laminæ of a gneiss. The lamination is in the vertical sense parallel with the walls of the fissure, but oblique to the walls from one side to the other ; the schistose parts of the dyke, as well as the central massive portion of it, contain a large proportion of carbonate of lime, causing a lively effervescence if the rock is immersed in muriatic acid ; usually also a certain quantity of magnetite and iron pyrites granules is found intermingled with the schistose part of the rock-belt, but in the central massive part of the dyke magnetite is very abundant, giving the rock a dark lead color, and imparting to it a powerful influence on the magnetic needle. This massive central part of the dyke is sub-crystalline, but earthy, absorbent, or porous ; it consists of the same gran-. ular feldspathic ground-mass as the outer, and is copiously inter-mingled with small flattened, lenticular bits of a green-colored fatty, talcose mineral, which becomes more visible if the surface of the rock is moistened ; pearly mica scales are an additional component, and some harder portions of the dyke-mass also contain radiated clusters of actinolite of pale green color. A similar narrow transverse rock-seam, richly impregnated with magnetite, occurs on the shore of the main-land near the quarter-post on the north line of Sect. 4 ; the rock-mass of this is harder, and actinolite is one of its principal constituents. Other magnetic and schistose dykes are found in the N.E. quarter of the S.E. quarter of Sect. 4, and one near the quarter-post on the south line of the same section, which latter intersects a dioritic dyke. Perfectly similar dykes can be observed in the N.W. quarter of the N.W. quarter of Sect. 9, in the S.W. quarter of the N.E. quarter of Sect. 10, at the N.W. corner of Sect. 18, the N.E. quarter of the S.W. quarter of Sect. 20 ; and in Michigan and Arch Streets of Marquette a similar dyke, not much over one foot wide, occurs. Also in Town. 48, R. 26, a dyke of this kind intersects the granite in the S.W. quarter of the N.W. quarter of Sect. 23, and in Town. 48, R. 27, in the S.W. quarter of the N.W. quarter of Sect. 19.

On the west side of Partridge Island is another dyke of this group, which consists principally of dark green silky-shining schists, which insensibly merge into rigid masses of asbestus ; the schists and the asbestus are in an extremely contorted, corrugated condition, and intermingled with siliceous seams and with a large proportion of sparry carbonate of lime as filling material of the interstices. With these schists occurs a seam of a dark basalt-like rock of aphanitic structure, and a narrow band of a compact rock richly impregnated with magnetite granules, and with ferrugineous calcspar crystals imbedded within a micaceo-feldspathic and partly actinolitic ground-mass. This dyke, about six feet wide, intersects a dark black basalt-like dolerite dyke of aphanitic grain, not far off from the water-line of the shore. A larger dyke identical with this one is on the north side of the island, which contains, besides the asbestine and actinolitic masses, thick seams of saccharoidal calcspar interwoven with asbestine fibres, and with well-formed large epidote crystals ; these rocks have some resemblance with certain seams of the serpentine formation, but contain no serpentine and no chrome-iron, which is a constant associate with the latter group.

CHAPTER IX.

ESSENTIALLY distinct from the described narrow transverse rock-seams, are these clefts in the rock-masses, subsequently replenished with crystalline mineral substances deposited there successively by percolating aqueous solutions. We find them in all parts of the Huronian series, and in the granites, retaining in general the same character, whether they occur in the higher or lower horizons. The commonest are veins of white milky quartz, which sometimes fills the fissures solidly without the intermixture of any other mineral. In other cases the quartz is associated with calcspar, or with a mixture of calcspar and sparry carbonate of iron. Not rarely red feldspar crystals and epidote crystals intermingle with the quartz and calcspar ; the quartz, epidote, and calcspar compose together fibrous bands with fibres transverse to the walls of the fissures, but this occurs only in narrower seams, not wider than a few inches. Frequently nodular concretions of iron and copper pyrites are intermingled with the quartz veins, and chlorite is almost constantly present as the last-formed deposit filling the interstices left between the other minerals. A more rare mineral is turmaline in the quartz veins ; it occurs in a black, fibrous, radiated masses. Quite common is large-leaved micaceous iron oxide in such fissures, and in a few instances botryoidal incrustations of the fissure walls with banded chalcedony occur. In several localities larger metalliferous quartz-veins have been discovered, which, besides the before-enumerated minerals, contain argentiferous galena associated with zincblende and copper pyrites. The Holyoke mines were opened in such veins, which, after expenditure of large sums of money, had to be abandoned again, as not a sufficient quantity of the valuable ores could be found.   A similar costly experiment, which likewise proved to be a failure, was made in the S.W. quarter of Sect. 27, Town. 48, R. 26, at the so-called Sedgwick mine, where a quartz vein carries a small quantity of copper pyrites.   Considerable test-pitting has also been done in examination of a quartz-vein containing carbonate of iron and some copper pyrites in Sect. 25 of the same township, a short distance north of the Morgan furnace, but with no better success.   A good many other localities could be enumerated in which explorers spent weeks and months of hard labor to follow such quartz veins, in which they discovered a few nodules of copper ore or galena.   The most promising veins of argentiferous galena have been discovered in the granite hills near the head-waters of the Chocolate River.   I have seen there, some years ago, many tons of pure lead-ore piled up on the side of the test-pits, but it seems as if these also are abandoned at present. It can safely be asserted, from precedent experiences, that the Marquette district is, with exception of its immense wealth in iron-ore, rather barren of metallic ores of another kind.

PART II.

MENOMINEE IRON REGION.

MENOMENEE IRON REGION.

GEOLOGY.

THE previous Report on the geology of the Marquette district was delivered to the Board of the Geological Survey in the fall of 1879.

After its acceptance the Board decided to defer the publication until I was ready to bring in another similar description of the Menomenee iron region, which, during the past few years, has with surprising rapidity grown up into a mining-centre equalling in importance the mining district of Marquette.

I was ordered, therefore, to spend the coming summer season in examination of said region, and to be ready to report on it at the end of 1880.

The results of this examination are given in the subsequent pages.

The area which had to be examined is very large, and much of it is as yet an unbroken wilderness, accessible only by slow, tedious travel. To accomplish this examination in the given time would have been impossible for me, if it was not for the most liberal assistance I received from the inhabitants of the district, all included, from the leading business men down to the ordinary laboring man. I feel it to be my duty to express here publicly my sincerest gratitude for all the acts of kindness I received from them, which I ·appreciate not only in the interest of science, but also individually I am thankful for the favors disinterestedly tendered to me as their fellow-man.

To learn the local distribution of the iron-bearing rock-series in the Menomenee River district, its structure, and its relative position to other rocks, was the principal object aimed at in my examination. I begin, therefore, with its description, abstaining for the present from an attempt to classify it with the subdivisions adopted for the Huronian group as it occurs in the Marquette district.

The Brien and Emmet mines, 33 miles due west of Escanaba, are the first discovered, and the most eastern mines in the district ; all the interval between them and the lake shore is covered with horizontal Silurian rock-beds and with drift-deposits, and no more outcrops of the Huronian formation can be found in this eastern direction ; also westward, the Silurian sandstones, and sometimes the younger calcareous strata, conceal much of the older rock-formations, frequently preventing the observation of the succession of beds, and being a great impediment for the explorer.

The mines are close to a swamp, on the south side of a chain of hills trending in west-north-west direction across the north part of Sect. 22, Town. 39, R. 28. The top part of the hills is formed of horizontal ledges of Silurian sandstones, which are to a great extent covered again with drift. The ore-bearing Huronian strata, scarcely seen in natural outcrops, are in the mining-pits uncovered to the amount of about four or five hundred feet ; they dip to the south under a high angle. The most southern and consequently highest strata of this succession of beds, observable in some test-pits on the land of Mr. Saxton, in the N.W. quarter of the N.W. quarter of Sect. 23, are white and red mottled hydro-mica schists, similar to the so-called soapstone of the Jackson mines of Negaunee. These are succeeded northward by a large series of well-laminated, mostly thin-bedded siliceous and argillitic rock-ledges, all of which are more or less intensely impregnated with hematitic iron oxide and with granular martite. Interlaminated between them occur seams of iron-ore of a reddish brown color, in sub-brecciated, porous, non-stratified masses, consisting of a mixture of granular martite with amorphous red oxide of iron, frequently also in part of the hydrated oxide. These ore-seams are evidently a secondary product of lixiviation of the strata by percolating water, concentrating and purifying the ore-particles, which percolation is proved by the abundant occurrence of druse cavities in the ore lined with crystals of calcspar, and with the most brilliant crystals of iron pyrites. The given description particularly applies to the eastern part of the mining location. to the Emmet mine ; the western openings, known by the name of

Brien mines, are in a somewhat lower horizon of the series, and work a different ore-seam. The ore mined there occurs also in irregular pocket-like seams ; it has a dark, blackish-gray color, is quite soft, friable, and consists of minute octahedric crystals of martite. The foot-wall of the ore is formed of a thick series of dark gray, thinly-laminated, argillitic, flaggy beds, richly impregnated with martite granules, and by insensible gradations merging into the ore. Farther north succeed red-colored, hematitic, argillaceous, and siliceous strata, of which little can be seen, on account of the Silurian sand-rock ledges covering them. In test-shafts sunk through the sandstones some distance west of the Brien mines, these lower beds are found to be very rich in martite and hematitic oxide throughout, and certain seams yielded 62 per cent, of iron by analysis, but for the present no actual mining for shipment of the ore has begun in these localities.

In the pits of the Brien mine a very good occasion is offered to observe the superposition of the Silurian sandstone over the nearly vertical Huronian strata.

The lower ledges of the sand-rock constitute generally a breccia by copious intermixture with angular fragments of ore and other rocks of the ore - bearing group. Deep clefts in the Huronian strata, widening below into large cavernous spaces, are seen here replenished with sand-rock, and the curious fact happened to the miner to find the horizontal Silurian ledges below in a shaft sunk through upright Huronian beds. The Silurian sandstone is sometimes deep red-colored by hematitic pigment, but the higher beds are usually not tinged, white ; it amounts on top of the hill to a thickness of at least 75 feet, and high bluffs of it occur near the north line of the west half of Sect. 22. The Silurian limestones above the sandstone formation (calciferous sand-rock) occur in outcrops on top of the hill near the quarter-post on the north line of Sect. 23, and in the test-pits opened in the N.W. quarter of Sect. 24 the same siliceous and dolomitic lime-rock is struck, which in certain seams incloses a large amount of concretionary masses of copper pyrites, by decomposition partly transformed into malachite and azurite. North of the Brien mines are, for quite a distance, no outcrops of Huronian rocks of any kind ; south of them, across the swamp, the surface is likewise covered with drift-deposits, but in some test-pits opened in the

S.E. quarter of Sect. 21 the hydro-micaceous white and red mottled schists, in connection with siliceous and argillaceous hematite ores, have been found. West of the Brien mines and of the exploring pits in the N.W. quarter of Sect. 22, the iron-bearing rocks are for several miles hidden from view by drift-deposits ; the first outcrop we find, by following the railroad, is a dark gray slate-rock exposed on the south side of the road in the N.W. quarter of Sect. 19. From here this slate-rock is traceable into the south half of Sect. 13 of the next Town. 39, R. 29, where a wide belt of the slates, alternating with quartzose seams, is exposed in the embankment of the Sturgeon River, within sight of the railroad bridge ; the strata dip south under a high angle, and strike west-north-westward. The drift-masses covering the slate-rock are full of siliceous flag-ore pieces. Examining the surrounding country northward, on the west side of the river, we find, a few hundred steps north of the railroad, a series of test-pits opened by Mr. Dike, in which clay-slates are uncovered somewhat softer than those in the river embankment, and lighter gray or bright red-colored by impregnation with iron oxide ; their dip is south, conformable with the others. From the position of the test-pits we must infer a great thickness of this succession of clay-slates ; farther north follows an equally large series of well-laminated siliceous and jaspery rock-beds richly impregnated with iron oxide, in the red amorphous condition, and in crystalline granular form, which latter imparts to them a dark gray color with a dull metallic lustre. Interstratified with these siliceous flaggy ledges are softer argillaceous seams, likewise rich in iron oxide ; and some seams occur which almost exclusively consist of minute crystalline grains of the oxide mingled with only a small proportion of argillitic or siliceous substance. Such seams are often several feet wide, and expand sometimes into pocket-like dilatations 20 and 30 feet wide, which constitute the valuable ore-deposits of this formation. The ore of all the mines in this range has a dark. blackish-gray color, somewhat glistening from the reflex of the minute crystals which compose the porous, rather soft mass, easily crushed into a sand-like powder by the pressure of the fingers, but exceptionally harder and compact masses of the ore occur, resembling the finer-grained specular ores (the so-called steel-ore) of the Jackson mine of Negaunee.

North of Dike's mines, along the east slope of the hill-range, are a number of other test-pits, all of which exhibit similar ferrugino-siliceous and argillaceous beds, occasionally inclosing a seam of higher graded ore. The whole series of the ore-bearing strata amounts to more than a thousand feet in thickness, and retains throughout the same general character, although a great many variations in the aspect and molecular structure of the ledges occur, which to describe would be a useless task. This ore-bearing series dipping to the south is conformably succeeded on the north side by siliceous limestones in thick massive ledges, amounting to a belt of over 200 feet in thickness ; they are exposed along the north slope of the hill-range which borders the south side of Pine Creek valley, and extend eastward across Sturgeon River through the north halves of Sects. 17 and 18, Town. 39, R. 28, where several parallel low ridges of the limestone project from the undulating drift-covered pine plains.

North of the limestone outcrops, on the west side of Sturgeon River, is the mouth of Pine Creek, surrounded on both sides by a broad belt of rolling hill-lands deeply covered with drift. On the east side of the Sturgeon River no natural exposures of rock are observable north of the limestone belt ; but in the S. E. quarter of the S. W. quarter of Sect. 7, Town. 39, R. 28, test-pits have been opened, not more than 300 steps north of one of the ridges of limestone, in which, under a cover of from 5 to 25 feet of drift, a large series of flaggy rock-beds, richly impregnated with bright specular iron oxide granules, has been found to succeed the limestones conformably, in descending order, as both of them dip under a high angle southward. These banded, flaggy rock-ledges, consisting of an arenaceous, quartzose, and partly feldspathic ground-mass, in intermixture with various proportions of the specular oxide, amounting to from 25 to 65 per cent of the rock-substance, by their bright metallic lustre, equalling sometimes that of the specular slate-ores of the Negaunee district, and by the large average percentage of iron in all the ledges, are very tempting for the explorer; but so far all the energetic efforts of the owners of this place to find a rich marketable quality of ore have been in vain. In such explorations frequently much money is thrown away uselessly, by misconception of the nature of the ore-deposits. Many of the miners who were trained in districts where the ore-deposits are found in fissure veins, firmly adhere to the prejudice that also in this part of the country an ore-seam of inferior quality near the surface may become very rich at a greater depth, which is often the case in fissure veins ; but here the ore-deposits are regular layers of oceanic sediments which once were horizontal, and most likely consisted of the same material in all parts of such a layer within distances not too remote. These beds we find now in an upheaved, often nearly vertical position ; we see cross-sections through a number of successive deposits exhibited at the surface, of which each layer may differ from the other, but the nature of every one of the layers will as a rule be the same in all its parts, be it near the surface or hundreds of feet below it. An explorer may therefore cross-cut a formation from one layer to the other, and reasonably expect to strike a rich ore-seam after he went through many poorer ones ; but to sink down parallel with an ore-seam of inferior quality in the expectation to find it changing into a rich ore, is folly. A narrow belt of ore may increase some in width if followed to a greater depth, but it will never improve in quality below if it is poor at the surface.

How wide this belt of iron-bearing strata is, and what kind of rock-beds succeed it, is not known, as north of the test-pits all the surface is covered with drift-deposits for the distance of a quarter of a mile, where we meet with high bluffs of quartzite, which form part of a belt of quartzite ledges, amounting to not less than a thousand feet ; their dip is in discordance with the iron-bearing rock-series. In the bluffs a quarter mile below the falls of Sturgeon River the quartzite dips north-east, and in some localities on the west side of the river the dip is north-west or north. The quartzite formation is, farther north, seen to repose inconformably on the granites, which form the bed of Sturgeon River at and above the falls. The granite and quartzite formations shall be considered in another place, as our present object is to examine the iron-bearing rocks of the south belt of this formation.

West of Dike's mines, located in the N.W. quarter of the N.W. quarter of Sect. 13, are the East Vulcan mines, opened along the south line of Sect. 11 ; another company also sunk a shaft close to them, in the N.E. corner of Sect. 14. The character of the formation is the same : an alternation of highly ferruginous, harder siliceous, and softer argillitic beds, interlaminated with various seams of iron-ore, is laid open for observation in the different mining-pits. One of these ore-seams, much wider than the others, but quite irregular in its diameter, consists of the before-described dark blackish-colored, soft, friable crystalline oxide, which is characteristic of all the mines in this range ; some of the narrower seams of ore are hard, compact, and resemble the fine-grained so-called steel-ore of the Negaunee mines. The strata are so near to a vertical position that it is often hard to decide which way they dip. North of the mines extend undulating drift-covered plateau-lands, on which Silurian sand-rock is found in patches to underlie the drift ; farther on, a steep descent is made into the valley of Pine Creek, through ravines washed into the drift, and near the base of the slope cliffs of the limestone formation project, showing a decidedly southern dip. South of the mines the hill-side is covered with drift, and slopes down to a swampy depression of the rolling, drift-covered plateau-lands, a broad belt of which borders the valleys of the Sturgeon and the Menominee Rivers. This plateau is underlaid by the slate-rock and quartzite beds mentioned before as being exposed in the embankment of Sturgeon River, in sight of the railroad bridge. Outcrops of them are observable near the quarter-post on the west line of Sect. 13, close to the railroad track, at which place crystalline diorites are inclosed within the ledges in apparent parallelism with them ; but I consider them as intrusive. The dip of all the beds is south.

Proceeding west, we find in the N.W. quarter of Sect. 10 and in the adjoining part of Sect. 9, the Vulcan mines, occupying the south slope of a prolongation of the same range on which the East Vulcan mines are located. The ore-formation is here much better exposed than in the other places, partly by artificial denudation in the mines, partly in natural outcrops. In the eastern pits, situated near the west line of Sect. 10, the strata are in a nearly vertical position, dipping south ; in the western pits, in Sect. 9 their dip is less steep, and in places an inclination of the beds is observable, deviating from a horizontal position only 20° or 30°. The ore mined in the different pits represents different seams, but the quality is in all much alike, the soft, easily friable, so-called blue ore of the miner. In the pit intersected by the west line of Sect. 10, the ore-seam, very changeable in its width, is inclosed between hard siliceous banded rocks resembling the jasper-banded, mixed

12

ore-beds of the Jackson mines of Negaunee, but the alternating bands of jasper and iron-ore composing this rock are not so conspicuous, as the jasper has a dark purplish and not a bright red color like these. In the pits in Sect. 9 a large series of intensely red-colored slaty argillitic beds forms the hanging wall of the ore ; these openings are north of the pits in Sect. 10, but nevertheless the strata seem to be above the others. On the higher part of the hill north of the mines, a large succession of highly ferruginous, siliceous, and argillitic thin-bedded or thicker banded rock-beds is exhibited in numerous test-pits. The top of the hill is covered with horizontal Silurian sand-rock. and in a test-shaft sunk there through the sand-rock, light-colored quartzites, in connection with white and red streaked hard micaceous argillites, have been brought to the surface, which seem to belong to the horizon of the limestone formation, although no calcareous rocks have been found in the shaft as far as it went. South of the mining-pits, along the slope of the range, here and there red and white blotched hydro-mica schists are exposed, similar to those found in the test-pits of Mr. Saxton, south of the ore-bearing rock-belt of the Emmet mines ; the base of the slope is formed of well-stratified sandy and gravelly drift-accumulations. Lake Hanbury fills out the bottom of a depression between the ore-bearing hill-range and another row of lower hills which rise with steep rock-bluffs from the south shore of the lake.

These hills, making part of the before-mentioned belt of drift-covered plateau-lands north of the Menominee River valley and west of the Sturgeon River, are formed of a large succession of dark blackish-colored clay slates, merging into various modifications of lighter gray-colored, partly silky-shining micaceo-quartzose and feldspathic schists, which contain a considerable proportion of carbonate of lime, or of sparry carbonate of iron, and of numerous interlaminated belts of dark-colored granular quartzites, composed of brightly glassy grains of quartz in intermixture with a micaceo-schistose ground-mass, and with a ferrugino-calcareous cement, which makes the rock hard and compact ; by exposure and lixiviation of the carbonates from the rock the outside becomes porous to the depth of from half an inch to an inch, and these pores are filled with brownish or orange-colored ochraceous iron oxide.

In the geological reports of Wisconsin, Major Brooks gave a lengthy description of the different ledges composing this rock-series ; he suggests a plication and repetition of the strata in this broad belt of exposures, amounting to over a quarter of a mile in width, which is probably the case, as beds of the same kind repeatedly occur when we go across this succession of beds, although no synclinal and anticlinal position of the ledges is observable. On the north side of the hills the dip of the strata is clearly southward, in the centre part of the outcrops they are nearly vertical, and on the south side of the hills, which present vertical escarpments of slate rock, in places a northern dip of the strata is observed ; this may, however, be merely a slight tilting over of the marginal vertical ledges, for want of support on the free side. South of these bluffs is the valley of a creek running east into Sturgeon River, which is the outlet of Lake Hanbury. Farther south, from the creek to the Menominee River, undulating drift-hills fill out this interval of something more than a mile, and no Huronian rocks are seen to come to the surface.

Returning to the iron range, we find the Curry mines in the S. W. quarter of the N. E. quarter of Sect. 9, in which a large seam of the soft blue ore occurs under similar conditions as in the adjoining Vulcan mines. Next to it, in the S. E. quarter of the N.W. quarter of Sect. 9, are the test-pits of Mr. Stephenson, in which the siliceous flaggy strata of the iron-formation, interlaminated with narrow ore-seams of a siliceous character, have been found, but going deeper with the pits, in nearly all of them the quartzose layers of the limestone formation were struck, and the place was then abandoned. Very few steps north of the pits the limestone formation is naturally exposed, and from there a chain of knobs of limestone trends in north-west direction diagonally across the N.W. quarter of Sect. 9, connecting with the limestone outcrops in Sects. 4 and 5, which form the foot-wall of the ore-formation in the Saginaw and Norway mines. The strata dip, conformably with the iron-formation, to the south ; the upper layers are quartzites rather than limestones, and have an unhomogeneous brecciated structure ; below them follow limestone beds of various shades of color, whitish or reddish, and more or less intersected by siliceous seams parallel with the bedding and transversally ; a large conglomeratic belt occurs in this association, composed of very unequal larger and smaller limestone fragments, of a partially angular, and in part rounded form, in intermixture with quartz fragments ; the cement of the rock is calcareous. The thickness of the limestone formation in this place amounts to not less than four or five hundred feet, and is probably much larger, if an accurate measurement should be made.

The higher hills of the iron range east of Stephenson's test-pits are interrupted here by a broad, swampy depression ; only the row of low limestone knobs crosses the swamp, and forms connection with the equally high range which rises on the opposite side, trending from there in the same north-west direction as the former eastern range.

On the slope of this west range are mines opened by four different companies in close proximity to each other—the Saginaw mine, in the S.W. quarter of the S.W. quarter of Sect. 4 ; the Stephenson mine, in the N.W. quarter of the S.W. quarter of Sect. 4 ; the Norway mine, in the east half of the S.E. quarter of Sect. 5 ; and the Cyclops mine, in the S.W. quarter of the S.E. quarter of Sect. 5. The strata laid open in the pits of the Saginaw mine dip with great regularity to the south, under an angle of from 60° to 70° ; well-laminated, thin-bedded, partly siliceous, partly argillitic beds, rich in iron oxide, inclose the ore-belt from both sides, which consists of the usual so-called blue ore. South of the pits the surface is deeply covered with drift deposits ; north of them are the shafts of the Stephenson mine, which, with the exception of an abandoned open pit, is altogether underground work. The ore-belt of the Stephenson mine likewise dips under a high angle southward, and not over 50 feet north of the shaft are outcrops of the limestone formation, conformably dipping under the ore-formation. Among the waste rock hoisted from the shaft are blocks of a crystalline, half-decayed, brittle diorite, in which the feldspar crystals and the hornblende are partially transformed into an absorbent kaolinitic mass retaining the shape of the crystals. The largest part of the waste rock is a dark-colored schist of chlorito-argillitic composition charged with granular martite ; some of it has an amygdaloid structure, and in place of the amygdaloid nodules are cavities left, filled with a pulverulent ochraceous residue. West of these mines, and in direct continuity with them, is the Norway mine ; it occupies the higher part of the slope, and all the work is done in open pits. The summit of the hills is formed of horizontal Silurian sandstones amounting to considerable thickness ; the lower part of the Silurian strata consists of a coarse breccia of the shattered ledges of the ore-formation, recemented on the spot by the Silurian sand washed into the interstices between the fragments. These brecciated masses covering the upright strata of the ore-formation, and filling, in wedge-like accumulations, deep ravines which existed between them, are well exposed in the mining-pits. Various belts of ore occur in the mines, and the intermixture of rock-seams between the ore-masses requires often much labor to separate them from the ore. North of the ore-bearing beds a limestone belt conformably underlies them, as in the other before-mentioned mine. The upper layers of the limestone formation are almost exclusively a quartz rock of brecciated structure ; farther north are purer, compact, fine-grained limestones, of red, white, and gray color, with interlaminated schistose seams of calcareo-hydro-micaceous composition, and of cherty bands. The thickness of this formation amounts to at least three or four hundred feet. North of the limestones follows a large series of light-colored reddish, or gray or greenish slaty argillites, with interlaminated arenaceous seams, and some of them rich in mica scales ; they seem to underlie the limestones conformably ; but for the present I will not attempt to solve this question, and go on westward with the examination of the ore-formation.

The Cyclops mines are on the same hill as the Norway mines, but represent a higher horizon of the iron-ore formation ; most of the rock-beds disclosed in the mine above and below the ore-belt are argillites, red-colored by hematitic pigment, or gray-colored by martite granules disseminated through the masses ; still there is one large siliceous rock-seam, of a compact jaspery texture, and richly impregnated with ore-granules exposed along the slope, some distance east of the western pits, and south of the ore-belt. The ore of the Cyclops mine is a very soft, friable blue ore of excellent quality ; the seam is unequal in its width—in places 30 feet wide, in others much narrower—and irregular in its course, as the strata inclosing it are considerably distorted by their upheaval.

The superposition of the Silurian sand-rock on the ore-formation is, in the west pit of the Cyclops mine, most beautifully exhibited ; the lower beds adapt themselves to the curved surface of a trough in the Huronian strata, and in the same measure as they fill up this depression they straighten and finally become perfectly horizontal ; the lower beds always inclose ore fragments and other rock pieces of the underlying formation.

West of the Cyclops mine the continuation of its ore-seam has been much hunted for, but so far without success. A great many test-pits were opened on both sides of the county road to Quinnesec, in the west part of Sect. 5 and in the east part of Sect. 6, in which the jaspery and argillitic strata of the ore-formation, with interposed seams of a hard siliceous ore of a dull metallic lustre, are found. In the test-pits opened by Mr. Curry in Sect. 6, on the higher part of the hill-slope, north of the road, strata of a lower position occur, lighter-colored than the others, and of more argillitic than siliceous character, amounting to a large succession of thinly-laminated flaggy layers, part of which contains very little ferruginous matter, but much the greater part of them is disseminated with small octahedric crystals of martite sparingly, or in proportions overbalancing the argillitic ground-mass—not enough, however, to give them value as an iron-ore in the present market. Other test-pits are on top of the hill-range, sunk through a capping of horizontal Silurian sand-rock, under which, regularly, cherty rocks and hard schistose argillitic strata of a sub-crystalline grain, and of pale whitish or reddish color, were found, which represent the upper horizon of the limestone formation.

Farther west, in Sect. 1 of the adjoining Town. 39, R. 30, many test-pits have been opened in the N.E. quarter of the section, but the drift-deposits and the underlying Silurian sandstones amount here to such a thickness that, as far as I can judge from the material thrown out of the pits, none of them was dug deep enough to reach the Huronian beds below the sandstone. Further on, in Sect. 2, nothing of the iron-formation can be discovered near the surface ; but a row of limestone bluffs commences not far from the east line of the section, on the north side of the county road, and extends without interruption to the N.W. corner of the section, which is located on the limestone cliffs ; south of the road are drift-covered pine-plains, with no outcrops within a mile's distance. The limestones dip to the south under an angle of about 70°. Some test-pits have been opened by Mr. Wendell about 30 or 40 steps south of the bluffs, in the N.W. quarter of the N.E.

quarter of Sect. 2, in which light reddish or gray-colored fine-grained, hydro-micaceous, sub-schistose, absorbent rocks have been dug out, associated with harder sub-crystalline compact ledges, more of a feldspathic composition, but evidently only a modified molecular form of the same material. In other pits nearer to the bluff, cellulose quartzites, red-colored by iron oxide, were found.

The mentioned limestone bluffs form the south edge of a large area, having limestone as a surface-rock, which embraces the largest part of Sect. 35 and the N.E. diagonal half of Sect. 34, Town. 40, R. 30, as far as it can be ascertained by outcrops; but it is very probable that the extent of this area would be much larger if the thickness of the drift-deposits covering the surface of Sects. 27 and 28 did not prevent the observation of the older rock-beds underlying them. The creek draining Lake Fumee intersects this area, and on both sides of it are fine exposures; it forms a cascade where it runs over the marginal ledges of the rock-belt. The thickness of this limestone formation cannot well be estimated, as it is folded into several successive synclinal and anticlinal arches, which folding is clearly exhibited in some of the low knobs projecting over the swampy ground in the S.W. quarter of Sect. 35; but commencing at the bluffs an eighth of a mile east of Quinnesec village, a measurement of the beds, so far as they succeed each other with undisturbed regularity along a wood-road which leads northward across the well-denuded strata, shows its thickness cannot be less than six or seven hundred feet. These limestones have great similarity with the Huronian limestones of the Marquette district; they are usually fine-grained, of conchoidal fracture; their color is reddish or whitish or gray; large belts of them are a breccia of sharp angular fragments of different kinds of limestone, or represent a shattered rock-mass recemented again without intermixture of foreign fragments. All of them are of dolomitic composition, and in a degree siliceous, often full of quartzose seams parallel with the stratification, or intersected transversally by an irregular network of linear cellulose veins; certain ledges of this rock-series are exclusively formed of a flinty quartz, and such are frequently in a brecciated condition, formed of fragments of various color; large blocks of this kind are quite common in the boulder-drift which covers the limestone area; very large ones lie on the road midway between Quinnesec and Lake Antoine.

The limestone bluffs abruptly terminate at the N.W. corner of Sect. 2, and disappear under the drift. Proceeding in the direction of their strike about 100 steps farther, we find, after crossing a ravine, at once exposures of the iron-bearing rock-series. We have now come to the location of the Quinnesec mines, situated in the S.E. quarter of the S.E. quarter of Sect. 34, Town. 40, R. 30. The limestone belt is, however, not interrupted here ; it only recedes, and, retaining its southern dip, continues onward north of the iron-formation, which composes a conspicuous chain of hills trending from here west-north-west. The ore-bearing strata of the Quinnesec mine dip northward, while in all the previously examined localities their dip was south, conformable with the dip of the limestones.

The succession of beds composing the ore-formation at the Quinnesec mines is not less than a thousand feet thick. It consists in the southern, as it appears the lower part of the series, of compact, even-bedded flaggy or banded thicker siliceous ledges, impregnated in the various beds with larger or smaller proportions of iron oxide, particularly with granular martite of metallic lustre ; among them are seams carrying as high as 60 per cent of the oxide, which are too narrow to be used. The sedimentary lamination and cleavage of the beds are generally parallel, but some of the seams, consisting of a hard hydro-micaceo-feldspathic substance, less impregnated with oxide, have a schistose structure, and their sedimentary lamination is oblique to the cleavage. North of this part of the series follow somewhat softer, ferruginous, argillitic, also well-laminated strata of a grayish color, in alternation with the siliceous ones. At this horizon occurs a belt of a porous, soft, well-laminated ore (the blue ore of the miners), amounting to from 10 to 20 feet ; north of the ore-belt ; the ferruginous flaggy layers continue for some distance, and farther off the limestones crop out, with a southern dip.

The top part of the hill is formed of Silurian sandstones, the lower beds of which are a breccia of ore-fragments. In the mining-pit the Silurian sand-rock is seen to fill out a deep excavation worn into the surface of the Huronian strata, just at the place where the productive ore-belt occurs ; the undermined sand-rock ledges, left without a support, commence to break down by their own weight, and make this part of the mine very dangerous. A short distance west and north of the mining-pits an exploration was made with the diamond drill, giving the instrument an inclination to the south. The drill went first through Silurian sand-rock ; then, for over 500 feet, through siliceous compact limestone strata ; next, a not very thick belt of light-colored argillites was penetrated, and last, the red-colored iron-bearing rocks were struck ; the entire length of the drill-hole amounted to 750 feet. South, at the base of the Quinnesec ore-range, are outcrops of gray-colored silky-shining schists in a vertical position, consisting of an interlamination of linear seams of quartz, and sometimes of granular feldspar, with a hydro-micaceous ground-mass. Farther south are drift-covered pine-plains, which terminate with steep bluffs at the Menominee River. South-east of Quinnesec, in Sect. 11, these drift-bluffs are half a mile off from the Menominee River, and in various places on top and on the slope of the terrace-land, slaty and quartzose rock-seams in a vertical position are exposed, striking in a west-north-west direction. This series of rocks, which amounts to a great thickness, consists of a variety of harder quartzose seams. Some are amorphous, flinty, black, and red mottled from intermixture of hematitic and magnetic iron oxide ; others are composed of granules of quartz, with glassy opaline fracture, which granules are imbedded in a schistose hydro-micaceo-chloritic ground-mass ; also gray-colored, saccharoidal, fine-grained quartz-seams occur. These are interlaminated between thick belts of hydro-micaceo-chloritic and more or less ferruginous schists or slates, part of which is silky-shining, quite fissile, inclosing lenticular narrow seams of quartz, perfectly identical with the above described schists exposed at the base of the Quinnesec ore-hills ; others are less fissile, much harder, more of a dull aspect, in which the quartzose and feldspathic constituents prevail over the chloritic and hydro-micaceous. These dark-colored slaty and quartzose rocks are equivalents of the quartz schist formation which composes the hills on the south side of Lake Hanbury ; in fact, they are a direct continuation of this rock-belt, which first is exposed in the S.E. quarter of Sect. 13 ; then crosses Sturgeon River, and shows itself again at the surface near the west quarter-post of Sect. 13 ; then along Lake Hanbury. From there it is traceable to the N.E. quarter of Sect. 17 ; thence an abundance of slaty fragments of this kind mingled with the drift-masses in Sect. 18, and in Sect. 12 of the next township, show its extension in this direction, and make the connection with the outcrops in Sect. 11 complete. In the S.E. quarter of the S.W. quarter of S. 12, T. 39, Range 30, are a few low knobs formed of a diorite-like crystalline serpentine rock, intensely charged with magnetite granules and with a smaller proportion of chrome iron. Seams composed of calcspar, of silky-shining white asbestine fibres, and of grass-green amorphous nodular masses of serpentine, occur in connection with the massive crystalline serpentinic rock. All the plateau-lands surrounding these isolated rock-bubbles are deeply covered with drift, full of the before-mentioned slate fragments, but a half mile farther south the dioritic or as some call them diabasic rocks, which form the bed-rock of the Quinnesec Falls, are extensively exposed in the hills bordering Menominee River, east of the falls. These will be specially considered in another chapter.

The ore-formation soon disappears under drift-deposits west of the Quinnesec mines, and following the line of its strike we meet with outcrops of the limestone formation, as, for instance, in a ravine in the S.E. quarter of the S.E. quarter of Sect. 33, a short distance from Dikey's farm-house. The limestone beds dip to the south, and alternate there with slaty seams of a silky lustre. From there we can follow limestone bluffs for more than a mile westward along the brow of the hills.

In Sect. 33 are, south of the limestone bluffs, drift-covered terrace-lands on which some test-pits have been opened, but the drift was found too deep to go through it without incurring a great expense. North of the bluffs the whole hill-side is riddled with test-pits. All of them went through drift-deposits of various thickness, and then struck the Silurian sand-rock. Its upper strata are generally not tinged, whitish ; the lower ones are often red, colored by iron oxide ; and the lowest part of the sandy sediments constitutes generally a breccia, formed of angular fragments of the different beds of the ore-formation, but particularly of rich ore-pieces ; cherty quartzose fragments are often abundant in it. Calcareous rocks not rarely occur in this lower horizon of Silurian deposits, formed of an agglomeration of good-sized rhombohedric dolomite spar crystals in intermixture with an earthy, hematitic, interstitial mass. Druse-cavities in this rock are lined with exquisitely fine crystals of the spar. Beneath the ore-breccia, in nearly all the pits carried to a greater depth, the siliceous beds of the Huronian limestone formation were encountered. In some pits opened near the quarter-post, on the line between Sects. 33 and 32, large accumulations of loose fragmentary masses of rich blue ore, as it occurs in the Quinnesec mines, were found under the Silurian sandstones, which at this locality project in a row of low cliffs on the higher level above the pits, while a short distance south of and below them the limestones crop out. These loose accumulations of ore cannot be transported from any great distance, as with them large bulky masses occur, composed of a great number of successive ledges, which have kept their original parallel contiguity with each other entirely undisturbed, and in consideration of all other circumstances observable, the greatest probability exists for the suggestion that the site of the ore-belt from which these masses come is north of the pits, and not a great way off from them. Going from these test-pits northward over the undulating plateau-like summit of the hill-range, we find it covered with drift, only occasionally the horizontal Silurian sand-rock ledges become exposed. At the base of the north slope of the range, near Lake Antoine, are several test-pits opened, in which, beneath the sand-rock, reddish-colored compact limestones, dipping under a high angle northward, are observable.

If we go from the test-pits on the west line of Sect. 32 a few hundred steps farther west, and thence take a southern course, we first come across a belt of limestone with ledges dipping south in steep inclination ; then succeeds another broad belt of reddish-colored and partly brecciated quartzites. It projects in high vertical bluffs along the hill-side. Descending over these cliffs we find a depression of the surface, and then ascend a rounded lower ridge composed of a large succession of siliceous flagstones richly impregnated with martite granules, some of which constitute regular flag-ores of high percentage ; they dip north, contrary to the limestone formation. An equally large succession of softer, more argillitic beds, cleaving parallel with the sedimentary striation, underlies them conformably, which, instead of the martite of metallic lustre, contain the bright red-colored form of iron oxide. Beneath them follow fine-grained hydro-mica schists, partly red, partly whitish colored, or irregularly blotched with white and red spots ; they correspond with the so-called soapstone of the miner, which occurred to us first above the ore-belt of the Emmet mines, and then in the Vulcan and other mines, always in a position seemingly above the productive part of the ore-formation, while here they are lowest. South of these outcrops, and partly artificial denudations, is a narrow swamp, and the hill rising on the other side is formed of drift-deposits ; but a short distance west of this place are the Keelridge mines, in which the same succession of rock-beds is exhibited, but the dip of the strata is there not so obviously northward, almost vertical. We find there the red and white blotched hydro-mica schists on the south side, succeeded by others gradually changing into gray-colored schists of a bright silky lustre, composed of an alternation of linear seams of quartz, and partially also of granular feldspar, with equally thin layers of hydro-mica of strong lustre, which is often increased by a corrugation of the substance into minute wrinkles. These schists are the same as those seen in outcrops at the base of the hills a quarter mile west of Quinnesec village, and they are the transitory link making connection with the slate-rocks on the south side of Lake Hanbury. To bring the described descending section through the ore-formation in the S. E. quarter of Sect. 31 and likewise in the Quinnesec mine, in accordance with the other previously made observations, we have to infer an overturned position of the strata, either in the one or in the other of these cases before described. The occurrence of large accumulations of loose angular fragments of ore and of other rock-beds connected with the ore in the above-mentioned test-pits on the west line of Sect. 32, on top and north of the limestone belt with southern dip, and beneath the Silurian sandstones which form the summit part of the hill-range, suggests an exposure of the ore-belt from which these fragments come, on the north part of this hill-range. A repeated plication of the strata is to be inferred from the fact that a mile farther north, near Lake Antoine, the slope and base of this same range is formed of limestone beds dipping to the north. The ore of the Keelridge mine is more siliceous than that of the Cyclops, Norway, and Vulcan mines ; it resembles the ore of the Emmet mine, both of which ores seem to occur in a higher horizon than the others. West and north of the Keelridge mine the surface is too much covered with drift to allow a special observation of the structure of the hill-range, but by test-pits opened here and there the extension of the ore-formation and the concomitant limestone formation with the range is demonstrated. In the N.E. quarter of the N.E. quarter of Sect. 31 north, far from the west end of the chain which commenced at the Quinnesec mine, is the so-called iron mountain, a spur of the higher main range consisting of a large succession of banded silico-ferruginous rocks, formed of alternating thin seams very rich in specular ore-granules which have a bright metallic lustre, and of others still disseminated with ore granules, but prevailingly quartzose ; some of the seams are schistose, like the specular slate-ores of the Negaunee district. The strata are almost vertical, with scarcely perceptible dip to the north. South of this series of lean ores, as they justly may be termed, are other rather argillitic than siliceous flagstones, not so rich in ore-particles as the others, but yet averaging from 20 to 40 per cent of the oxide.

Another spur adjoins the iron mountain on the north-west side, on which the Chapin mines are located. The strata in this spur are conformable with the others, dipping northward ; they are more of an argillitic character, but rather compact, not clay-like, abundantly disseminated with comparatively large crystals of martite, and inclosed between them is a belt, 30 feet wide, of a pure, soft, porous, dark blackish colored ore, composed of glistening octahedric martite granules. North of it are again argillitic strata, but they have not been intersected much in the mine, and are not exposed at the surface. About a quarter of a mile north of the Chapin mine are large bluffs of vertical ledges of limestone, striking in the west-north-west direction of the range. In the direction of their strike are other limestone outcrops, in the swamp near the railroad track, in the centre of the S.W. quarter of Sect. 30. These continue across the road, and limestone ledges are denuded on the hill-slope near the branch road leading to the Ludington mines, in the S.E. quarter of Sect. 25, Town. 40, R. 31 ; on the north side of the pits of the Ludington mine the limestones and siliceous cherty layers making part of it are laid open by test-pits. Farther west, in the valley of the Menominee River, we see them in the bottom of a test-pit opened in the S.E. quarter of the S.E. quarter of Sect. 23. The ore-hill on which the Ludington mine is located is actually a continuation of the Quinnesec ore-range, but is severed from it by a broad swampy depression. The strata are in the mine almost vertical, faintly dipping to the south : the ore is a fine quality of the soft blue ore, in a belt of about 10 feet thickness ; the hanging wall of the ore is formed of gray-colored rather soft argillitic flaggy rock-beds, very rich in ore-granules ; the beds forming the foot-wall are more of a siliceous character, likewise richly impregnated with iron. Following the south line of Sect. 25 of Town. 40, R. 31, we find, not far from the quarter-post, in test-pits, red-colored sericite schists uncovered, which dip to the south. Very few steps south of the test-pits, within the limits of Sect. 36, are low rounded hillocks formed of diorite, partly of massive, partly of schistose structure, and in the superficial parts in a disintegrating, crumby condition. On the north side of the soft, red-colored sericite schists, which occupy quite a broad belt of surface, succeed harder quartzose schists, likewise deep red-colored by hematite, and north of them the briskly ascending hill-slope is composed of a very large succession of nearly vertical silico-ferruginous banded rock-beds, which correspond with the ledges exposed in the Ludington mine. The banded structure principally depends upon a more or less intense impregnation of the siliceous ground-mass, with granules of mar-tite in the successive sedimentary laminæ of the rock ; this ground-mass is not always siliceous, but is often replaced by a kaolin-itic substance. The summit of the hill, which forms a very prominent landmark, is composed of horizontal Silurian sand-rock ledges amounting to over 100 feet in thickness. The lowest beds of the sand-rock are, as usual, a coarse breccia of fragments of the ore-formation, recemented by the sand-masses washed over them. The north slope of these hills and the rolling lands surrounding their base are deeply covered with drift, only in the N.E. quarter of the S.E. quarter of Sect. 24, a belt of schist, with interlaminated seams of quartzite, comes to the surface, and is also still better exposed in a cut of the railroad south of the bridge across the out-let of Lake Antoine. These schists, as far as the exposures go, about 300 feet in thickness, strike west-north-west, in conformity with the general direction of the different rock-formations com-posing the ore-range, and their position is upright, with no definite inclination to either side ; they are dark gray colored. One portion of the series is a fine-grained, hard clay-slate, banded with thin, closely crowded, interlaminated quartz-seams of lenticular structure, wedging out at both ends, and intimately united with the interstitial slaty seams. Another sort of the schists is composed of dark micaceous or hydro-micaceous scaly ground-mass in intermixture with minutely granular saccharoidal quartz-seams in a gneissoid manner, or filled with larger glassy grains of quartz, irregularly dispersed within the micaceous body substance. Interlaminated with these schists, which are partly much corrugated by the uplift, occur belts of light-colored granular quartzite, from 1 to 8 and 10 feet in thickness.

As no other characteristic rocks are seen in contiguity with this rock-belt, its position in the series is doubtful, but its lithological character has the nearest resemblance to the slaty rock-series on the south side of Lake Hanbury. A mile north of the railroad cut, and about 150 steps below the bridge across the Menominee River, is a broad belt of slates or schists exposed in the embankment, and in the bed of the river, amounting to more than 500 feet in thickness, which consist essentially of the same micaceous scaly ground-mass as the schists in the railroad cut ; they have a much brighter silky lustre, and the described interlaminated seams of quartz are in them much more delicate, linear. Certain beds in the slate rock-formation of the Lake Hanbury series, in the exposures of Sect. 11, Town. 39, R. 30, near the foot of the terrace, and others in the S.W. quarter of the N.W. quarter of Sect. 29, Town. 39, R. 28, are almost identical with them. Some of the silky-shining, less fissile schists on the south side of Lake Hanbury are in substance and in aspect very similar to these schists, called in the Wisconsin Reports Phyllite, according to Wichmann's determination. The strata under consideration are in close proximity with the diorites and dioritic schists, exposed right under the bridge and above it, but they are in evident discordance with them. The dioritic schists dip to the south, the so-called phyllites dip to the north. I am fully convinced of their being a co-ordinate member of the Lake Hanbury rock-series, of which they represent the higher part, while the series exposed in the railroad cut are lower beds of the same group of strata.

North of the Menominee River, in Wisconsin, and along its course on the Michigan side up to Badwater village, diorite and dioritic schist is the exclusive surface-rock, ignoring the drift-deposits which cover a large part of the indicated area. Eastward from the railroad bridge a chain of diorite hills is traceable for a distance of six miles through the north half of Sects. 18, 17, 16, and 15, into the N.W. quarter of Sect. 14, Town. 40, R. 30. North of this chain of diorite exposures are widely spreading undulating highlands, completely covered with drift, but in all probability underlaid partly by diorite, partly by granite. South of the chain we find all along it the iron-formation, though rarely in natural outcrops, as heavy drift-masses and the Silurian sandstones cover the concerned area, but a great many exploring pits have been opened in the south part of the above-named sections, which demonstrate this fact. In test-pits opened in the south half of the S.E. quarter of Sect. 18, near Moon Lake, a large series of fine-grained sericite schists were brought to the surface. They vary in color from whitish gray to red and purple; some are harder than the others, and all have a dull satin lustre. Their dip is southward. North-east of these pits, in the S.W. quarter of Sect. 17, on the higher part of the hill-slope, are other test pits, in which a very large succession of well-laminated banded silico-ferruginous rock-beds with southern dip is uncovered. All are abundantly interspersed with martite granules, but particularly the northern lower part of the group of strata is very rich in iron oxide of a bright metallic lustre. Some of these richer beds resemble the specular slate-ore of the Negaunee mines, but no seam free enough from siliceous matter to be valued as a marketable ore was discovered in this locality. Ascending the top of the hill, we find it covered with horizontal Silurian deposits, through which a great number of test-shafts have been sunk by different parties, which uniformly had the result of meeting with a deposit of a rich soft hematite ore, mingled with hydrated grape-ore concretions, beneath a cover of from 20 to 40 feet of the Silurian sand-rock, which, as usual in its lower ledges, had the character of a breccia of ore-fragments. These hematites are, as it appears, a horizontal deposit of Silurian age, probably derived from the washing of the ocean waves over cliffs of the exposed Huronian ore-bearing rock-beds, and deposition of the iron mud particles in close proximity of them. Similar Silurian hematite deposits of great purity I have also found to occur in other localities, as, for instance, in a test-shaft of Mr. B. Brien, opened in the

N.W. quarter of Sect. 22, Town. 39, R. 28, where these horizontal sediments lie right on the upright ledges of the ore-formation. Such ore-beds have of course a limited local extent, and cannot as safely be relied upon as an ore-seam interstratified with the Huronian formation, but I wonder that all the parties that opened the test-pits in Sect. 17 suspended their work in disappointment, for hematite deposits amounted in every shaft to a sufficient thickness to be profitably mined. From the S.W. quarter of Sect. 17 the ore-formation continues without interruption diagonally across the north half of Sect. 20. Wood's mines are opened in the S.E. quarter of the N.E. quarter of Sect. 20, on the slope of a steep high hill covered with drift deposits, and formed on the summit part of Silurian sand-rock amounting to a considerable thickness. The strata dip, as in the other localities, under a high angle southward. A belt of soft blue ore, resembling the blue ore of the Vulcan or Chapin mine, from 20 to 30 feet in thickness, has for its foot-wall hard siliceous rock-beds richly interspersed with ore-granules, and for a hanging wall a series of argillitic beds in various modifications, which likewise are freely charged with martite granules and with amorphous hematitic oxide. Next to the mine, siliceous slate-ores of great lustre came out of a test-shaft, which must have a position a very few feet off from the ore-belt, but in the mine such ledges are not seen.

East of the Wood mines, in the S.W. quarter of the N.W. quarter of Sect. 21, are other test-pits on the slope of the same hill. A shaft sunk there to the depth of 80 feet struck on the bottom the siliceous, cherty beds of the limestone formation ; all above them was Silurian sand-rock, constituting with its lower beds a breccia of ore-fragments, limestone, and quartz pieces. From here to the west end of Lake Fumee, which is the direction of the strike of the formation, no more outcrops occur ; drift-deposits form the surface crust to a considerable depth on all this interval, but undoubtedly the iron-bearing rocks are continued in this direction, as in various spots in the line of strike a very strong attraction of the magnetic needle is perceptible. One of such spots, on which the needle is at once reversed with its north end to the south, is in the S.W. quarter of the S.E. quarter of Sect. 21, on a road branching off from the Lake Antoine road, about 150 or 200 steps from the forking.

13

Near Lake Fumee, in the north half of the N.E. quarter of
Sect. 27, and in the N.W. quarter of Sect. 26, extensive explorations have been made along the slope of a high ridge, the top part
of which is formed of Silurian sand-rock, and above it by a thick
series of dolomites, representing the calciferous sand-rock formation.   In the test-pits near the edge of the swamp in Sect. 27,
the strata dip under an angle of about 45° south-west ; the uppermost layers are thin-bedded flags, or thicker rock-seams, light
reddish-colored or mottled with white.   Some have an earthy,
argillitic fracture, others have compact crystalline grain.   They all
consist of a minutely scaly hydro-micaceous ground-mass in intimate intermixture with granular feldspar, which in the harder
forms of crystalline fracture prevails over the hydro-mica, a proportion of larger whitish scales of mica is always mingled in.
Some sub-porous ledges, resembling argillite, are abundantly disseminated with glassy quartz-grains, and in all of them are
octahedric crystals of martite sparingly dispersed.   Certain of the
harder, thin, flaggy beds are on the bedding plains covered with a
coating of hydrated iron oxide in dendridic ramifications of great
beauty, distantly resembling fern-leaves or fucoid branches.   The
lower part of the formation is composed of well-laminated, dark-
colored hard quartzose rock-beds, impregnated with granular martite, which gives the richer seams a bright metallic lustre, and
some of them constitute a hard, fine-grained specular ore of laminated schistose structure.   These siliceous lower beds of the ore-
formation are succeeded by light-colored compact quartzites full
of cleavage seams, causing them to break into even-bedded sub-
rhomboidal small fragments.   Other beds of the quartzite are
more massive, or cellulose quartzites occur, full of sparry seams,
which are partly sparry carbonate of iron of brownish or blackish
color through the whole substance, or also white rhomboidrical
dolomite spar or ordinary calcspar ; usually all the three kinds of
spar occur together.   I consider this quartzite to be identical with
the upper quartzose beds of the limestone formation, and not
equivalent with the great quartzite formation exposed at the falls
of Sturgeon River.   Quartzites analogous with those found in the
test-pits are found naturally exposed a mile south-east from there,
in association with the characteristic calcareous beds of the formation.   They form a row of low hillocks which diagonally inter-

sects the south half of Sect. 25 ; the south-east corner of the section is located on one of these hillocks.   From there across the north part of Sect. 31, in Town. 40, R. 29, no outcrops are observable, but a large, broad belt of limestones, dipping under a high angle southward, intersects the north half of Sect. 32 from west to east, forming a ridge about three quarters of a mile long, with rock bluffs on its south side all along it. · Some of the strata are quartzitic ; others constitute a coarse breccia of compact granular limestone fragments of light color, cemented by a dark-gray siliceo-calcareous interstitial mass ; still other ledges are a quite pure granular compact dolomite. East of this ridge is a swamp, and farther on, to the bed of Pine Creek, all the surface is deeply covered with drift.   This limestone ridge, surrounded on both sides by low swampy lands, is directly north of the limestone belt which underlies the ore-formation at the Norway and Stephenson mines, a little over a mile apart from it, with a swamp valley between them.   Both belts dip to the south.   We must therefore either suggest a rupture of the rock-belt in the intervening space, or an intervening synclinal trough connecting the two.   The same correspondence in dip exists between the limestone bluffs on the roadside near Quinnesec and the equivalent quartzose beds on the north side of Lake Fumee ; but in that case we can prove by natural exposures the occurrence of a repeated plication of the rock-belt in the intervening space.   Besides the locality already mentioned in which this plication of the beds is seen, there is another one handy for observation in the S.E. quarter of the N.E. quarter of Sect. 34, on the roadside to Lake Antoine, where the limestones dip northward in anticlinal position with the more southern outcrops.   An anticlinal position exists also between the limestones exposed in the south slope of the Quinnesec ore-range and those on the north slope of the range dipping under the bed of Lake Antoine, and great probability exists for the occurrence of a synclinal trough of limestone in the place where the basins of Lake Antoine and of Lake Fumee are now.   The identity of the ore-formation of the Quinnesec mines with the ore-bearing rock-series in the Wood mines and in the test-pits on Lake Fumee, is in any case to be considered as an established fact, by their general lithological similarity, and by the relative position which they hold to the limestone formation.

Recapitulating the so far ascertained facts, we have become acquainted with three distinct groups of rock, one succeeding the other conformably, or at least in direct superposition on the other. The most southern, seemingly uppermost, is a series of dark gray-colored slaty or schistose beds, with inter-laminated quartzose belts, amounting to a thickness of perhaps over two thousand feet, which I will call the *Lake Hanbury slate group*. A second group next succeeding it consists in the upper part of light red, or whitish, or gray-colored hydro-micaceous and argillitic strata ; in the lower, of siliceous beds richly impregnated with iron oxide in the amorphous hematitic condition, or in the crystalline form of martite, with metallic lustre, which lower series incloses seams almost exclusively composed of martite granules, constituting the economically valuable ore-deposits. This group I will name the *Quinnesec ore-formation ;* it amounts to a thickness of not less than one thousand feet, but locally perhaps it is much thicker. The third group is formed of a series of light-colored quartzite and limestone beds of a siliceous character, usually in part of a brecciated structure, and also amounting to at least one thousand feet in thickness, which I will call the *Norway limestone belt*. All these strata are upheaved in a certain axial direction, which is about west-north-west, and dip southward, if we consider them as a body, and overlook folds of the strata and other local irregularities. According to this, we had to take all the rock-beds which come to the surface north of the three mentioned successive rock-groups, and dip in the same southern direction, as older than they are, and all those on the south side of them as younger, if they are in a conformable position with them. As natural as this rule is in principle, as difficult it often is to determine the relative position of the rock-beds to each other, we have rarely the opportunity to see the strata in their succession without frequent interruptions, in which covered intervals, by existing plications or by a fault, the order of things may be totally changed without an indication of such a change on the surface. Moreover, the position of the strata is generally so near to the vertical that it is often arbitrary, if we decide which way we descend or ascend in the series of deposits, and if we expect to be guided by the character of the rock in decision of the relative age of the strata, we often find ourselves involved in the greatest perplexity, as the endless variety of schistose beds of lower and higher position in the stratified series is only a modified form of the same hydro-micaceous ground-mass mingled with quartz or feldspar or iron oxide, or with all of them in different proportions and in different molecular condition ; schists supposed to be perfectly identical may come from horizons widely apart, with thousands of feet of sediments of another kind between them.

Inquiring what kind of rock-beds succeed on the north side of the limestone formation, we have only a few localities to resort to by which this question can be solved to satisfaction, as most universally the northern edge of the limestone formation and the underlying rocks are hidden by Silurian sandstones or by drift deposits. I have mentioned the occurrence of a large succession of siliceous specular flag-ores on the north side of a limestone belt in the S.W. quarter of Sect. 7, Town. 39, R. 28, which dip southward under the limestone, which is only about 200 steps distant from the test-pits, and likewise has a southern dip. The ore-bearing flags come on the east side of Sturgeon River, close up to its bed, but neither in the river bed nor on its west side the continuation of this ferruginous rock-belt has been discovered, although a number of test-pits have been sunk into the drift-masses which cover the surface on the west side of the river ; they had to be abandoned on account of the, water before they were deep enough to meet with solid rock-ledges. Also farther west, along the valley of Pine Creek, no rocks lower than the limestone come to the surface south of the quartzite bluffs, which follow the north side of the valley at about a half mile's distance in its lower part, but farther up come close to the creek-bed

The next locality from which information about the succession of beds may be expected is north of the Norway mines, of which I have likewise previously spoken, saying that a series of reddish or gray, or greenish-colored micaceo-argillitic and partly arenaceous schistose beds seem to underlie the limestones conformably, which are well exposed there in close contiguity with the ore-formation. A ditch has been dug from the engine-house of the Norway mine toward the swamp on the north side of the hill, which commences next to the limestone, and after intersection of some Silurian sand-rock beds on the surface, cuts through the above-mentioned micaceous slaty argillites crossways for the distance of over 200

steps ; the same beds are also uncovered in several test-pits
opened a very few steps north of the cliffs of limestone, projecting
over the surface on the east side of the mine.   The beds dip under
a high angle to the south, as the limestones and the ore-formation
do, and from one end to the other of this extensive succession no
material change in the character of the beds can be perceived.
Farther northward is a broad swamp, and no outcrops or test-pits are
found there, but making a circuit around the slope of the hill-side,
we come, near the slaughter-house, which is about a quarter mile
direct north of the mentioned ditch, to other test-pits, in which
similar micaceo-argillitic schists are dug out.   Crossing there the
creek, we find in the S.E. quarter of the S.E. quarter of Sect. 32
a number of test-pits, in which likewise a southern dip of the strata
is observed.   The most southern ledges exposed are siliceous
flags, somewhat micaceous, and impregnated with martite granules
in moderate quantity ; associated with them are slaty argillitic
beds of a greenish-drab color, harder than ordinary argillites, and
of a fine-grained sub-crystalline fracture.   Then follows a large belt

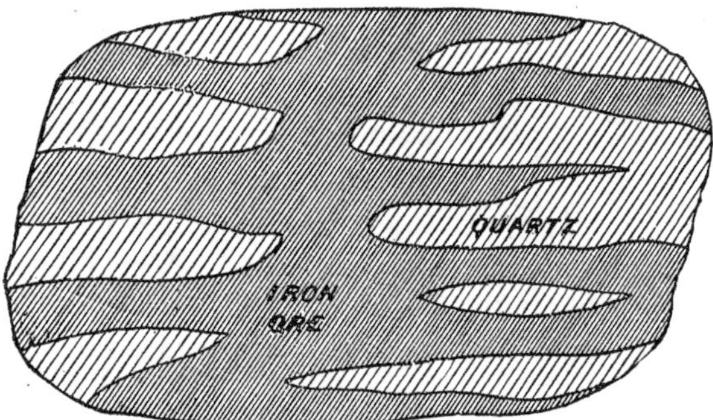

of thick-bedded quartzose ledges, all highly ferruginous ; some are
regularly banded, consisting of alternating narrow seams of a pale-
colored jaspery quartz, and of a compact siliceous blackish-colored
iron-ore, with a smooth flinty fracture.   These beds strikingly resemble the jasper-banded ferruginous beds of the McOmber mine
of Negaunee, and sometimes a broader seam of comparatively pure
ore is found interstratified with jasper-banded layers.   Other massive quartzose ledges are peculiarly striped and mottled by dark
reddish brown or purplish seams of compact siliceous hematite,
which pervade the non-tinged quartzitic ground-mass in a very
irregular branching and anastomosing manner in some parallelism

with the stratification ; some of the seams wedge out, and others run transverse to the stratification. Most likely this peculiar distribution of the oxide in the rock-mass is the result of infiltration of the once porous sand-rock mass with iron, favored perhaps by existing cracks in the rock.

North of this quartzose iron-bearing rock-belt is a belt of graphitic schist about 8 feet wide ; then follow banded micaceous quartz schists variegated with gray and red stripes, and north of them are light whitish-colored hydro-mica schists mottled with red blotches. Farther north, almost to the middle of the section, these siliceous, argillitic beds continue, and at one time again ore-bearing siliceous beds and belts of graphite are met with, which indicates a repetition of the strata, but all seem to succeed each other uniformly, with a southern dip, as far as the exposures allow us to see. A swampy creek valley runs through the middle of the section ; going across the swamp we find the above-described limestone ridge, whose ledges, as stated before, have also a southern dip. I have remarked that there must be either a synclinal trough, or a rupture of the rock-belt between the two opposite limestone ridges. The occurrence of entirely different rock-beds on the south side of the Norway limestone ridge, than we find on its north side, allows the suggestion of both cases.

Suppose we were at the Norway mines, on the apex of an anticlinal arch of the limestone formation, so compressed as to make the anticlinal sides parallel with each other, and the ore-formation to be the next incumbent younger deposits, we should necessarily expect to find on the north side of this fold, next to the limestone, the iron-formation again, which on the south side of the arch lies directly on the limestone. The micaceo-argillitic beds which we find there are very similar to the hydro-micaceous, or argillitic beds found on the south side of the ore-formation, but it is most unlikely that on the interval of 20 or 30 steps, between the two sides of the limestone crest, so sudden a change would occur, which would bring these beds in contact with the limestone and cause the elimination of the ore-bearing rockbelt a thousand feet in thickness. The similarity exists also between the beds next to the limestone belt only and those south of the ore-belt. The strata exposed farther north essentially differ. The ore-bearing rock-belt found there is unlike the Quinnesec ore-formation, and in its next proximity a seam of graphitic schist occurs, of which not a trace can be observed on the entire range from the Brien mines to the Ludington. Supposing instead of an anticlinal arch, the existence of a rupture of the limestone belt in this locality, these northern exposures had to be considered as a series of lower beds, but the reappearance of a similar limestone belt three-quarters of a mile north of them, which dips south in conformity with the others, would in this case be a circumstance difficult to explain. The hitherto described rock series of the Menominee iron range allows a much more simple and harmonious explanation of its structure if we suggest a synclinal trough of limestone in this place and revert the generally observed order in the superposition of the rock-beds, considering the most southern, apparently highest rock-beds of the Lake Hanbury series as the lowest, directly succeeding above the diorites south of the Menominee; next higher would be the iron formation and highest or youngest the limestone formation and strata north of it. This order is actually exhibited on the east side of Sturgeon River in the S.W. quarter of Sect. 7, T. 39, R. 28, also in the S.E. quarter of Sect. 32, T. 40, R. 30, and in the Chapin mine and Quinnesec mine. In all other described localities, according to this theory, which I believe to be the fact, the strata have been placed in an over-tilted position by the upheaval acting most powerfully from south to north, whereby the limestones came to lie beneath the others, and were by me at first mistaken for the oldest in the succession. North of the limestone ridge in Sect. 32 are rolling, drift-covered lands and swampy low grounds adjoining Pine Creek, on which no exposures of rock-ledges can be discovered ; but crossing the creek we are very few steps off from the base of vertical walls of white compact quartzite ledges, standing in upright position ; they are of great thickness. Next, north of these bluffs, the granite is seen in close, but, as it appears, discordant contact with the quartzite. If we follow the creek on its south side farther to the west up stream, we have to the left a high drift-covered hill-range : with very steep bluffs slanting down to the bed of the creek. At the place where the north line of Sect. 29 intersects it, we leave the creek and follow the section line westward to the corner, a distance of about 500 steps ; here we find a number of test-pits opened, in which a large succession of slaty rock-beds in alternation with quartzite seams has been uncovered, beneath a surface crust of drift from 4 to 8 feet in thickness. The strata strike in the usual west-north-west direction, and are vertical. The slaty layers vary considerably in molecular structure, but may with propriety all be called sericite schists. Some are impalpably fine-grained ; the scaly nature of their ground mass is only visible under the magnifying-glass, and the silky lustre, proper to all sericite schists, is rather dull. Others are coarser, scaly and of bright lustre ; in their hardness also is a great difference—some are easily scratched with the finger-nail, others are extremely rigid and hard ; the prevailing color is a dark sub-metallic gray, others are red-colored by hematite. The quartzite seams, interlaminated with the slates, are granular in structure, red-colored by iron oxide, and some of them are intimately intermingled with *hydro-micaceous*, or, what is the same, *sericitic* scales, often in addition with true mica, in hexagonal tabular crystals. The sericite schists must amount to a very great thickness, as we meet with outcrops of them over a space more than a quarter mile in width, transverse to the direction in which they strike. No iron-ore of any value has been discovered here. South-west, in the centre of Sect. 30, is a high ridge covered with strata of Silurian sand-rock over 100 feet in thickness ; the lowest beds are full of ore-fragments, and on the top of the hill dolomitic sandy limestone beds overlie them. This ridge is in the line of strike with the high ridge on the north side of Lake Fumee. On its south-west side are the before-mentioned hillocks, intersecting the south half of Sect. 25, composed of quartzite and siliceous limestone. The Silurian sandstones are here found also at the base of the hills covering the limestone, and in the lower beds very rich in ore-fragments of bright metallic lustre. Considerable work has been done in this place, opening test-pits in search of the ore-belt from which these fragments come, but so far not with the hoped for success. North of the high ridges, capped with Silurian dolomites and sandstones, the sloping interval between them and the bed of Pine Creek is covered with drift, and has no outcrops of quartzite or Huronian limestone, as it is represented on Major Brooks' map ; but farther west we find some exposures of rock which are of peculiar interest, as they represent another horizon of sediments than those previously observed, likewise formed of limestone beds, differ-

ent from the Norway limestone belt. In the north half of the N.E.
quarter of Sect. 14, Town. 40, R. 30, near Merriman's camp, are
at the base of the hills, and particularly on both sides of the creek,
which flows along the north line of the section and enters there
into Pine Creek, large exposures of crystalline dolomitic limestones
of coarser or finer grain.   Some are white, saccharoidal, like Italian
marble ; others are rose-colored or darker red ; all copiously intermingled with silvery white mica scales.   Still others are dark greenish and purple-colored by additional admixture of chlorite and of
hematitic iron oxide ; also quartz-seams of fine-grained saccharoidal structure often pervade the calcareous mass, and ledges occur
in which the sparry carbonates are intermingled with a large proportion of chondrodite.   The sparry carbonate of iron replaces
sometimes partially the dolomite and calcspar.   Narrow, soft shaly
seams, mostly composed of mica, argillite, and hematitic iron
oxide, are at times interposed between the limestone ledges, which
dip under a high angle to the south.   The thickness of this limestone belt is not less than 500 feet.   Above it succeeds a large belt
of a reddish-colored granular quartzite 60 or 80 feet wide, which
contains little cubes of iron pyrites abundantly disseminated, and
certain seams of the rock-belt are composed of brown-colored
sparry carbonate of iron, in cellulose intermixture with quartz.
South of the quartz are again more impure micaceous and ferruginous, somewhat porous lime-rock beds with quartz-seams, inclosing
concretionary masses of hard hematitic iron-ore.   Farther south,
but not disclosed in immediate contact with the former, follows a
large series of dark lead-colored hard sericite schists, like some of
those found in the test-pits at the N.W. cor. of Sect. 29, T. 40, R. 29.
Some of the schists on the south side of the belt are black, colored
by graphite.   Exposures of this graphitic variety are in the N.W.
quarter of the S.E. quarter of Sect. 14.   The limestone belt can
be traced along the north side of the before-mentioned creek into
the N.E. quarter of the N.W. quarter of Sect. 14 ; farther on, in the
N.W. quarter of the N.W. quarter, is a diorite hill which forms
the terminal point of the diorite chain, extending from the twin
falls of the Menominee River eastward.   I have yet to mention
the occurrence of large boulders in close proximity of the limestone
outcrops near Merriman's camp, which consist of a magma of crystals of feldspar, quartz, black hornblende, or in its place chlorite

in intermixture with rhombohedric, ferruginous dolomite spar crystals, in such an abundance as to be one of the most conspicuous constituents of the rock which, on exposure, by lixiviation of the spar, becomes full *of little cavities, filled with ochraceous iron oxide. As accessory minerals in the rock occur principally magnetite, iron pyrites and copper pyrites in small, well-formed crystals. The feldspar is flesh-red orthoclas, but also anorthic feldspar seems to be present. The color of the rock is dark greenish-black, speckled with the white dolomite spar crystals of brilliant lustre. Other portions of the rock are almost destitute of hornblende and chlorite, and resemble an ordinary flesh-red granite. A boulder perfectly identical with these I found on the road-side, half a mile east of the Commonwealth mine in Wisconsin.

The eminently calcareous nature of this rock, and the abundance of boulders of large size in this locality, make me suppose a relationship between them and the limestones, but I have not been able to find an outcrop of the rock in place.

South-west of the above-mentioned graphitic schists, in the S.E. quarter of the S.W. quarter of Sect. 15, are in test-pits exposures of intensely red-colored sericite schists of soft clay slate character, and of sericitic quartzose rock-seams, containing a large percentage of granular martite, which I suppose represent the strata north of the Norway limestone belt. The whole surrounding country is so completely covered with drift, that nothing definite can be learned about the structure without resorting to the pick and shovel, or to the drill.

On several previous occasions the occurrence of a large quartzite formation north of the iron-bearing rocks and of the limestone formation, was mentioned ; we have learned that north of the Norway limestone belt a large series of sericite schists of various color and hardness follows, which incloses graphitic seams, and an ore-bearing belt, which in this part of the district is not productive, but incloses, farther west, masses of pure ore in really astonishing quantities. This series of sediments is, according to my previously given views on the sequence of the strata, a younger group next succeeding the limestone. Which position the similarly situated limestones near Merriman's Camp occupy I am so far unable to determine.

Between the limestone outcrops of Merriman's Camp in Sect. 14

and the quartzite bluffs north of them, lies a valley over half a mile in width, which is deeply covered with drift-masses, extending close up to the base of the bluffs, and so we find it in all other localities along the valley of the Pine Creek, which follows for over ten miles a course strictly parallel with the trend of the quartzite formation, sometimes passing close by the high rock-walls of the quartzite, at other times a short distance off from them; but never had I the opportunity to see this quartzite in contact with any rock-beds deposited above it, except the loose drift-material. The first exposures of this large quartzite belt, in places over a thousand feet in thickness, occur in the S. W. quarter of Sect. 10, Town. 39, R. 28, which locality is something over a mile direct north of the Brien mines; it can be traced from there in a continuous chain of exposures to the falls of the Sturgeon River, but merely the crests of the upheaved ledges project over the drift-masses, which occupy most all the surface, and nothing can be seen of other strata connected with them. On the map of Major Brooks, south of the falls, is a belt of limestone delineated, following the trend of the quartzite formation in close proximity, of which I could not see the smallest sign from one end to the other of its purported extension. At the falls of the Sturgeon River is one of the best opportunities to see the quartzite formation in its grandest display, and in its contact with the granitic rocks, found on the.north side of all the length of the quartzite chain, in juxtaposition with it.

The bed-rock of the falls is granite, which evidently forms here an arched, bubble-like protrusion, dipping in all directions ; the sedimentary strata above this bubble have likewise been pushed aside with the same irregularity. They have in places become entangled between the granite, and seem to dip under it, but the same ledges are seen in another place dipping in a different direction, and to lie above the granite. The granite is a granular magma of ill-defined crystals of red feldspar and quartz, in intermixture with various proportions of a black, sometimes scaly, sometimes columnar mineral, with brightly shining cleavage, of which it is doubtful to say, whether it is black hornblende, or black mica, without a microscopical examination. According to the quantity of this mineral in the composition, the granite occurs in all shades of color, from dark blackish to flesh-red. It has sometimes a banded gneissoid structure, but generally not ; quite frequently it is intermingled with fine scales of sericite, and iron pyrites is also a common accessory mineral. Interstratified with the granite are belts of dark diorite-like rock, consisting of quartz, white, probably anorthic feldspar, and of a large proportion of black mica. This rock generally contains a good proportion of carbonate of lime, and often considerable quantities of cubes of iron pyrites. Some of such seams have a thinly laminated schistose structure, and are almost exclusively composed of the black mica, with only a small proportion of feldspar and quartz granules. There are other broad belts of rock, partly parallel to the granite ledges, partly intersecting them transversally, which consist of a genuine diorite formed of dark green hornblende crystals and of white anorthic feldspar. One of such diorite belts, of considerable thickness, which crosses the river a quarter mile above the falls, is in its superficial part in a state of decomposition, which allows one to crush the rock with the hand into a heap of sandy crumbs; the decomposition goes on concentrically. The rock is seen to segregate into globular masses, which easily are taken out of the surrounding crumby bed-rock, and show, when broken in two, a hard unaltered nucleus, which eccentrically becomes softer and softer. Above the falls, not far off from this dioritic transverse belt, is a doleritic dyke strongly magnetic; the exterior part of this dyke is a black aphanitic compact mass resembling basalt; the central portions of the dyke are a magma of distinct crystals of black augite and of white glassy feldspar. This is one of the very few instances in which a doleritic dyke occurred to me in the Menominee district, while such dykes are abundant in the Marquette region. In intimate, seemingly conformable contact with the granite occurs a series of schistose beds, which are exposed at the foot of the falls in an almost vertical position, but they seem to be in an anticlinal position on the two sides of the river. On the west side are stratified red-colored feldspathic rocks, crowded with granules of magnetite and with iron pyrites in small cubes; with them occur narrow seams of a rich granular magnetic ore contaminated with iron pyrites. This belt amounts to about 8 or 10 feet, and the strata dip under the granite. Next and below it is a rock-belt, 10 feet wide, of schistose, feldspathic and sericitic beds; then comes a seam of compact, finely granular red feldspar 20 feet wide, which incloses sparingly disseminated octahedrons of magnetite and little cubes of iron pyrites. Under it succeed silky-shining gray sericite schists, with a feldspathic ground-mass ; then a break in the formation occurs, and the same feldspathic sericite schists dip in an opposite direction, away from the granite, and farther on in this direction we soon come to quartzite ledges, apparently incumbent on them. On the east side of the river we find similar, hard sericite schists, with interlaminated granular feldspar seams, and with several belts a coarse conglomerate rock formed of red granite pebbles and of white quartz pebbles, some of them opalescent. The cement is the schistose sericite. Some of the granular feldspathic beds of the schists are distinctly ripple-marked. Going across this schistose belt, which amounts to about one hundred feet, we come again unto granite, which seems to be in conformable contiguity with the schists. We have here evidently a series of sedimentary beds deposited on a granitic substratum, which during the upheaval became wedged in between the plastic granite mass, tilting and overlapping them locally so as to appear as the lower beds. At the base of the Sturgeon River falls is a kettle-shaped dilatation of the valley, surrounded on the east and west side by steep hill-sides formed of quartzite ledges, amounting, as I have stated before, to the thickness of at least one thousand feet ; they dip under a high angle north-eastward. The ledges are thick, compact, of a finely granular saccharoidal fracture of white color, often very plainly ripple-marked. Above the falls, on the east side of the river, the quartzites are in direct but discordant contact with the granite, without the intervention of the above-described sericitic schists. The lowest beds of the quartzite are there in a degree schistose by the intermixture of linear seams of hydro-mica with the quartzite ground-mass ; not all of the beds in that locality are white ; some are pale reddish ; also lively green-colored ledges occur there, and in several other localities west of the Sturgeon River falls, from which an uninterrupted series of large rock-walls of quartzite can be followed across the north half of Sect. 7, and diagonally through Sects. 1 and 2 of Town. 39, R. 29 ; then they disappear temporarily under the drift. We meet again with large bluffs of quartzite near the north line of the N.E. quarter of Sect. 33, Town. 40, R. 29, which we may follow along the bed of Pine Creek into the south part of Sect. 20 ; then comes another interruption, but high bluffs of the quartzite are again encountered in the N.E. quarter of Sect. 13, Town. 40, R. 30, which continue north-westward into the N.E. quarter of Sect. 3. On the north side of the quartzite we find all along the granite in close proximity with it, which alternates with large bulky belts of a dark blackish-green colored hornblende rock, consisting of a magma of hornblende crystals with white granules of quartz, and in part of feldspar. North from there, for miles, nothing but granite is to be seen, if the drift deposits allow any rocks to come to the surface. I made several trips across this granite area, which, in places where the granite actually forms the surface, is a very rugged country, a continued alternation of precipitous rock-ridges with intermediate swamps and windfalls. The granites are of a much more perfect crystalline structure than those at the Sturgeon River falls, and contain an abundance of bright scales of black mica. Gneiss of micaceous composition, in coarser and finer grained varieties, is very often associated with the granite, or replaces it in some localities entirely; and equally common are belts of hornblende gneiss of a black glistening aspect which occur conformably interlaminated with the granite, or with the, mica gneiss of a lighter reddish-gray color.

In the north half of Sect. 12, Town. 41, R. 30, occur also belts of black mica schists in the granite, which contain regularly disseminated lenticular or globular concretionary masses of granitic composition, varying in size from that of an apple to that of a hazelnut, but in the same bed always of equal size ; they are not pebbles, as they are imperfectly defined from the surrounding schistose mass. Similar strata I found subsequently farther north in various places. The dip of these granites and gneisses in the north half of the Town. Tier 41, and in the south half of Tier 42, is almost invariably to the north. In Sect. 12, near the locality in which the concretionary mica schists occur, I found a doleritic dyke dividing into many branches of an irregularly geniculated course, some of which are not more than an inch or two in width. The smaller branches consist, as it is usual, of an aphanitic black basalt-like mass ; in the broader seams the rock-mass is formed of microscopically discernible crystals of black augite and of white glassy feldspar. With the exception of the before-mentioned doleritic dyke met with at the falls of Sturgeon River, this is the only one which I found in the Menominee district, as far as I went over it.

Within this area of granites we find again the iron-bearing formation well developed in two parallel ranges, the southern of which passes through the centre of the north halves of Town. 41, Rs. 28 and 29 ; the northern, called the Felch Mountain range, runs along the south line of Town. 42, across Rs. 28, 29, and 30. The southern I have only transiently examined. In test-pits opened on the east line of Sect. 18, Town. 41, R. 28, at the base of the north slope of a drift-covered body of hills, filling out a large elbow of the west branch of Sturgeon River, I saw thick ledges of quartzite dipping under a high angle northward, and above them a series of micaceo-argillitic schists intensely red-colored by hematitic pigment ; work had been commenced but shortly before the time of my visit, and not much could yet be seen, as all the surface is covered with drift.

Farther northward, in Sects. 8 and 9, a number of other test-pits have been opened. The surface is covered with boulder drift, and under it Silurian sand-rock ledges in all the pits were first encountered ; the lower part of them generally constitutes a breccia filled with iron-ore fragments of the same character, as we find them inclosed in the analogous rock-beds in the vicinity of Quinnesec. Beneath this brecciated rock silico-ferruginous flaggy strata have become uncovered, dipping under a high angle northward ; they are in the superficial parts much shattered, and the limited extent of the openings does not allow to see much of the succession of beds, but the material thrown out of the pits resembles the siliceous rocks, connected with the Quinnesec ore-belt ; and the narrower seams of ore associated with the siliceous beds, resemble likewise the blue ore of the Quinnesec mines, and are partly soft, friable, partly harder, approaching specular ore. North of the test-pits, in Sect. 5, is granite, the surface rock, interlaminated with large belts of gneissoid hornblende rock, dip north. In the S.E. quarter of the N.W. quarter of Sect. 33, Town. 42, R. 28, on the east side of the trail leading to Mr. Curry's test-pits on Felch Mountain, we pass a short ridge composed of granite and gneissoid hornblende rock ; the strata dip north-east. About 50 steps north of the bluffs of granite, opposite to them and separated by a swampy depression, are rock-bluffs formed of a large succession of limestone beds of white color, and of coarse-grained sparry crystalline structure. The lime-rock is full of tremolite crystals, singly dispersed through the mass, or in clusters and seams almost entirely composed of the white, silky-shining tremolite, which partly occurs in colorless, translucid columnar crystals, partly in a radiated fibrous form. The thickness of the limestone is not less than 200 feet ; it dips north-west. Under the limestone are conformable beds of compact granular quartzite, with distantly dispersed crystals of green hornblende within its mass, besides crystals of magnetite and iron pyrites. Intermediate between the quartzite and the limestone are seams of dark green, well-crystallized hornblende in intermixture with crystals of diallage, which seem to be a product of metamorphosis of the hornblende, as some of the crystals exhibit the only partially completed metamorphosis. Also narrow seams of a brightly shining black mica occur in this association. The quartzite reposes directly, but inconformably, on a belt of hornblende gneiss 50 feet wide, which is in close contiguity with the granite, and runs parallel with it. North of the limestone follows another thick belt of quartzite, somewhat red-colored and in part cellulose, and this is overlaid by a very large succession of micaceous schists, composed of good-sized mica-leaves in gneissoid intermixture with narrow seams of granular feldspar. The schists very readily decompose into a crumby mass. Above them follow harder siliceo-argillitic beds, richly impregnated with iron, in which on this hill-side much test-pitting has been done, but no ore-seam of value has been discovered at this horizon. The highest part of the hill-side is formed by a large belt of a thick-bedded, compact, dark-colored quartzite about 150 feet wide, which projects in high walls along the edge of the plateau-like summit of the range. This quartzite, richly charged with martite granules, averages about 40 per cent of iron throughout its whole bulk, and incloses narrow seams of a very rich compact ore of metallic steel color, besides concretionary, almost chemically pure oxide-masses of solid crystalline tabular form, like the ore of the island of Elba.

At the base of these bluffs of quartzite are, in several places of the hill slope, exposures of a fine-grained glistening black hornblende rock in immediate contact with the quartzite. South of the main range, in the centre of the N.E. quarter of Sect. 32, is a smaller ridge separated from it by a swampy depression, which on the north side is intersected by an exploring trench extending from the base to the top, in which a succession of about 300 feet of

14

flaggy siliceous beds, in alternation with argillitic seams and thicker quartzite belts, has been laid open. A great proportion of them is rich enough in granular martite to be called a lower graded ore, but no higher graded ore-seam was found. On the crest of this hill at the end of the trenches, we find the ferruginous beds, which dip to the north under a high angle, in contact with a large belt of white crystalline limestone, full of radiated fibrous tremolite crystals in some parts, in others quite pure ; farther down the south slope of the hill all the surface is deeply covered with boulder-drift. On the north side of the large ferruginous quartzite belt of the main range Mr. Curry has made extensive explorations in the N.E. quarter of Sect. 32, Town. 42, R. 28. In the numerous test-pits is a great variety of quartzose and of argillitic rock-beds uncovered ; most of them are richly impregnated with iron oxide, and several larger seams of a good quality of iron-ore are found interlaminated with them. An ore-belt is opened in a test-shaft about 50 feet north of the large quartzite belt, in which a soft crystalline blue ore, very similar to the Quinnesec ore, is found ; farther north is a broad belt of a harder ore in a partially decomposed, hydrated condition, of ochraceous aspect on the outside ; bright red-colored earthy hematite ores occur also in valuable quantities. In the north half of the N.W. quarter of Sect. 32 are other test-pits, in which about 400 feet of rock-beds are laid open in trenches, of which about one quarter represents a good salable ore ; the other three quarters are to a great extent rich enough in ore-particles, to be called siliceous low-graded ore-beds, and only the smallest part consists of purely quartzose beds ; the strata dip north, but are almost vertical. South of the ore-hill is a large swamp. The ore of this locality is partly a soft blue ore, like that of the Vulcan mines ; partly compact and hard, but also of the dull metallic bluish color of most of the Menominee ores. North of Curry's test-pits, on the dorsal undulation on which the camp is located, the Silurian sand-rock, which forms the capping rock in most of the test-pits, is found too thick for the explorer, and nothing is known of the strata succeeding farther north. The surface slopes from Curry's camp northward into a ravine which, followed for a third of a mile eastward, brings us to a swampy valley whose north side is formed of granite hills, with well denuded rock-ledges, on which hills the quarter-post of the north line of

Sect. 33 is located. We see there coarsely crystalline granite, formed of large feldspar crystals, in intermixture with white mica leaves and quartz crystals, and finer grained belts of laminated gneissoid structure repeatedly alternating with dark blackish-colored gneissoid hornblende rocks ; dip northward, nearly vertical. Following the north line of Sect. 32 west, we walk over horizontal ledges of Silurian sand-rock unto the middle of Sect. 31, where, near the north quarter-post, a large belt of quartzite comes to the surface, which dips north, and on its south side we find red-colored arenaceous mica schists conformably underlying. Farther on are no more outcrops along the section line, which runs over the highest part of the hill-range, except Silurian rocks. At the base of the hills, close to the Sturgeon River, the iron-bearing Huronian beds are naturally exposed in the S.W. quarter of Sect. 31, and in the adjoining part of Sect. 36 of the next western town range, and a number of test-pits opened in these localities has much improved the opportunities for observation of this group, which there consists of a large succession of well-laminated, partly flaggy, siliceous, and in a degree feldspathic beds, copiously disseminated with granular martite of metallic lustre ; also schistose micaceo-argillitic beds, impregnated with hematite and with martite, are found associated with the siliceous layers ; they all dip under a high angle to the north. Some of the seams are rich enough to be used as an ore, but further explorations will have to prove whether they are large enough to be practically valuable. South of these exposures, on the other side of the Sturgeon River, all the surface rock is granite ; on the north side high bluffs, tower above them composed of Silurian sandstone at the base, and on the top of dolomitic limestone beds of the calciferous sand-rock formation, which contain many but very indistinct remains of shells ; these bluffs continue across the centre part of Sect. 36. North of them is a large plateau covered with the Silurian rocks, and above them with large masses of drift. After crossing the Sturgeon River in the centre of Sect. 35, we find on the south side of the valley, along the slope of the hills, outcrops of massive quartzites dipping north under a high angle. Near the S.W. corner of Sect. 26, Town. 42, R. 29, Mr. Wheeler has opened test-pits in a large series of argillitic, also harder sub-crystalline feldspathie schists, full of brightly-shining white mica scales, part of which schist, is intensely red-colored by hematite ; other ledges are pale red or even white, free of iron pigment. The schists lean in a nearly vertical position on the north side of the before-mentioned quartzite belt. No iron-ore was discovered here in any of the pits, and at present, as I suppose, the work in this place has been given up. Similar micaceous schists were observable in the before-described outcrops in Sect. 36, on the north side of Sturgeon River, where they had a position lower than the siliceous ore-bearing beds. The quartzites and micaceous schists we found exposed near the quarter-post on the north line of Sect. 31, Town. 42, R. 28, also represent an identical horizon, but in this latter locality the quartzite lies above the mica schist, in Wheeler's test-pits below it.

North of Wheeler's camp, across the river, Mr. Kempt has made explorations in the north half of the S. W. quarter of Sect. 26, and in the south half of the N. W. quarter of the same section. Ascending from the river, after leaving Wheeler's camp, over a talus of drift-masses, we first encounter bluffs of hornblende gneiss in connection with micaceous gneiss-beds in considerably corrugated condition, which rock-belt stands vertical ; across it we find a swampy depression, and farther on, on the rising ground, we see in a row of test-pits over a quarter mile long, systematically dug in a transverse direction to the strike of the formation, a large succession of earthy-looking, absorbent partly schistose and well-laminated rock-beds uncovered, which, on closer examination, are found to be decomposed granites of various grain, gneisses of micaceous and of hornblendic composition, and mica schists. In all of them the original constituent minerals are yet well recognizable, but the feldspar and the hornblende have been changed more or less completely into a soft kaolinitic, minutely scaly substance ; the mica resisted better the decomposing influences, but lost considerable of its lustre ; the quartz is unaltered. The iron of the hornblende and in the mica is often but not always changed from the protoxide into the hematitic oxide, which imparts to these beds a resemblance with the ferruginous argillites of the iron-bearing rock-series. Some of these rocks inclose also dispersed grains of magnetite, or even a narrow seam of magnetite may occur, but from all I could observe I consider this group of decomposed granites as barren of valuable ore-deposits. The circumstance that the gneissoid rock-belt south of the weathered series is in a perfectly fresh, unaltered condition, is remarkable, as this process of decomposition has indiscriminately affected all the rocks north of it, within the distance of half a mile, and perhaps much more. An entirely similar series of decomposed granitic rocks, mica schists, and hornblende schists can be observed in other test-pits, opened by Mr. Kempt in the north half of the S.W. quarter of Sect. 14, Town. 42, R. 30 ; here also a wide belt, comprising many different strata, is uniformly affected by these decomposing influences ; south of them are unaltered granites. The two localities are in the same line of strike with each other, which is the general direction of all the formations in this part (west-north-west), and it is probable that a continued belt of granitic rocks in this decomposed condition extends from one place to the other.

West and south of Wheeler's camp, across the central part of Sects. 34 and 33, no other rocks but Silurian sand-rock ledges can be seen at the surface. In the S.W. quarter of Sect. 32 we find again a great many test-pits opened near the so-called Wood's camp. Next south of the creek which passes below the camp are red-colored quartzoso-argillitic mica schists, in which a seam of a peculiar rock is inclosed, consisting of large thick plates of white mica over half an inch in diameter, in intermixture with vitreous quartz in such a mode as to show the contemporaneous crystallization of both minerals, precluding a sedimentary agglomeration of the already formed crystals ; were any feldspar present I would not hesitate to declare it a coarse-grained granite, but none is to be discovered within the mass. These mica schists dip under a high angle to the north. South of them is a belt of compact thick ledges of a light-colored reddish granular quartzite with a glassy fracture, about 120 feet wide, which incloses irregular seams wedging out or locally dilating, in which the quartzite mass is richly disseminated with middling coarse martite granules of metallic lustre ; and narrower bands 6 or 10 inches wide, exclusively formed of the granular oxide, are usually associated with these quartzose, ore-bearing portions of the rock-belt. It is to be regretted that the quantity of this most excellent ore is too small to pay for its mining. South of this quartzite belt, which also contains conglomeratic ledges, follow again quartzoso-feldspathic mica schists, mingled with more or less hematitic pigment in alternation with narrower quartzite belts, which repetition of mica schists and quartz ledges continues southward for several hundred steps ; then we come to other deep test shafts, from which green-colored mica schists, almost completely formed of mica leaves, have been hoisted, in association with micaceous dark-colored quartz schists, and with other coarsely granular quartzose seams, some of which consist of a mixture of quartz-granules with about an equal bulk of octahedric crystals of martite of the same size as the quartz-granules ; in others of these seams the quartz-granules are in intermixture with kaolinite and with large white mica leaves. Not far south of this place the granite crops out. On the north side of Wood's camp the Silurian sandstones are very thick, and no test-pits have been sunk through them down to the Huronian beds. In the adjoining Sect. 31 still more extensive explorations are going on at present, under the auspices of different mining associations. The principal facts resulting from all these works I will condense in the following remarks : In the south half of Sect. 31, near the south line of the section, are outcrops of quartzite and of micaceous quartz schists, which are the lowest beds observable ; a short distance south of them the granitic rocks occupy the surface exclusively ; above them follows a large series of other rather soft mica schists, more of an argillaceous than a purely quartzose character, and generally also impregnated with hematitic iron oxide. Some are extremely fine scaly, resembling the sericite schists of the upper part of the Quinnesec ore-formation ; others are formed of comparatively large scales of white mica, mingled with the ferrugino-argillitic and siliceous ground-mass.

About in the same horizon with the mica schists occur dolomitic limestones of a reddish-drab color, with a sandy granular fracture ; some beds are thick, compact, others are thin, wrinkled ledges interwoven with linear streaks of mica scales. Not far apart from them is the position of other crystalline limestones of white color, which contain an abundance of fibrous radiated crystals of tremolite ; these are identical with the limestones found beneath the ore-formation at Felch Mountain. In the same part of the series occur white schistose quartzites of silvery lustre, from interlaminated linear seams of minutely scaly snow-white mica. This lower series of quartzite, mica schist, and limestone strata occupies a belt

nearly a half mile in width ; they all dip under a high angle northward, but the exact order in which the beds succeed each other is
not so fully understood as it would be desirable. Most of our information has to be obtained from the scattered pits of the explorer, and natural exposures are not only rare, but generally exhibit only a certain rock-belt for itself, and not larger sections
through the beds connected with it above and below. With this
lower rock-series I have yet to mention a peculiar kind of celluloso-
porous rock, like burr-stone, which comes from the bottom of a
test-shaft near the centre of Sect. 31, on the south side of high
bluffs formed of the upper part of the ore-formation, presently to
be described. The color of this rock is varying from pale whitish-
red to bright brick-red, or also to a darker brownish-red. It consists of a minutely granular feldspar throughout, or the red feldspar
forms a botryoidal incrustation of a skeleton of quartz-granules ;
the larger cellulose spaces of the rock are filled with a scaly
kaolinite, or also with ferruginous matter. In the higher part of
the shaft and in the neighboring pits not as deep, occur, next
above this cellulose rock, rather soft, crumby arenaceo-argillitic
beds, very rich in granules of specular oxide, but not enough to
impart to them the quality of a high-graded ore. These beds are
seen to dip under the harder silico-ferruginous ledges, which rise
on their north side into a stair-like succession of bluffs, and
amount to an aggregate thickness of a good many hundred feet as
far as their succession is observable, the end of which we cannot
see, as the top and the north slope of the hill are covered with
Silurian sandstones, and with the higher calcareous ledges of the
calciferous sandstone formation. This upper series of quartzose
beds is throughout richly impregnated with specular ore-granules ;
richer seams in alternation with poorer ones give the rock the
banded aspect of the mixed jaspery ore-beds of the Negaunee
mines, but their color is dusky purple instead of the bright cinnabar color of the Negaunee jasper-ores, and the siliceous ground-
mass is not of a jaspery nature, but consists of granular quartz,
often in intermixture with feldspathic or other aluminous accessory
constituents. In the very great number of test-pits opened in this
rock-belt, which is the only promising depository of valuable
seams of ore in this iron range, some few seams large enough and
of sufficient purity to be mined as an ore have been discovered,

but generally these immense quantities of iron oxide combined with the rock-masses are not concentrated into seams of larger size, as the miner wants them, but are either uniformly dispersed through a siliceous ground-mass, not in a quantity to overbalance the siliceous matter enough, to make it harmless in the smelting process, or the really pure seams of ore are narrow, constantly alternating with low graded quartzose seams which make them unavailable for practical use. There is no particular horizon in this large succession of iron-bearing rock-beds, in which an ore-seam could be expected in preference to another ; throughout the whole era in which these sediments were forming, never a lack of iron oxide existed which would have prevented the formation of an ore-belt, but the formation of such a belt depended only from a proper sifting of the heavier from the lighter molecules, induced by temporary and local conditions favoring this sifting process, which did occur at various times and in various places within restricted limits. A rich seam of ore, found in a certain position in one place, is therefore not at all a reliable proof of the occurrence of a similar seam in a correspondent position in a continuation of this group of ledges a quarter mile off from that spot ; this may be so sometimes, but just as often it will happen that we meet with a low-graded, worthless siliceous ore in the place of the rich. Geology teaches the miner where to hunt for a thing and where not, but there is another factor in such calculations, which the wisest scientist cannot foretell. Nature is no stereotype impression after a certain mould ; we have to study it in every place for itself, and where our wisdom will not reach, the pick and shovel, handled by a crafty arm, often will.

Exposures of the before-mentioned limestones inclosing tremolite crystals, are found at the base of the bluffs, formed of the upper siliceous division of the ore-formation in the S.W. quarter of the N. E. quarter of Sect. 31. A belt about 60 feet wide projects there, with vertically erected ledges. Next north and south of them are argillitic mica schists of red color, and a few steps farther on the north side the banded siliceous lean ores begin to emerge. A similar limestone exposure is found a quarter mile east from this place, also on the south side of the banded lean ores. The other red-colored dolomitic limestone, intermingled with micaceous seams, occurs in the bottom of test-pits opened in the

N.E. corner of the S.E. quarter of Sect. 36, Town. 42, R. 30. Going westward on the road across Sect. 36, we see on the north side a number of other test-pits opened in the banded siliceous lean-ore belt ; to the left, in the south half of the S.W. quarter of Sect. 36, we see on the top of the hills large exposures of quartzite, which dips in different directions, and on its north side is a thick belt of micaceous quartz schists splitting in very even slabs, covered with large silvery mica scales on the cleavage plains. This schistose belt amounts to several hundred feet, and its beds stand vertical. North of it I notice a limestone belt indicated on Major Brooks' map, but I did not go to the spot to see it. I found, however, a large exposure of the white tremolitic limestone, near the centre of the west half of Sect. 34 and the micaceous quartz schists in contact with it. Leaving the S.W. corner of Sect. 36, and passing with the road across Sects. 2 and 3 of Town. 41, R. 30, we see on both sides large granite exposures ; farther on, toward Badwater village, all the surface is covered with boulder-drift, but in a trip which I made across the centre of Sects. 17, 16, 15, 14, and 13, of that town, I found everywhere the granite to underlie the drift-masses. In the S.E. quarter of Sect. 17 are large bluffs of quartzite near a little lake, but I have not followed them to examine their extent.

Below Badwater village are exposures of schistose and massive diorites in the bed of the river, and high bluffs of them are near the mouth of the creek entering Menominee River at the N.W. corner of Sect. 32, Town. 41, R. 30. Before we follow these exposures and others below, I will lead the reader some distance up stream, to see an interesting series of sedimentary rock-beds, whose relative position to the other strata we have become acquainted with, I have so far not been able to ascertain positively. According to Major Brooks' views, these represent the upper horizon of the Huronian group, equivalent with the staurolitic mica schists of the islands in Lake Michigamee and the next lower strata. The lithological character of the mica schists, which occur at the falls of the Michigamee River, and also near the mouth of Brule River at its union with Paint River, is indeed very similar to the mica schists in Michigamee Lake ; but I leave this question open until I have had a chance to examine this group of rocks, and their connection with other rocks in the Menominee region more carefully, than by mere reconnoitring, as, for lack of time, I had to do this first time I saw them.

Rowing up the river from Badwater, we find the first rock-exposures near its intersection by the west line of Sect. 30, a short distance north of the quarter-post ; in the bed of the river and in the embankment of both sides the strike of the strata is north-north-west, their dip under a high angle west and correspondingly south. Lowest are greenish-gray colored schists composed of a gritty ground-mass of feldspar and quartz granules in intermixture with sericite, which gives it a silky lustre. Next above follows a large belt of a compact rock, cleaving in very even-faced rhomboidal blocks, partly of reddish, partly of greenish-gray color, with a gritty granular fracture. It consists of a quartzoso-feldspathic sub-crystalline mass, intimately mingled with glistening, very minute scales of sericite, or also perhaps chlorite in the greenish-colored ledges. Above this belt follow again sericite schists of dark gray color, some soft, very fissile, and much corrugated into larger plications, and also into very minute parallel wrinkles, visible on the glistening cleavage plains of the schists ; others of the strata are harder and less fissile by the larger proportion of quartzose and feldspathic substance in their composition ; some of the beds are also richly impregnated with hematitic pigment. These last-described beds are exposed on the Wisconsin side of the river. Farther up are for a while few exposures on the river, but the compact quartzoso-feldspathic rock-ledges are in several places seen to crop out farther back on the hill-sides of the Michigan shore. In the S.E. quarter of the S.E. quarter of Sect. 23, near the east line of the section, a large dioritic, or may be diabasic belt projects in cliffs at the water's edge ; it is a dark black rock, consisting of black hornblende crystals and of white semi-translucid feldspar crystals plainly discernible with the naked eyes. On the opposite Wisconsin shore are other outcrops of black, compact rocks of granular structure, composed of white quartz granules in intermixture with a very large proportion of black magnetite crystals, which compose at least half the bulk of the material. The compass needle is strongly attracted by it.

A short distance above, on the Michigan side, and on the group of islands in the north half of the S.E. quarter of Sect. 23, are again large exposures of the compact quartzoso-feldspathic rocks and sericitic schistose layers identical with those first encountered near the west line of Sect. 30 ; they strike north-west, and dip southward. Farther on, in the S.W. quarter of the N.E. quarter of this same section, are large bluffs of an equivalent but coarser-grained rock, which shows more plainly than the others its origin from a sedimentary sand-rock ; it has a glistening glassy fracture, on which large quartz-grains of an opaline milky hue are discernible among others perfectly translucid. Other high cliffs of the same kind of rock, associated with seams of schistose structure from inter-mingled sericite, occur on the Michigan side in the N.E. quarter of the N.E. quarter of Sect. 22 ; they strike east and west, dip south. After passing from here a bend of the river, we find a short distance off other large exposures on the Wisconsin side, which differ con-siderably in aspect from the former, but essentially consist of the same feldspathic quartzose granular ground-mass in intermixture with much sericite, which gives to all the beds a schistose structure, but the principal difference consists in a large proportion of sparry carbonate of lime combined with the rock substance, and also in separate seams of saccharoidal grain. These schists exhibit a much distorted, corrugated, or a shattered condition ; they are hard, not fissile, and resemble certain schists found in connection with the dioritic rock-group near the upper Quinnesec falls.

Higher up, on the Wisconsin side, in the N.E. quarter of the N.W. quarter of Sect. 22 (according to the Michigan town sub-division), are very compact massive rocks of a greenish-gray color, and a minutely crystalline grain, which I consider to be diorite, as small hornblende crystals are plainly discernible constituents of the rock-mass, which, like the other beds of the mica schist series, contains sericitic or micaceous scales intermingled.

Onward comes another group of islands, and from there up to the falls of the Michigamee River are, on both sides of the river, continued exposures of the mica schist formation, with inclosed large belts of the harder quartzoso-feldspathic and micaceous com-pact rocks. The strike of the formation north of the islands is east-north-east, dip south ; the same strike and dip of the strata is observed at the falls of the Michigamee. It would be a useless repetition to give a special description of the rocks at the falls of the Michigamee, or of those above the islands near the quarter-post, between Sects. 15 and 16. They agree perfectly with the before-described equivalent beds first seen on the west line of Sect. 30, Town. 41, R. 30, but are much more extensively exposed, and the micaceous schists are more even-bedded, richer in mica, and consequently have a much brighter silvery lustre than in the more southern exposures. Entirely similar rocks as those at the Michigamee Falls are found near the mouth of Brule River, at which locality the immense thickness of the formation can be observed by climbing from the river-bed across the strata up to the top of the hills. The strata dip under a high angle to the south, toward the hills on the other side of the Brule, which on their south side consist of diorite ; the north slope of them I have not examined.

From the falls of Michigamee River I followed the Menominee River farther on upward, which bends from here south-west. About 200 steps west of the fork of the two rivers commences, on the Michigan side, a long series of exposures of schistose beds, differing from the mica schists at the falls, and evidently representing another horizon of the same group of sediments, as a considerable similarity exists in the nature of the rock-material ; but as in this locality the strike and dip of the strata changes so very often, and frequent interruptions in the exposures occur, it is hard to determine the order in the succession of the beds, without making more detailed examinations of the surrounding country, than I had the time to do. The strata at the falls strike west-south-west and dip south ; the strata in the exposures a few hundred steps west of the forking of the rivers strike west-north-west, and dip north ; and soon after we find the strata to dip south, retaining the same direction in strike with the others ; subsequently we find, at the first rapids we meet, the strike of the strata to be north, and the dip in some places west, in others east. The schists are associated with massive dioritic rocks, which come to the surface in various places, evidently from beneath the schists. The schists themselves vary considerably ; a part of them is fine-grained, quite fissile, even-bedded, or corrugated, silky-shining, of lighter or darker gray or greenish-gray color, and consists of a homogeneous finely granular feldspathic and quartzose ground-mass, intimately mingled with the impalpably fine sericitic or micaceous scales. Other schistose beds connected with the sericitic are harder, less fissile, and less homogeneous, usually darker greenish colored and of little lustre ; the sericite is in them replaced by a coarser scaly dark green mica, and in part sometimes by chloritic scales ; also the feldspathic and quartzose ground-mass is coarser grained, or forms separate lenticular seams, interlaminated with the micaceous. Some of them are disseminated with crystals of carbonate of lime, or calcareous seams are interlaminated, and other portions of the schistose layers are found impregnated with hematitic iron oxide. The diorites in these exposures are dark blackish-colored, sufficiently coarse-grained to distinguish the component minerals, of which the dark fibrous hornblende prevails considerably over the feldspar. All contain also a small proportion of carbonate of lime, besides micaceous scales, and an intermixture of granular quartz is often observable. I went as far as to the centre line of Sect. 17, where both sides of the river are bordered with dioritic rocks, and then returned, seeing that I had to make good many further researches before I would attempt to express a positive opinion regarding the relative age of this group of rocks. Major Brooks asserts the identity of these mica schists and quartzoso-feldspathic gneissoid rocks with the staurolitic mica schists of Michigamee Lake. As the next lower strata, younger yet than the Lake Hanbury slates and the Quinnesec iron-formation, which, as we learn from his report, are placed above the Norway limestone belt, he considers the dioritic rocks exposed at the Twin falls, at the Quinnesec falls, and lower down the Menominee River, giving as his reason the parallelism of the dioritic rock-belt with the ore-formation, which dips to the south in conformity with the diorite on its south side. For the same conformity in dip, Major Brooks declares the granites and gneisses north of the Felch Mountain ore-range as younger than the ore-formation, which like them dips northward ; but their superposition on the ore-formation is nowhere observable ; on the contrary, the south side of the ore-range exhibits in several places the direct superposition of the ore-formation on the granite. This fact is known to Major Brooks, but he solves the dilemma by identifying the granites on the south side of the Felch Mountain ore-formation with the Laurentian ; those on the north side, he claims, represent the youngest Huronian rocks. How he could do so I cannot conceive, as the concerned granitic and gneissoid rocks north and south of the ore-formation are so absolutely identical, that no one who ever sees them can doubt for a moment the equality in the age of these rocks. Moreover, this identification of the northern granite with the upper Huronian, and of the southern with the Laurentian, implies another abnormity ; groups of rocks, usually separated from each other by thousands of feet of intervening strata, are in this case thought to be in immediate superposition, which does sometimes occur, but not in coincidence with another improbability like the one stated in this instance.

Examining the relative position of the dioritic rock-series to the iron-formation in the southern part of the district, we find these two groups rarely in contact, and then usually so incompletely exposed as not to allow the positive observation of their stratigraphical relations. The diorite belt exposed at the Twin falls, which has as far as ascertainable a southern dip, extends without interruption for six miles eastward from the river, and on the south side of this belt we can observe all along the iron-formation, likewise with a southern dip. The contact of the formations is not seen, on account of the deposition of Silurian sandstone ledges and of heavy drift-masses over the surface.

Following the western extension of this diorite belt into Wisconsin, we find it there, in the centre of Sect. 8, Town. 39, R. 19, in direct contiguity with the ore-formation of the Commonwealth mines, which, as above stated, has its position above the Quinnesec ore-formation ; but in this instance also of well-exposed contact nothing definite can be made out, as the strata adjoin in a vertical position. South of the Ludington mines I mentioned on a previous occasion the occurrence of sericite schists, belonging to the lower horizon of the ore-bearing formation which dip to the south, and near by, south of them, in the N.W. corner of the N.E. quarter of Sect. 36, Town. 40, R. 31, we find low hillocks of diorite, but there also nothing can be proved ; the dioritic rocks generally play the part of an intrusive rock with regard to the strictly sedimentary rock-beds of the Huronian series. A superposition of the diorite formation on the Lake Hanbury rock-series, which adjoins it the whole length of the Menominee valley from the upper Quinnesec falls to the Sturgeon falls, asserted by Major Brooks, is not observable ; the nearly vertical strata of both formations are even never seen in contact. There is always quite a large covered interval between them. The nearest exposures of the two groups are observable in Sect. 26, Town. 39, R. 29, where, in the centre of the section, a hill is formed of the vertical ledges of ferrugino-siliceous flagstones and slaty beds representing the Lake Hanbury series, and about two or three hundred steps from these exposures we find, on the south side of the road to Menominee, small hillocks of diorite. Major Brooks has identified these slates with the iron-formation of the Commonwealth mine, but I see no justifiable reason to do so. The Commonwealth ore-formation, wherever it occurs, is invariably connected with graphitic schists, of which in the Lake Hanbury series none are found. Giving a description of a cross-section from the Norway mines northward, I have previously stated the occurrence of graphitic schists, in association with iron-ore seams beneath the limestone formation, but according to my theory actually above it, which position I assign also to the Commonwealth ore-formation, on the strength of its lithological similarity with the rock-series north of the Norway mines; the limestones are rarely seen in that district. Still there are on Brule River, south-west of Chicagon Lake, large bluffs of limestone to be seen in close connection with exposures of this ore-formation, and evidently beneath it.

My reasons for holding the dioritic rocks south of the iron-formation as older than the latter, are based on the lithological similarity of this formation with the dioritic group of the Marquette district, and on the degree of metamorphism exhibited by the two groups, the dioritic and the iron-bearing. In the great succession of strata commencing with the Hanbury slate group and upward, we rarely find a bed so much altered that its sedimentary structure is altogether obsolesced, and the majority of the strata shows it very plain, while in the dioritic rocks, considered to be the younger, a stratified structure is also recognizable, but not one of these thousands of feet of ledges exhibits its original sedimentary lamination with any degree of distinctness like the others ; they have evidently been transformed under co-operation of heat, and partially brought into a plastic condition, which is shown by the extreme corrugation and mode of intermixture of these rock-masses, of which effects the other rock-groups do not exhibit near as high a degree. It would be very strange, then, if the lowest beds, nearest to the focus of the central heat, should have been so much less affected by these altering influences, than those pretended to be the higher upper strata of the rock crust. One might object : If the diorites are the older beds, why don't we find them just as well developed on the north side of the upheaved beds, between the quartzite and the granite? The sandy and conglomeratic nature of many of the strata of the quartzite and iron formation proves them to be shore deposits, while the dioritic group consists only of the finer material of deep-sea deposits, which explains the point in question. Moreover, the dioritic rocks are not altogether missing on the north side of the ore-formation, as we can see by the occurrence of the six-mile-long chain of diorite extending eastward from the Twin falls. A similar discrepancy between the rocks underlying the ore-formation on the two opposite sides of its exposure, is seen in the Negaunee district. On the south margin, at the Cascade and Palmer mines, it rests directly on the granite, while on the northern exposures the diorite underlies it in great thickness.

The equal dip of the strata to the south in these adjoining formations is not necessarily a proof of the younger age of the most southern beds. The whole succession is so near to a vertical position that in many instances it has to be left uncertain which way they dip, but suppose their dip is conformably to the south ; the upheaval of the diorites by the eruption of the still more southern granite masses pushing the whole incumbent rock-series north, until all tipped over, is the hypothesis by which I explain the order in the succession of beds as an inverted one, the seemingly lowest beds being actually the youngest. But let us go and see these rocks from place to place, instead of making general speculations. The large body of dioritic rocks exposed in the Menominee River and its embankments below Badwater village, and continued to the upper and lower Twin falls and to the four-foot falls near the railroad bridge across the Menominee, have all one common character ; they are dark greenish-gray or blackish-colored, partly schistose, and even slaty, partly massive, coarser or finer grained crystalline rocks, consisting all of a feldspathic ground-mass in intermixture with a dark green mineral, recognizable in the coarser grained rocks of crystalline structure, as hornblende, and in addition to it, with a minutely scaly mineral considered to be chlorite, but often nearer to mica or hydro-mica.

By differences in the proportions and in the molecular condition of these three components, a great variety in the aspect of these rocks is caused.

The micaceo-chloritic constituents are more abundant in the schistose strata, than in the crystalline massive form of the rock, which is generally middling fine-grained, not much differing from the diorites of the Marquette district. The hornblende crystals are somewhat fibrous, of bright lustre ; they overbalance in quantity the white feldspathic ground-mass most generally, wherefore the rock has so dark a color; still pale green beds of finer grain also occur in which the feldspar considerably prevails over the hornblendes. Iron pyrites granules are constantly found dispersed through the mass ; less common is the intermixture of magnetite granules.

Among the rock ledges exposed at the lower Twin falls I observe a thick belt of an aphanitic compact rock with flinty fracture, which consists of a pale green amorphous feldspathic ground-mass, semi-transparent in thin splinters, impregnated with an abundance of very minute chloritic or hydro-micaceous scales, so distributed in layers as to give the rock on cross fractures a most minutely lineated structure, parallel with the bedding ; by cleavage cracks the rock divides into rhomboidal blocks with very even surfaces. The dip of the strata at the lower Twin falls is to the south, but in places the position of the beds is vertical ; at the upper Twin falls the dip is northward, also nearly vertical. At the upper Quinnesec falls the dip of the strata is southward, in correspondence with the west-north-west trend of the formation, and approaching a vertical position. In the most northern exposures on the Michigan side, below the falls, are dark green-colored, partly schistose, partly massive crystalline rocks, not differing from the dioritic rocks of the Twin falls or the four-foot falls ; north of them are drift-covered terraces which extend for over a mile northward to the foot of the Quinnesec ore-range. On their south side follows a large series of much lighter-colored, grayish-green, in certain seams porphyritic schists, inclosing well-formed orthoclas crystals within their mass ; they are composed of a granular feldspathic body-substance in intermixture with an abundance of hydro-micaceous (paragonitic) scaly seams, and with a considerable proportion of carbonate of lime ; also dimly defined pale green horn-

15

blende crystals are intermingled. A part of these ledges occurs in more even-bedded flaggy layers, which are the ones exhibiting the porphyritic character most distinctly.

Other beds, generally much corrugated, consist of an irregular wedge-like intermixture and alternation of micaceo-feldspathic seams and sparry laminæ ; still others are obscurely schistose, hard bulky rock-masses of the same micaceo-feldspathic and calcareous composition, in which large milk-white, ill-defined sub-globular concretions of feldspar are dispersed, which make them resemble a conglomeratic rock, and certain beds are crowded with poorly defined light green hornblende crystals. Next to them follows, on the south side, a belt about 100 feet wide, of very well stratified thinly laminated rocks of silky lustre ; some are gray., much corrugated, and consist of greenish-white semi-translucid laminæ of feldspar composition of one or two millimetres' thickness, in alternation with equally thin seams of hydro-mica. Here and there are quartz-grains as big as a lentil or pea wedged in between the laminæ ; they have no crystal facets, are rounded on the surface, and coated over with hydro-mica. Another series of beds intimately connected with them has a pale red color, consists of the same alternation of laminæ of feldspar and hydro-mica, but the feldspar is orthoclas ; the intermixture of quartz-grains is in them more abundant than in the former, and in the micaceous part of the laminæ are numerous clusters of fine needles of black turmaline ; also larger red feldspar crystals are sometimes observable. Another modification of the same schistose rock-belt is harder, less fissile, still consisting of a succession of thin laminæ with large quartz-grains wedged in between them ; their color is dark gray, variegated with red ill-defined blotches, which mainly are formed of granular red orthoclas. We are now right under the falls. A large massive belt of diorite, on the south side of the before-described schists, crosses here the river-bed ; it is not a single thick belt, but a succession of belts with interlaminated schistose seams, similar to the sparry calcareous schists below the falls. The massive diorite has, as I stated before, the same composition as the schists ; the larger portion of the rock is a magma of ill-defined granular crystals of white feldspar, with pale green hornblende crystals, and always with some proportion of the micaceous scales and of calcspar intermingled. Its color is light greenish-gray, of a dull non-reflecting granular aspect ; other portions of the rock are formed of well-defined crystals, with brightly glistening facets. If the feldspar prevails the diorite is white, dotted with green ; if the hornblende prevails the ground color is green, speckled with white. These *diorites* are, in the Wisconsin Reports, described under the name of *diabase,* as by microscopical examination of some hand-specimens the discovery was made that augite besides hornblende was one of their constituents, in combination with anorthic feldspar. A number of Diorites from the Marquette region are also on the same ground pronounced to be Diabases. This is true with the specimen described by M. A. Wichmann from the Washington mine, but it is an essentially different rock from the other diabases he describes. We meet in the Marquette district with many dykes of augitic rock, some with large crystals of augite readily discernible with the naked eyes ; they are, how-ever, of a much later origin than the dioritic rocks of that region. I have not made a microscopical examination of the dioritic rocks of the Menominee region, but I was able to find in almost every exposure of this kind of rocks, specimens of a crystalline grain coarse enough to see with the naked eyes, or with an ordinary magnifying-glass, the component minerals, and in every instance I could fully convince myself of the presence of hornblende in these so-called diabases as one of the main constituents, by the bright cleavages of the crystals intersecting each other under an angle of 124° ; and only in a few instances, in rock-masses which were in a state of beginning decomposition, I could observe a secondary transformation of former bright hornblende crystals, into opaque crystalline masses, which cleft by crushing them into nearly cubical little fragments supposed to be augite.

The beds of diorite and interstratified dioritic and calcareous schists exposed at the upper Quinnesec falls in uninterrupted continuity of succession, amount, with exclusion of the beds below the falls, to about 700 feet. After a short interruption of the out-crops, we find, higher up in the river-bed, the succession of strata continued by other schistose beds, scarcely differing from the former, and inclosing from time to time belts of compact crystalline diorite. One of these belts of diorite, cropping out at the base of the rapids a half mile above the falls, is the most beautiful variety of this rock I have seen ; it consists of brightly pale green, quite large hornblende crystals, imbedded within a granular milky-white interstitial ground-mass of feldspar. The rapids in this place are occasioned by a succession of about 400 feet of thinly laminated schists, quite variant in molecular structure, but not so much in general composition. Some of the beds are smooth-bedded, very fissile mica schists, of dark greenish-gray color, with great lustre ; other micaceous strata are not fissile, unhomogeneous, curly masses, formed of an aggregation of nodular rounded crystals of white feldspar of orthoclase and of quartz, imbedded within a schistose ground-mass composed of bright blackish mica scales and of sparry carbonate of lime. Another variety of the schists, formed of micaceo-feldspathic thin laminæ, resembles a conglomeratic rock from lenticular masses of quartz abundantly wedged in between the laminæ ; other similar micaceous seams regularly alternate with narrow bands of granular quartz. Also dark green chlorito-micaceous belts occur in this succession, which by gradations merge into a crystalline chloritic hornblende rock

Beyond the rapids I did not examine the rocks of the exposures found some distance above. This whole large series of rock-beds, exposed at the upper Quinnesec falls, evidently represents one inseparable group of altered sedimentary deposits formed from bottom to top of the same material, in different molecular form and different proportion in the intermixture of the component mineral substances. This composition and structure also agrees with the dioritic rock-series of the Marquette district, as near as it can be expected in places remote from each other, which similarity is for me a strong inducement to consider them as analogous and contemporaneous formations. In the hills south of the falls, a quarter mile from the river-bed, the dioritic group is exposed in a row of vertical walls and in single cliffs ; one of these localities exhibits the intersection of the massive crystalline diorite by a granitic dyke. This granite consists of a minutely granular, almost flinty ground-mass of feldspar composition, in which dimly defined large red crystals of feldspar and of quartz have segregated, besides scantily disseminated linear interrupted seams of dark micaceous scales. The larger outcrops of granite indicated on the map of Major Brooks I failed to find, in the hurried way I went over the drift-covered surface of this broken country. The rock-series at the lower Quinnesec falls is a direct continuation of the rocks at the upper falls. North and above the falls are dark green diorites and dioritic schists, as on the north side of the Menominee below the upper falls, and the same as at the Twin falls. The lighter white and greenish speckled diorites, interstratified with schists of micaceo-feldspathic composition in intermixture with a large proportion of sparry carbonate of lime, are exposed at the falls, several belts of the crystalline rock above, and another large one at the foot of them. The schists occur in a good many variations, as at the other exposures. From the lower Quinnesec falls down to the sandy portage rapids in the N.E. quarter of Sect. 24, Town. 39, R. 30, an uninterrupted row of high rock-walls forms the brow of the hills on the Michigan side, which are composed of the same, partly schistose, partly crystalline massive dioritic beds ; large exposures are also half a mile north of the river in the knobs projecting over the drift-covered terrace-lands in the central part of Sect. 14. At the upper end of *sandy portage rapids* commence exposures of hard, thinly laminated micaceo-feldspathic schists like those at the foot of the upper Quinnesec falls, but of a darker greenish color ; dispersed through the substance are nodular masses and streaky seams of red orthoclas. Farther on, the schists change somewhat in structure, but not materially in quality ; they are in a vertical position ; several belts of massive rather dark green colored and comparatively fine-grained diorite are interstratified between them. The schists amount to 400 or 500 feet in thickness. By following the river downward we find, south of the former, much lighter whitish or reddish gray-colored delicately laminated micaceo-feldspathic schists of a sub-porous absorbent nature, and of gritty instead of lubricous feel ; portions of this schistose series of beds are in a state of decomposition, and disintegrate into loose argillitic sand-masses, or into small splintery fragments. These light-colored schists extend across the river to the Wisconsin side, which side I have not farther examined. The same kind of schist is observable lower down the river, at Devil's Gut. From there are, for some time, no more outcrops to be seen on the Michigan side of the river, until we have passed the mouth of the Sturgeon River. A few hundred steps below it a belt of serpentine about 50 feet wide, associated with asbestine and sparry seams, crosses the river obliquely ; lower down, after short interruption of the exposures, another belt of serpentine, about 100 feet wide, is visible in the bed of the river, but only at low water these beds are accessible. They consist of a dark greenish black serpentine, translucid in thin splinters, with a green color ; it contains magnetite granules in considerable quantity, and gives with the blowpipe reaction of chrome. Nothing definite can be seen in these two exposures, in which relation the serpentine is to the dioritic rock-group, which forms the hills on the Wisconsin side at that place ; but farther down, above Sturgeon falls, if we follow a small creek which enters the river not far from the quarter-post on the west line of Sect. 26, we come to the base of bald rock-knobs, consisting of a fine-grained diorite, speckled with large and small white dots of nodular segregations of feldspar within the grayish-green dioritic ground-mass, which massive rock-belt is intersected by a dyke of serpentine about 40 feet in diameter, sharply defined from the diorite, and plainly exhibiting its intrusive nature ; it strikes from north-west to south-east, about parallel with the large diorite belt of the falls, which is about 300 steps south of the serpentine dyke. The serpentine is dark blackish green, full of cleavage cracks, causing it to break into very irregular sharp-edged fragments ; the surface of these fractured faces is generally covered with a thin cuticle of silky-shining asbestine fibres ; other portions of the serpentine are intersected by a great many sub-parallel and sometimes anastomosing seams of chrysotil of bright satin lustre. The Sturgeon falls are occasioned by the same rock barrier, which is broken through by the Menominee River at the upper and lower Quinnesec falls. The rocks of all the three falls are perfectly similar. We find here again the light-colored white and greenish-gray speckled diorite of a more or less perfect crystalline structure, massive or schistose, and then pervaded in all directions with narrow seams of calcspar ; sometimes also veins of white dolomite-spar, a foot or more in width, occur. Near the base of the falls a broad belt of thinly laminated, silky-shining hydro-micaceo-feldspathic schists, like those at the two other falls, is exposed, succeeded on the south side by another diorite belt ; all the beds dip south-west under a high angle. East and south-east of the falls, the country bordering the river is extremely broken, full of large exposures which represent this dioritic rock-formation, showing its very great thickness and a great variation in the structure of the rocks, although nearly all are composed of the same constituents in different proportions and different molecular form. The order in which the various beds succeed is not clearly observable, but it appears the dark green, fine-grained diorite, speckled with comparatively large white crystals of feldspar, distantly dispersed, and quite obvious from a distance, which incloses the serpentine dyke, is one of the lowest of the exposed strata. To about the same horizon belongs the dark blackish diorite exposed in low hillocks on the west side of the road to Menominee, in the N.E. quarter of the S.W. quarter of Sect. 26. A part of the rock is almost aphanitic ; another is composed of quite large crystals of dark brownish green hornblende, with scarcely any feldspar in the combination. The lighter white and gray-speckled diorite, which forms the barrier rock at the falls, occupies the central part of the formation. A very fine variety of this rock, of a most perfect crystalline structure, occurs in the S.E. quarter of the N.E. quarter, and in the N.E. quarter of the N.W. quarter of Sect. 35. The upper horizon of the group is formed of light greenish-gray colored schistose or massive very hard felsites, the schistose form of which contains a good proportion of hydro-mica in intimate intermixture with the feldspathic ground-mass ; frequently also these felsites are porphyritic by segregation of red feldspar crystals within the body mass, which porphyritic masses resemble a granite, and probably are identical with the granite mentioned as occurring in this vicinity by Major Brooks. Iron pyrites is the never-missing accessory mineral in the composition of all these rocks.

Below Sturgeon falls we find large exposures of the porphyritic felsites, partly of non-stratified massive, partly of schistose structure, as we follow the river across Sect. 1, Town. 38, R. 29, and Sect. 6, Town. 38, R. 28 ; lower down the exposures are for a while interrupted, and the embankment is formed of loose drift-masses, but some distance off from the river-bed, on the road leading to Menominee, the drift-polished rounded heads of the underlying dark green crystalline diorite can often be observed in the cuts of the road. A half mile below Holmes Creek, in the S.E. quarter of the N.E. quarter of Sect. 20, Town. 38, R. 28, we find on the Michigan side, in the river bluffs, a large succession of well-stratified and banded silico-ferruginous rock-beds exposed, dipping under a high angle east-north-east ; they are considerably corrugated, or shattered and recemented into a breccia, consisting of alternating narrow seams of chalcedonic, or also porous cherty quartz, once little colored, whitish or grayish, and then again brightly red or brownish red-colored, by impregnation with hematitic iron oxide ; some larger belts of glassy quartz occur interstratified. Above and below this rock-belt, which amounts to several hundred feet, are felsitic rocks in contiguity with it, which on the line of contact are likewise impregnated with hematitic oxide by secondary infiltration from the ferruginous beds, as it appears, as the more distant parts of these are not charged with iron. The incumbent beds are dark greenish-gray, schistose, porphyritic felsites ; the imperfectly schistose structure is produced by interrupted linear fibroso-scaly seams of hydro-micaceous and augitic composition, permeating the felsitic ground-mass ; the underlying beds are of non-stratified massive structure, light gray colored. Those next the siliceous iron-colored strata are in a state of commencing decomposition ; they are absorbent, porous by partial transformation of the felsitic ground-mass into kaoline. The originally white-colored rock is mottled with large dark red blotches by infiltration of these parts with hematitic pigment. Below these porous weathered beds are hard compact felsites of a uniformly light gray color ; they contain always some proportion of carbonate of lime, which makes them effervesce with acids, and inclose, sparingly dispersed, small black octahedrons of magnetite, or perhaps titanic iron, as they resist the action of acids. Lower down the river these massive felsites, of great thickness, are in contact with pale green, fine-grained homogeneous greenstones, which seem to be a modification of the felsite only, but are by insensible transition also connected with the dark green crystalline diorite, which forms, close by, large islands in the river, and is seen in a much greater display at the Quiver falls, also called Pemenee Bon Won falls. At the lower end of the largest of the islands, the pale green aphanitic greenstones are well exposed in association with a fine-grained crystalline diorite of green and white speckled color ; there also masses of the aphanitic greenstone, porphyritic by red orthoclas crystals, abundantly disseminate through the mass. At the Quiver falls large hillocks of rock rise with vertical walls from the middle of the river-bed, dividing the stream in three arms, which wind themselves through narrow chasms in the mural rocks, and finally rush down over stair-like offsets in the cliffs to a 60 or 70 feet lower level.

The rock composing the cliffs at the Quiver falls is a dark greenish-gray colored fine-grained diorite. Portions of the rock have a peculiar concretionary structure by segregation of globular nodules in the mass, densely crowded together as in an oolite, only of much larger size, from a small hazelnut to a hickorynut ; they consist of a granular red orthoclas in intermixture with quartz. By decomposition of the rock these balls readily separate from the surrounding diorite mass. Below the Quiver falls the exposures of diorite continue for about a half mile downward in this grand style ; then for several miles only here and there the rock comes to the surface in little islands in the river, or locally projecting above the drift-covered valley. In the north part of Town. 37 we find again rapids, and with them also large exposures of very coarsely crystalline, dark blackish-colored hornblende rocks, much differing in aspect from the diorites of the Quiver falls. One variety is a black glistening rock composed of a magma of granular crystals of white feldspar and black hornblende, in which mass large crystals of the hornblende are segregated, but inseparably amalgamated with the inclosing ground-mass, as being formed by the parallel arrangement of the smaller crystals into compound larger ones. Another very beautiful variety is composed of large blackish-green hornblende crystals of great lustre, in intermixture with a small proportion of red orthoclas crystals. A third variety consists of similar large crystals of hornblende in peculiar intermixture with the feldspathic constituent of the rock. Both minerals permeate each other in the crystals in a mode as if a process of paramorphosis from one into the other were going on. Interstitial between this magma of crystals is a purplish red, dull, earthy-looking but hard mineral matter, principally composed of hematitic iron oxide, which imparts to the rock a showy, variegated aspect ; black mica-leaves are sparingly intermingled. In contiguity with these coarsely crystalline diorites we find in this locality quartzite beds and cherty argillitic stratified rocks richly impregnated with hematitic iron oxide, which in all probability are analogous with those occurring up the river near Holmes Creek.

About three quarters of a mile below these outcrops are the Pemenee falls, where an immense body of dark-colored feldspar porphyries comes to the surface in bold cliffs, in the river, and on the borders of the river-bed. The exposures begin a half mile above the falls ; the rock is here a genuine granite, composed of a magma of indistinctly defined crystals of red feldspar, with a granular quartzose and partly feldspathic ground-mass, which is pervaded with streaky interrupted linear seams of a dark-green chlorite-like mineral, so often found substituted for mica in the granites of the Marquette district. From this granitic form of the rock, all transitions into an aphanitic homogeneous mass, with a flinty conchoidal fracture, are observable ; but this aphanitic dark blackish-colored ground-mass always incloses distantly disseminated, well-defined crystals of orthoclas, or sometimes amygdaloidal rounded nodules, formed of crystalline orthoclas, and, examined with the magnifying-glass, appears no more homogeneous ; the light-colored feldspathic susbtance, and the dark-colored chloritic or also augitic or hornblendic components of the mass are segregated to a certain extent into delicate linear seams, which sometimes impart to the rock a sub-schistose structure. This lineated structure of the rock becomes obvious to the naked eyes on weathered surfaces, and proves to full satisfaction the lava nature of this rock ; the serpentine torsions and convolutions of these lineations exhibit the flowing motion of the once liquid mass as clear as we see it exhibited in the banded slags of an iron furnace. At the base of the falls I found, in contiguity with the porphyritic rocks, lighter-colored sub-schistose felsite porphyries similar to those·associated with the diorite at the Quinnesec or Sturgeon falls ; an exposure of the coarsely crystalline dark-colored hornblende rock, found a mile above the Pemenee falls, is observable below the falls in the river-bed. A short distance below the falls the rock disappears under the drift ; about a mile below, near the Pemenee farm, we can see in the river-bed an outcrop of a fine-grained dark greenish-colored diorite, which differs from the crystalline fine-grained variety of the porphyry at the falls only by the segregation of hornblende crystals in the mass. I returned to Quinnesec from the Pemenee farm, as I was not prepared to go farther down the river, but from notes made on a former trip ten years ago, I know the occurrence of porphyritic and granitic rocks similar to those at the Pemenee falls, at the Muscongo rapids ; they come there in close contact with well-laminated

schistose beds, and with coarsely crystalline and aphanitic dioritic rocks.   Farther down, at the so-called chalk hills, we
find the hematitic quartzites and argillitic strata once more
associated with the diorite, as we saw it in two other localities
above mentioned.   It does not appear in any of these exposures
as if valuable deposits of iron-ore were to be found in this group
of rock-beds, but it is of great scientific interest to find out by
future examinations in which relation these beds are with the
dioritic rocks—whether they are a regular link belonging to this
group, or whether they are deposits of a younger age incumbent
on them, which during the upheaval became entangled between a
fold of the dioritic and felsitic rocks.   The lithological character
of this ferruginous rock-belt is unlike the ore-formation of the
Quinnesec mines.

Reviewing what we have seen of the formations along the
Menominee River, said to be the youngest of the Huronian
group, I again point out the great similarity in the composition
and structure of this very large series of rocks with the dioritic
formation of the Marquette district ; also its intersection by the
serpentine group, which in the Marquette district is under similar
circumstances associated with the diorite formation.   Further in
favor of this analogy is the intersection of the Menominee diorites
by porphyritic granite in dyke form, as is the case with the
diorite group of Marquette.   These porphyritic granites are on
their part in close relationship with the felsite porphyry of the
Pemenee falls, merging by insensible gradations with the granite,
which is only a more completely crystallized form of the same lava-
mass.   On the other hand, there exists not the slightest resemblance between the dioritic rock-belt of the Menominee River and
those rock-beds of the Marquette district which represent subdivisions 15 to 20 of Major Brooks.

The exact order in which the different rock-masses composing
the dioritic formation succeed each other—whether the dark green
diorites of the Twin falls and in other places are the lowest, and
the lighter colored diorites at the Quinnesec falls the higher ones
—is at the present state of our knowledge uncertain, but it is most
likely the case ; so the dark-colored coarsely crystalline hornblende rocks exposed a mile above the Pemenee falls may be
older beds than those at the Quinnesec falls.   The massive belts

of this series of altered sedimentary rocks, interlaminated with the schistose members, can, as I think, not all be considered as regular links in the stratified succession ; some of these, and particularly the larger masses, as they occur at the Quiver falls, I believe to be intrusive, in the same qualified sense in which I have considered some of the massive dioritic rock-belts of the Marquette district, and still in another sense they represent only a more altered portion of the stratified beds connected with them. Considering the granite on the south and west side of Menominee valley as an eruptive rock, like the porpyhry of the Pemenee falls, I can agree fully with Major Brooks in this part of his chronological system ; these rocks undoubtedly came to the surface after all the other Huronian strata of sedimentary origin were formed, as their eruption to the surface caused the upheaval of the others. I therefore have always represented the dyke granites of the Marquette district as actually the youngest rocks in the group, but I suppose this was not the original meaning of Major Brooks' system. In all his stratigraphical descriptions, he has not made a proper distinction between sedimentary succession and interstratification, counting up the beds just as they came in a cross-cut ; his Groups VII., IX., and XI. are a proof of this assertion.

It still remains for me to give a description of the country west and north-west of the Quinnesec mining district, which is equally important by its wealth in iron-ore, and even supersedes the other in the size of its ore-belts. One of the largest ore-deposits discovered is the Commonwealth mine ; it has a seam 162 feet wide, of a compact, solid, high-graded ore, in which only a few narrow bands of a more siliceous character occur, which are well defined and easily separable. The Commonwealth is on Wisconsin territory, south of the Brule River ; but also on the north side of the river, in Michigan, several equally large belts of the same kind of ore have been discovered, besides a great many smaller ones, and constantly new discoveries are made by hundreds of explorers roaming over this promising wilderness.

I have previously made the statement that the ore-formation of the Commonwealth mine represents a higher horizon than the Quinnesec ore-formation. Major Brooks places the Commonwealth ore-deposits into the upper part of the Lake Hanbury slate series, but while he considers that as one of the upper members of the Huronian series, I place it, on the contrary, below the Quinnesec ore-formation.

The abrupt termination of the Quinnesec ore-formation, on the east side of the Menominee River, near its junction with Pine River, is very singular. We see for the last time the limestones underlying the Quinnesec ore-formation uncovered in test-pits in the S.E. quarter of Sect. 23 ; and right across the river, in Sects. 21 and 20 of the Wisconsin town subdivision, Town. 39, R. 19, occur the characteristic sericitic and plumbaginous schists of the Commonwealth ore-formation ; the strata strike in the usual west-north-west direction, and dip north in an almost upright position. Some layers are slaty, very delicately laminated, soft argillitic-like, and fissile ; silky-shining, gray, or intensely red-colored ; others, mostly gray-colored strata, are harder, and consist of granular layers of feldspar in seamy intermixture with sericeous scales. With them occur black plumbago schists, containing irregular glassy quartz bands. No iron was found in the test-pits, which are not far off from the bed of Pine River. The higher part of the hill-side is deeply covered with drift. A mile north from here, in the centre of Sect. 8 of the same town, are, on the height of the drift-covered plateau, the previously mentioned knobs of diorite which form a continuation of the outcrops at the Twin falls. On their south side we find, in immediate contact with them, vertical strata of a greenish-drab colored, rather hard but absorbent schistose rock, weathering rusty brown, and breaking into uneven angular shelly fragments. It consists of a half-decomposed kaolinitic granular feldspar mass, abundantly intermingled with micaceous, or probably chloritic scales. These are succeeded by other somewhat softer micaceo-argillitic beds of an imperfect schistose structure, not cleavable into even slaty pieces ; their color is ash gray, or purplish gray, or deep red. With them occur more micaceous or sericitic beds, with a slaty cleavage ; the thickness of these strata is hard to be estimated, as they are only uncovered by test-pits. To these follows a large succession of red-colored quartzose beds, partly banded and compact, partly cherty cellulose ; interstratified with them occur argillites of a seamy or irregularly dotted variegated lighter and darker greenish and purplish color, produced by a streaky and corrugated intermixture of the variously tinted clay masses. In this association occur seams of iron-ore in different degrees of purity. Some are more or less contaminated with siliceous or also argillitic matter. The pure ore forms a compact, amorphous, fine-grained mass, with a sub-conchoidal fracture without lustre ; its color is dark reddish or purplish brown ; scraped with the knife it gives a bright red streak. With these compact hematitic ores are cellulose concretionary ore-masses associated, which consist partly of a fine-grained compact martite with sub-metallic lustre, partly of hydrated oxide under the form of grape-ore ; and not rarely in the cell-cavities of this mixed mass fine large black crystals, like the crystallized iron oxide of the island of Elba, are found attached to the side-walls, or grow out from the surface of a stalactitic stem of the hydrated ore, which proves the formation of these crystals contemporaneously and after the formation of the stalactites.

The Commonwealth mine is about five miles north-west from the test-pits I have just described. One can see from here the spot where it is located. The ore-formation extends, in all probability, from here without interruption to the Commonwealth mine ; but the surface is so generally covered with drift that only by boring or digging is information obtainable about the underlying rocks of any part of this country. The Commonwealth mine is in Wisconsin, and fault may be found if I enter into a detailed description of it ; but if we want information about the geology of a district we cannot mind State boundary lines ; we must pick up information where we best can ; and here is certainly such an occasion. The Commonwealth mine is not far from the centre of Sect. 34, Town. 40, R. 18 (Wis. Surv.) ; it is on the plateau-like summit part of a ridge, declining on the north side toward the Menominee River, just about three miles south of the mouth of the Michigamee River. The south side of the ridge slopes down to the Pine River, distant about four miles. Under a cover of from 4 to 8 feet of drift, the ore-bearing rock-series can be found most everywhere on the summit part of this ridge ; the strata are near to a vertical position, and dip south. A belt of solid hard ore 162 feet wide is uncovered in the mine, which was incidentally mentioned before ; its stratification is very obscure. The extremely fine-grained brownish or blackish purple compact mass, with a dull clay-like fracture, exhibits to the observer the aspect of an extremely fine hardened mud-mass, with the same irregular cleavage into angular small fragments as a piece of dried clay would ; by shrinkage of the indurating mud-mass, a great many fissures and little druse-cavities formed within the rock-mass, which are filled or coated over with crystals of dolomite-spar, or with brilliant crystals of iron oxide, or with bright purple scales of micaceous oxide, or with the hydrated grape-ore. The homogeneity of the substance is also frequently interrupted by a partial transformation of the amorphous oxide into a minutely granular crystalline form, with a dull metallic lustre. Portions of the ore-belt are locally found shattered and recemented into a breccia by feldspathic or argillitic seams of reddish or whitish green color, and interstratified with the ore-mass are a few narrow belts of banded ferruginous quartz-beds. South of this ore-belt is a large series of well-laminated schists, blackish-colored by graphita, with interlaminated quartz-seams ; some of the schists are so richly impregnated with graphita as to deserve attention regarding their economic value ; most of them, however, are very impure, siliceous, or clayey. The thickness of these plumbaginous schists with quartzose seams is very great, as can be observed in the ravines on the south side of the mines, but excepting these, all the other surface south of the mines is deeply covered with drift ; therefore, no estimation can be made how far these quartzoso-plumbaginous schists may extend southward, and what other kinds of strata succeed them. North of the ore-belt, consequently beneath it, are dark-colored hard siliceous and partially argillitic schists and flaggy layers, richly impregnated with iron oxide ; they inclose another seam of good iron-ore about four feet wide. Farther down the slope succeed other dark greenish or brown-colored schists of a siliceo-argillitic character, some with an even slaty cleavage, others cleaving very irregularly into uneven slivers ; certain layers are rich in sericitic scales, all contain much iron in the state of protoxide, but become rusty ochraceous by exposure. The larger portion of these schists contains an abundance of lenticular concretionary masses of iron pyrites, which by their decomposition cause the schists to open their laminæ in the above-mentioned slivered mode, and the surfaces of the cleft, still closely coherent slivers, become incrusted with a brightly shining glassy varnish of hydrated oxide of iron of a dark blackish brown color, often also lively iridescent ; the little cavities left after the decomposition of the pyrites are filled with brownish yellow ochre. This kind of schists is very characteristic for the Commonwealth ore-formation, as much so as the plumbaginous schists ; they occur everywhere as far as this formation extends, and form the largest bulk of this rock-series ; they cover the surface of a great many square miles north of the Brule River and south of the Paint River, and by their occurrence the explorer generally knows that he is on ground where an ore-belt can be expected ; but he would be greatly mistaken, if he thinks to find the ore-deposits equally distributed in this formation in a certain fixed position. There were certainly periods during the time of the deposition of this group of sediments in which more molecules of iron oxide were carried by the turbid waters which made the sediments, than at others, and the prospects of success in such a horizon are for the explorer generally much better than in another ; but one must never imagine that at such a time a uniform sheet of irony deposits formed all over the then existing ocean bottom ; the materials were distributed by the currents according to their specific gravity, and according to the velocity and transporting power of the currents ; while here all circumstances favored the formation of an ore-deposit, in another place, not a great way off, a stronger current may have prevented the deposition of any sediments, or only allowed the coarser sandy grains to settle down. North of this great belt of schists, which incloses from time to time quartzose arenaceous seams or lenticular masses of quartz, or also a narrow seam of ore, we find another series of dark plumbaginous quartz-schists with interlaminated black and white banded quartzite ledges, which are well exposed in some shafts near the new-built dwelling of Captain Tobin, the superintendent of the Commonwealth mine, to whom I am greatly indebted for favors and assistance in the prosecution of my work. Some distance east and north of this locality, near the quarter-post on the east line of Sect. 34, are test-pits in which, under a cover of Silurian sand-rock, fine-grained, silky-shining, grayish or intensely red-colored sericitic slaty argillites are uncovered ; they dip under a high angle southward, and consequently must be considered as the lower members in the described succession. We find similar beds exposed a short distance farther east, in a brick-yard near the road-side. Farther north are no more exposures. Other test-pits on the south side of this road, in Sect. 35, struck in part soft black plumbago schists, and in part the same sericitic argillites as those near the quarter-post ; these two kinds of schist alternate with each other several times, and amount to great thickness, as they are met with everywhere over a space a quarter of a mile wide.

This whole formation, above and below the ore-belt, amounting to not less than 2000 feet of strata, consists throughout of the finest mud-sediments, which have retained their delicate sedimentary lamination most perfectly, even in the slaty rock-beds, whose cleavage is generally parallel with the bedding, and not transverse to it, as in other slate-rocks. West of the Commonwealth mine, in the centre of the S.E. quarter of Sect. 33, on the south slope of the hill-range, is a large belt of the same ore, as we see it in the mine, naturally exposed ; the higher part of the ridge north of this ore-mass is formed of nearly vertical ledges of ferruginous and of graphitic quartz-schists. The extension of this large body of ore in east and west direction has not been fully examined yet. In the S.W. quarter of Sect. 32, near the west line, in a number of exploring pits, a large succession of quartzite beds of various character, interstratified with seams of a rich coarsely granular, somewhat magnetic ore of metallic lustre, has been exposed ; some of the quartzite beds inclose a large proportion of the crystalline coarse ore-granules ; others are purely quartzose, also banded beds of alternating ore and quartz-seams occur, and with them fine-grained dark greenish or blackish siliceo-feldspathic, very compact hard rock seams, which contain a large proportion of iron. In the western pits are well-laminated hard hydro-micaceous feldspathic schists exposed, some of which are beautifully mottled with copper-colored irregular blotches on the dark purplish gray ground-mass ; others are light greenish yellow, and resemble the novaculitic schists of the Marquette district. The strata are nearly vertical, seem to dip southward ; on their south side, in test-pits and by natural exposures, the plumbago schists interlaminated with quartz seams are to be observed, and on the north side of the exploring pits red and grayish purple sericitic slaty argillites occur, similar to those on the north side of the Commonwealth mine. About a quarter mile farther west, in the S.W. quarter of Sect. 31, south of the road, are high bluffs of a compact light reddish-colored quartzite.

The Florence mine, situated in the S.W. quarter of Sect. 21,

16

Town. 40, R. 18, corresponds with the Commonwealth mine in the character of the ore-belt and the rocks associated with it, as well as it can be expected in localities two or three miles apart ; the strike of the formation is about the same as that of the Commonwealth, but its dip is opposite, northward. The ore-belt is considerably shattered on the surface, but is also very large, over a hundred feet wide. A part of the ore is very compact, finely granular, of dark steel-gray color, with a dull metallic lustre. The largest quantity of the ore presently mined is a compact amorphous dark shattered mass, full of fissures and little cavities filled with soft ochraceous oxide of yellow color, or incrusted with grape-ore. Larger stalactitic masses of hydrated grape-ore are quite abundant, and these grape-ore stalactites are often covered with black solid crystals of oxide, and with micaceous iron oxide, transparent with deep purple color. Interstratified between these ore-deposits are some quartzose seams and a belt of green and red mottled rather hard and compact argillite. South of the ore-belt, therefore beneath it, follows a series of siliceous ores, too low-graded to be used, and then succeed the hard dark blackish-colored and rusty yellow or brown weathering siliceo-argillaceous, pyritous schists, varnished over with a glassy coating of hydrated oxide of iron, which I have described as occurring north of the Commonwealth mine, and which, to avoid the lengthiness of description, I will in future only call *pyritous schists*. Above the ore-belt, on the north side of the hill, are graphitic schists with quartz seams, and abundantly disseminated with iron pyrites. Farther north the strata are hidden by drift-deposits, but west of the mine is a large number of test-pits partly opened by the Florence Mining Company, partly by Mr. Harvey in Sect. 20 and Sect. 17. The graphitic schists are there not immediately on the ore-belt, but red iron-colored micaceo-argillitic or harder feldspathic schistose, or slaty beds intervene. The ore-belt of the Florence mine does not seem to extend in this direction in equally large dimensions, but narrower seams of rich ore, interstratified with leaner siliceous ores and with quartzite seams, are found in its place. North of the graphitic schists succeeds a large series of sericitic schists, some dark red-colored with hematite, others lighter grayish, or almost white ; their ground-mass is partly a hard granular feldspathic mass, partly kaolinite. These strata resemble the sericite schists north of the Commonwealth mine, which appear to be below the ore-formation, while those are clearly above it. Two different belts, a lower and a higher, of deposits of this kind seem to exist, but possibly they may represent the same horizon, and have come into such positions by plication or an overturn of the strata. I have so far not been able to decide this question, but as the miner is often guided in his explorations by these schists, it is of great practical importance to ascertain positively whether there are two distinct horizons of schists so similar to each other, or only one.

A very interesting field for observation of a different, most likely lower, horizon of the Commonwealth ore-formation is found on the north and west sides of Keyes Lake, in Sects. 25, 24, 23, 27, and 28, in Town. 40, R. 17. Besides a good many natural exposures, the great number of test-pits recently opened there have brought to light a great variety of rock-beds, but the order in the succession of these strata is not clearly recognizable, as the denudations by the test-pits are too much disconnected, and the frequent change observed in the dip of the strata indicates the existence of many plications of the rock-beds, causing their repetition in the different localities. We observe, in the S.E. quarter of Sect. 25, a large belt of vertical quartzite ledges over 200 feet in width, which can be traced to extend in a north-west direction across Sects. 24, 13, and 12, to the Brule River. A part of this rock is compact, light-colored, and resembles the quartzite exposed at the falls of the Sturgeon River, but the much greater portion of the rock occurs in thinly laminated schistose, very compact thick ledges, which schistose structure is due to the copious intermixture of linear hydro-micaceous laminæ with the granular quartz-mass. On the south side this quartzite belt is adjoined by an equally large succession of alternating quartzose and actinolitic seams of a dark color, in rough, irregular, somewhat shattered and recemented layers ; the quartzose seams are partly compact in banded, streaky, or reticulated seamy intermixture with granular magnetite, or uniformly disseminated with larger or smaller proportions of it, partly porous saccharoidal, particularly the narrow bands of quartz wedged in between the actinolitic rock-masses. The actinolite forms very tough uneven layers, composed of a dense agglomeration of globular clusters of radiated, delicately fibrous crystals, generally blackish-colored by intermingled granules of magnetite, but not rarely it is not tinged, whitish, of silky lustre. Single radiated globular masses of actinolite are often seen dispersed within the substance of the sandy quartz-seams, in contact with an actinolite seam. South of this actinolitic rock-belt, which occasionally incloses narrow seams of granular magnetic ore, succeed hard dark blackish-colored, fine-grained slaty rocks in various modifications ; their black color is due to graphitic matter, partly to granular magnetite, which usually is found dispersed through the siliceo-feldspathic hydro-micaceous ground-mass which composes all of them. Farther west and north, but south of the quartzite belt, in Mr. Burt's test-pits, in the S.E. quarter of the S.W. quarter of Sect. 24, we find a large succession of quartzose and argillitic, rather hard rock-beds, all of which are more or less richly impregnated with hematitic oxide ; associated with these are black plumbaginous schists of soft or harder siliceous nature. The strata in this location dip north, and in some test-pits they are almost horizontal ; in others they are steeply inclined.

Interlaminated with these beds are various smaller seams of valuable iron-ore, in compact aphanitic masses of blackish purple color, or in the form of grape-ore, in partly hydrated, partly not-hydrated condition ; also actinolitic seams richly impregnated with iron, and usually in a porous, earthy, decomposing condition, are found in these test-pits. In the S.W. quarter of the S.W. quarter of the same section white and reddish speckled porous kaolinitic beds of considerable thickness are found in the bottom of the pits, which might represent a decomposed dioritic rock. The most promising iron-ore seams are found in the test-pits of Mr. Tobin, in the N.W. quarter of the S.W. quarter of Sect. 24, where, in association with the quartzitic and argillitic ferruginous beds, rich layers of an earthy compact hematitic ore occur, in which a great quantity of large octahedric crystals is disseminated. As in the same mass also dim fibrous crystal groups of actinolite, transformed into a soft yellow ochraceous substance, are found imbedded, it becomes evident that the amorphous red hematite, inclosing the crystals, is a product of alteration of the rock by higher oxidation of the ground-mass, which has not yet affected the crystals. In the S.W. quarter of the S.E. quarter of Sect. 24 occur compact sub-magnetic ore-seams of dull metallic lustre, imbedded within actinolitic quartz schists, which evidently represent the fresh unaltered condition of these hematitic earthy ores, with inclosed magnetite crystals; the steel-gray minutely granular mass exhibits the large octahedric crystals plainly. A short distance north of these test-pits the mural walls of the large quartzite belt ascend to form the summit of the range ; north of the quartzite are no more rock exposures. In test-pits opened in the S. E. quarter of the N. W. quarter of Sect. 25, the schists of this ore-bearing group are intersected or interlaminated by a doleritic rock-seam in a softened, decomposing condition, which totally differs from the dioritic rocks of this region, and completely resembles the doleritic dyke-rocks of the Marquette district ; the augite crystals are dark brown, not fibrous, but like basaltic augite ; the feldspar crystals have lost their glassy lustre, and have become pale brownish by imbibition of hydrated iron oxide. The denudations are not sufficient to see whether this dolerite belt is parallel with the strata, or whether it intersects them transversally. In the S. E. quarter of the N. E. quarter of Sect. 23 are other test-pits, opened by the Union Iron and Steel Company, in which generally light whitish or greenish-gray and red-colored sericitic and argillitic schists, associated with graphitic belts, have been found, but no promising seams of iron-ore.

Following the road from Keyes Lake to Wakefield's explorations, we see near the south corners of Sects. 25 and 26 exposures of highly ferruginous actinolitic schists, inclosing granular quartz-seams. Farther on, near the quarter-post, on the south line of Sect. 26, these schists are in close contact with a fine-grained dark greenish-black colored rock, consisting of a minutely granular feldspathic ground-mass of a pale whitish color, in intermixture with a scaly mineral, which is probably chlorite, and with a great abundance of small needles of black turmaline. Farther on, near the N. E. corner of Sect. 34, the graphitic schists are well exposed, and south of them follows a large succession of the actinolite schists with quartzose sandy seams, and with others of a compact magnetic ore, of partially actinolitic structure ; all these beds are so near to a vertical position, that nothing definite can be said about their dip. Going here off from the road in a north-west direction, we come over swampy grounds, with numerous exposures of dioritic rocks projecting above the surface in low hillocks ; they consist of quite large, well-discernible crystals of green hornblende, with an interstitial white feldspathic mass. In the S.W. quarter of the N.W. quarter of Sect. 27, test-pits are opened in actinolitic schists in a vertical position, which are interlaminated with quartzite seams and cellulose cherty belts, besides narrow seams of a compact crystalline, somewhat magnetic, iron-ore, which thin flaggy ore-layers inclose quite a number of brownish red garnet crystals. The actinolite schists in this place have been cross-cut by trenches about 150 feet, which at each end struck a belt of diorite in close contact with the vertical rock-ledges ; the portions of the diorite next to the actinolite schists are in a weathered, friable condition ; farther off the fracture of the diorite is bright, fresh, perfectly similar to the diorite outcrops in the swamp. In the adjoining part of Sect. 28 are other test-pits, in which the actinolitic schists come likewise in contiguity with the dioritic rocks, believed by Major Brooks to be incumbent on the schists, but evidently intrusive masses, which is clearly evinced by the occurrence of a belt of ferruginous actinolite schists 150 feet wide, intermediate between two large bodies of diorite, on the other side of which again the actinolite schists come to the surface. From all observations I had occasion to make, I infer the age of the actinolitic rock-series to be older than that of the productive ore-belt of the Commonwealth mine, but both belong to one and the same group of deposits.

Going north of Florence we find, on the north-west shore of Fisher Lake, outcrops of a fine-grained massive, and partly schistose diorite ; all the surrounding country is covered with drift. On the road leading to the Brule River similar diorites are seen extensively exposed on the height of the hill-range in Sect. 16. The very steep descent to the river is all drift-covered in the place where the road goes, but farther east the slope toward the river is full of rock-cliffs, as I could see from the opposite side.

I have mentioned the occurrence of large exposures of mica schists, and of harder, compact, fine-grained gneissoid rocks in Sect. 12, on the north side of Brule River, near its junction with Paint River ; we leave these on our east side and follow the road westward, parallel with the course of the Brule. For six miles nothing but sand or boulder-drift is to be seen, while we pass over the undulating highlands bordering the river ; finally, in Sect. 31,

Town. 42, R. 32, after crossing a small creek and ascending a very steep hill-side, we find it composed of the schists, which for brevity's sake I proposed to name *pyritous schists* on a previous page. They are almost vertical, and dip on different parts of the hill in different directions. Onward to Brown's trading-post, in the N.E. quarter of Sect. 36, Town. 42, R. 33, we see on every hill-slope of the very broken country these schists exposed, until we have descended into the valley of the Brule. Taking from here a northern course, we find the schists again exposed, or merely covered by a thin coating of soil, on the brow and summit of the hills in Sects. 25, 24, and farther north ; in fact, ignoring the loose driftmasses, these schists form the exclusive surface-rock of the town we are in, and of the adjoining towns, with very few exceptions, where in circumscribed narrow spots lower rock-beds reach the surface. The extension of these steeply upheaved beds over so large an area naturally implies their often repeated plication, which folds are not only often obliterated by compression of the curved sides into a parallel, conformable position with each other ; but even where this is not the case, the loose superficial masses of drift and soil hide the beds so much that in any of the exposures we find or make by artificial denudation of the beds, we can rarely make conclusions on the succession of the beds from their dip in a certain direction, as we have rarely occasion to observe the complicated flexions of the strata, which reverse the order of things at once ; and therefore we have in most instances to decide by the character of the rock-beds whether we ascend or descend in the series by going in a certain direction.

Passing on the road northward across Sects. 25 and 24, small outcrops of the schists and interlaminated jaspery quartzose seams frequently occur ; particularly well they are exposed in a ravine in the N.E. quarter of Sect. 24, where the beds are quite ferruginous and gave inducement to the opening of some test-pits in this place, but no ore-seam of any value could be found. Subsequently testpits were opened by Mr. Porter 400 or 500 steps south-west of that locality, in which graphitic schists interlaminated with banded quartzose ledges of ferruginous character occurred ; the strike of the strata is north-west, their dip under a high angle north-east. From these pits a row of other pits and trenches was dug southeastward, crossways to the formation, in which a variety of siliceous, argillitic, and graphitic beds, amounting to a very great thickness, were intersected, all of which contained a larger or smaller proportion of hematitic oxide, and some narrower seams of a fair quality of hard ore, similar to the Commonwealth ore, had been found inclosed at the time I visited the place ; and later, after my return to Ann Arbor, the proprietors informed me of their final success in discovering, by extending the test-pits still farther south, a large belt of a compact dark purplish brown aphanitic ore of an excellent quality, as the specimens sent to me prove it.   North of Porter's pit, near the line between Sects. 24 and 13, we have to descend into a swampy valley, in which several low hillocks project, which are composed of a fine-grained massive diorite.   Leaving the swamp and ascending the hills farther north, we meet, in the north half of Sect. 13, again with the ferrugino-siliceous schists and banded jaspery beds we found near Porter's camp.   East and west of us are crests formed of the nearly upright ledges of this rock-series ; arrived at the top, in a saddle-shaped, swampy depression between these crests, we discover a hillock, about 12 feet high, rising from the middle of the low ground, covered with quite thick deposits of bog iron-ore, and coming up to it we find it composed of solid iron-ore, the same as the Commonwealth ore, in intermixture with some jaspery seams confined to a certain limited part of the ore-belt, which strikes approximately north and south.   The width of this ore-mass is about 70 feet ; the length of the exposure 300 or 400 feet ; south, in the direction of its strike, we find only the ferruginous quartz schists ; north is a swamp ; and east and west the same kind of ferruginous quartz schists occurs, which generally forms the surface of the country.   This ore outcrop, claimed to be first discovered by Mr. Jac. Armstrong, one of the prominent explorers of this region, is named by him, on account of its large size, the Mastodon mine.

West of the Mastodon mine, near the S.E. corner of Sect. 11, Mr. Bond has opened test-pits in this siliceo-ferruginous schist-series ; the strata are in places vertical, in others they dip south, and locally I found them almost horizontal.   The southern strata near the corner of the section are principally banded, fine-grained, or flinty siliceous rocks, some of which bands are richly impregnated with iron oxide of dark brown color on the outside ; the inner, not-weathered parts are blackish, as they contain the iron oxide in a not-hydrated magnetic condition. These beds inclose irregular seams of a good quality of ore, like that of the Mastodon ; but none of those I saw were large enough to be of great practical value. In the north part of the section the structure of the rocks is more slaty, in a degree argillitic, yet rich in iron ; but no ore-seams are found in it. From Sect. 11 I went north-east into Sect. 1. Near the S.W. corner of Sect. 1 are quite extensive exposures of these slaty ferruginous strata to be seen in the bed of a creek ; they dip south, or are vertical. All the surface of Sect. 1 is composed of the same siliceo-ferruginous slates and schists, in alternation with large belts of graphitic schists, and occasionally a narrow seam of hematitic ore is encountered, but none of any larger bulk has been found, although a great amount of work has been done here by explorers. North of Sect. 1, in the N.W. quarter of Sect. 31, Town. 43, R. 32, Mr. Sheldon and Mr. Schaefer have had more success in their explorations ; a very large body of ore-beds, amounting to over 150 feet in diameter, has been uncovered there, which resembles the ore of the Commonwealth mine, but is less free of siliceous seams interlaminated with the ore-mass ; some slaty strata, almost rich enough in iron to be used as an ore, are exposed on the north side of the ore-belt, but no other rock-beds are denuded there in connection with the ore-belt, which stands vertical. In the bed of the creek crossing the south part of Sect. 31, and of Sect. 36 of the next township, are outcrops of a middling coarse-grained crystalline diorite ; the hill-sides round it are all drift-covered.

From these northern exploring pits I returned to Porter's camp, in the N.E. quarter of Sect. 24, and went from there across to the N.W. quarter of Sect. 23, where likewise some explorations for iron-ore have been made, but the drift-deposits are there most too thick for the explorer ; some of the pits had to be dug through 60 feet of this loose material before the rock-ledges were struck ; the work has for this reason been abandoned. The extension of the schists of the iron-formation over this part of the country is fully evinced by the rocks thrown out of these test-pits, and by several natural exposures found there. Farther west, by following the road to Lake Chicagon, from time to time rock-ledges of the same kind are found locally denuded from the drift, which generally forms the surface of the surrounding lands. Such exposures are met with in Sect. 28, on the brow of an extremely steep hill-side sloping down to Armstrong's Creek. The schists in upright position form the higher part of the slope, and the basal portion is formed of bulky dioritic rock-masses. From there to Chicagon Lake, and thence to Iron River, in Sect. 36, Town. 43, R. 35, along the road no rock-ledges can be seen at the surface, formed of a coarse boulder-drift in which granitic and dioritic blocks largely prevail over other kinds of rock. In the valley of Iron River we find the iron-formation again well exposed in the hill-sides bordering it. In several places larger masses of ore were naturally exposed, which discovery attracted a number of exploring parties, who are at present earnestly at work in digging test-pits. The explorations of Mr. Sheldon are going on in the west half of the north-west quarter of Sect. 36 ; the strata are there considerably shattered at the surface, and it is difficult to ascertain their exact strike and dip, but in the bottom of the pits they are more regular, and dip under a high angle north-eastward. A large mass of iron-ore, entirely similar to the ore of the Commonwealth mine, is naturally exposed in the S.E. quarter of the N.E. quarter of Sect. 35, but following the line of strike of this mass, which is approximately north and south, parallel with the course of the river in this place, we soon lose sight of it, and test-pits opened in the same direction did not meet with a similar ore-mass. Above and below this seam of ore are siliceo-ferruginous and partly argillitic strata of great thickness ; below it are, conspicuous, in particular, banded layers formed of alternating seams of white, or gray or brownish flinty quartz, and of others consisting of a fine-grained, compact, more or less siliceous ore. These flinty ledges are often brecciated, but do not represent an accumulation of different kinds of rock-fragments cemented together, but merely the shattered flinty quartzite strata, which often are not much dislocated, and have often the corresponding broken ends of the fragments right opposite to each other ; their interstitial cement is a granular quartzose mud-mass, impregnated with hematitic oxide, or almost totally consisting of the oxide.

In the test-pits farther up on the river side, in the N.W. quarter of the N.W. quarter of Sect. 36, which are opened in a somewhat higher horizon of the series, argillitic strata prevail over the siliceous ; some are well-stratified banded ledges, variegated by the alternation of non-tinged whitish or greenish seams, with others intensely red-colored by hematite ; others are of uniform color, red, or gray from impregnation of martite granules, or black from graphita in their composition ; also mottled argillites are found in this association of brecciated structure, or else consisting of an imperfect intermixture of argillitic masses of different color, when in a plastic condition. Interstratified with these occur hematitic ore-masses, in pockets rather than in regular seams, and also un-homogeneous in their mass, as if crushed and baked together again ; a part of the hematite-ores is soft, paint-like; another part is a hard, compact, amorphous mass, with intermingled crystalline ore-granules, and coated over with oxide crystals on the walls of little cavities in the ore. The massive ore-belt naturally exposed in Sect. 35 has its numerous irregular druse-cavities lined with brush-formed clusters of needle-shaped crystals of goethite, which are translucid, with a brownish purple color, similar to the color of iron mica in thin leaves ; other cavities are incrusted with ordinary hydrated grape-ore. By going direct east from this natural ore-exposure unto the plateau-like top of the hill-range, we find a large belt of vertical ledges of a fine-grained, compact siliceous rock of a sub-schistose structure, which incloses a large proportion of disseminated minute granules of magnetite ; its color is almost black, which may in part be due to an intermixture of fine molecules of graphita. Noteworthy is yet the occurrence of large rounded chunks of a high-graded schistose specular ore in the drift-masses, which are foreign to this ore-formation, and must have been transported from some northern locality representing another group of ore-bearing rocks, similar to those of the Marquette district.

On the west side of the river, opposite the described test-pits in Sect. 35, are high bluffs, some distance backward from the river channel, formed of the dark blackish-brown siliceo-ferruginous schists, with slivered, uneven cleavage, interlaminated with more compact ledges of the same silicco-ferruginous composition, which series of rocks is all over the country characteristic of this formation, and composes the largest bulk of it. The strata are almost vertical. A half mile north of these bluffs the river bends at a right angle to the west across the centre of Sects. 26 and 27. In some parts of the generally drift-covered hill-slope, on the south side of the river, we find the flinty siliceous rock-beds, banded with seams of siliceous iron-ore and brecciated, corresponding with those first described, as occurring below the large naturally exposed ore-belt on the other side of the river ; the interstices between the siliceous fragments are usually filled with seams of grape-ore ; the strata dip under a high angle south, and on their south side a thick series of light yellowish-colored fine-grained calcareous quartzite strata succeeds them conformably.

South of Mr. Sheldon's location Mr. Wood has opened test-pits, in the S.W. quarter of the S.W. quarter of Sect. 36 ; the strata are, as in the other location at the foot of the hill-slope, a banded, partially brecciated flinty quartz rock, recemented by ferruginous matter of greater or lesser purity. Above are rich deposits of ore, in irregular pocket-like, dilating and contracting seams, the ground-mass of which ore is amorphous, compact, hard, like the ore of the Commonwealth, but full of druse-cavities lined with a thick incrustation of ordinary hydrated grape-ore, or of the darker-colored goethite, or with thick rhomboid crystals like the Elba island ore, or with all the three forms of the oxide at the same time. Large bulky masses of this ore are exclusively formed of long stalactitic stems of goethite, or the ordinary grape-ore ; some with the lustre of a mirror, others with velvet lustre. Above the ore, on the higher part of the hill, are argillitic and graphitic schists, associated with the quartzose seams ; farther on, near the edge of the summit plateau, are the dark rusty-colored ferruginous quartz schists, typical of this iron-formation. The recognition of the order in the succession of the beds, which in different localities so little corresponds, is almost impossible, on account of their imperfect denudation and the great dislocation of the strata by plication. Examining the west side of the river, down stream, along the section line between Sects. 1 and 2, Town. 42, R. 35, I found the ferruginous schists, seen in the river bluffs in Sect. 35, again exposed in the N.W. quarter of the N.W. quarter of Sect 1 ; but farther south all the surface is covered with drift. On the line between Sects. 11 and 12 no outcrops can be discovered. Going from the S.E. corner of Sect. 11 to the centre of the N.W. quarter of Sect. 13, a low undulating elevation striking north-west is found to be composed of a gray and white speckled diorite, very similar to the diorites of the Quinnesec falls. Taking from the diorite ridge a north-north-east course through the swampy valley of the river, and crossing it, we find bluffs of the ferruginous schists interlaminated with quartz-seams, inclosing narrow bands of siliceous iron-ore. These slate exposures can be followed all along the west line of the N.W. quarter of Sect. 12 into the S.E. quarter of Sect. 1, where the strata strike west-north-west, and dip toward the south. From here I went across the north part of Sect. 7, where the ferruginous quartzose schists are again exposed, but the surface of the greatest part of the hill-lands over which I passed, striking northward for the wagon-road to Mr. Sheldon's camp, is covered with drift. I mentioned on a former occasion the occurrence of large limestone bluffs on Brule River, in Sect. 19, Town. 41, R. 16, of the Wisconsin Town Maps. The limestones, of a siliceous character, in thick massive beds, amounting to a belt of 400 or 500 feet, have a vertical position ; south of them are no exposures. The rock-ledges disappear under drift-masses, but at a distance of about a quarter mile south of the limestone another parallel undulating ridge is composed of a peculiar dark-colored rock, consisting of an aphanitic feldspathic ground-mass, intimately mingled with a minutely scaly, hydro-micaceous or chloritic mineral, in which mass glassy grains of quartz are abundantly dispersed, besides amygdaloidal masses of ferruginous calcspar and of single feldspar crystals. North of the limestone bluffs are also no other rock-strata seen in contiguity with them, but across the river on the Michigan side the schists of the iron-formation, in a vertical position, are well exposed. The limestone bluffs extend on the Wisconsin side about three quarters of a mile down the river, and then, after a short interruption of the outcrops, we find the ferruginous and graphitic schists with flinty quartz-seams extensively exposed in the river-bed, and in the embankments on the Wisconsin and Michigan sides. Some distance lower down the river massive and schistose dioritic rocks come to the surface ; they form high bluffs on the Michigan side, in the N.E. quarter of Sect. 23, and are traceable for quite a distance northward off from the river. The massive dioritic beds are fine-grained, pale greenish or dark green, by chloritic intermixture ; they inclose an abundance of small calcspar crystals within their mass, and weathered surfaces of the rock are therefore full of little cavities, once occupied by the spar.

I have come now to an end with the record of my explorations in the Menominee River district during the summer season of 1880. Within the given time I was unable to see the whole of this interesting country; and even the part I did see, I could not always examine with the accuracy, necessary for a complete understanding of the order in the succession of the greatly dislocated rock-beds of certain localities; and with the best will to make an exhaustive examination of such places, it could not have been successfully done, without having first acquired the knowledge of the general structure of the whole district, which to obtain was my present object. Having quietly looked over and described the results of my examinations, I see now clearly the deficiency of my information in certain points, some of the wants in knowledge could have been supplied at the time I made the observations; but an observer seeing new things of interest often becomes so absorbed by the thing itself, that he forgets to inquire into the relations it has to others surrounding it, because he is not aware at that moment of their importance.

Having described the rocks of the Marquette district and of the Menominee iron region in two independent chapters, it remains for me to answer the very important question, What relation exists between the rocks of these two districts? In accordance with the generally adopted opinion of geologists, I consider the upheaved stratified rock-series of the Marquette district, which reposes on granitic rocks, and is overlaid by horizontal Silurian sandstones, as analogous with the Huronian group of the Canadian geologists. I leave it undecided whether an analogy exists between the granites of the Marquette region and the Laurentian rocks of Canada; but I claim the granite-belts interstratified with the Huronian formation as decidedly younger, than most of the strata of this series.

The analogy between the rocks of the Marquette region and those of the Monominee iron region is likewise generally admitted; the two regions are in direct continuity, and only 60 miles apart; still very few of the rock-beds of the two are identical, and even the different groups of strata do not exactly correspond.

The dioritic rock-group of Marquette, as has been previously stated, is considered by me as the analogon of the dioritic rock-series exposed in the different falls of the Menominee River, for reasons already stated. The felsite porphyry of the Pemenee falls I compare, in its relation to the dioritic group, to the intrusive granite-belts of the Marquette district. An analogon of the iron-formation of Marquette is found in the Quinnesec iron range. The quartzite formation of the Teal Lake range, and the quartzites connected with the ore-bearing rock-series, might be compared with the great quartzite formation of the Sturgeon River falls. The occurrence of a large limestone formation above the Quinnesec ore-formation, which has great similarity with the limestone formation exposed in connection with the quartzite ranges south of Marquette, seems to be contemporaneous with these, but the limestones of the Menominee district are always separated from the quartzite by a wide interval, while the limestones of Marquette are inseparably connected with the quartzite formation merging with it. The ore-deposits of the Taylor mine, S. C. Smith mine, and of the lately opened Northampton and D'Alaby mines in the Marquette district, which occupy the higher part of the fifth group in my adopted system of subdivision of the Huronian group, are evidently analogous with the Commonwealth ore-formation, and the actinolitic part of that series of strata finds its counterpart in the actinolite schists underlying the Northampton ore-deposits and overlying the quartzites of the Michigamee and Spurr mines. The Lake Hanbury series occupying the place of the lower actinolite schists below the ore-belt of the Washington and Republic mines has no lithological resemblance with these beds.

Whether the Felch Mountain ore-formation is analogous with the Quinnesec ore-formation, and the crystalline limestones, charged with tremolite crystals, correspond with the limestone formation connected with the Quinnesec ore-belt, I am not ready to decide; the similarity of the rocks of these two ore-formations is much greater, than it is between either of them and the Commonwealth ore-formation. I desist for the present from an attempt to make more special identifications, as by future examinations much is yet to be learned, before the suggested analogies can be proved. A forcible systematizing, as has been attempted in a tabular exhibition of the equivalency of Huronian rock-beds, in my opinion, does more to confuse a person than it helps to enlighten him.

Printed in France by Amazon
Brétigny-sur-Orge, FR

48269743R00152